AN ENGAGEMENT WITH PLATO'S REPUBLIC

The authors, distinguished Oxford teachers and scholars, have succeeded admirably in their goal, to help readers 'feel the force' of Plato's arguments. Their humane and patient book encourages us to engage with Socrates and Plato, still the founding teachers in the Western tradition of political and moral philosophy, whether or not Plato infuriates or persuades his modern readers. It is refreshing to be invited to 'grapple with the text' and to be guided by the authors to a place where we can think on the great issues of politics, justice and morality with clarity and confidence.
Mark Morford, Professor of Classics Emeritus, University of Virginia, USA

A truly engaging study. Anyone who teaches the Republic *as living philosophy should have this book at hand. It is the essence of two careers spent teaching the* Republic, *lively, contentious, and delightful to read. The style is as fresh as that of the best recent philosophy, and the issues addressed are of contemporary interest. There is no stale air here; all is fresh and invigorating. Lucas and Mitchell waste no time with Plato's arguments when they are bad, and spare no effort in support of his arguments when they are good, especially when Platonic arguments rightly undermine contemporary fashions such as pluralism.*
Paul Woodruff, Department of Philosophy, The University of Texas at Austin, USA

This book encourages today's students to engage in Plato's thought, grapple with Plato's arguments, and explore the relevance of his arguments in contemporary terms. A text only comes alive if we make it our own; Plato's great work the *Republic*, often reads as though it were addressing the problems of the day rather than those of ancient Athens. Treating the *Republic* as a whole and offering a comprehensive introduction to Plato's arguments, Mitchell and Lucas draw students into an exploration of the relevance of Plato's thought to our present ideas about politics, society and education, as well as the philosophy of mathematics, science and religion.

The authors bring the *Republic* to life. The first chapters help the reader to make sense of the text, either in translation or the original Greek. Later chapters deal with the themes that Plato raises, treating Plato as a contemporary. Plato is inexhaustible: he speaks to many different people of different generations and from different backgrounds. The *Republic* is not just an ancient text: it never ceases to be relevant to contemporary concerns, and it demands fresh discussion in every age.

to

A.D. Woozley and R.M. Hare

Our tutors in philosophy,
who are in no way responsible for our opinions,
but whose standards of thinking we have endeavoured to uphold

An Engagement with Plato's Republic

A Companion to the *Republic*

BASIL MITCHELL
formerly Nolloth Professor
of the Philosophy of the Christian Religion, Oxford University

J.R. LUCAS
formerly Fellow and Tutor of Merton College, Oxford

ASHGATE

Published by
Ashgate Publishing Limited
Gower House
Croft Road
Aldershot
Hants GU11 3HR
England

Ashgate Publishing Company
Suite 420
101 Cherry Street
Burlington, VT 05401-4405
USA

Ashgate website: http://www.ashgate.com

British Library Cataloguing in Publication Data
Mitchell, B. G.
  An engagement with Plato's Republic
  1.Plato. Republic
  I.Title II.Lucas, J. R. (John Randolph), 1929-
  321'.07

Library of Congress Cataloging-in-Publication Data
Mitchell, B. G. (Basil George), 1917-
  An engagement with Plato's Republic / B.G. Mitchell and J.R. Lucas.
    p. cm.
  Includes index.
  ISBN 0-7546-3365-9 (alk. paper) -- ISBN 0-7546-3366-7 (pbk. : alk. paper)
  1. Plato. Republic. I. Lucas, J. R. (John Randolph), 1929- II. Title.

  JC71 . M575 2003
  321'.07--dc21

2002026232

ISBN 0 7546 3365 9 (BC)
ISBN 0 7546 3366 7 (PBK)

Typeset by J.R. Lucas, helped by Sebastian Rahtz and Cliff Webb, of Merton College, Oxford

Printed and bound in Great Britain by MPG Books Ltd, Bodmin, Cornwall

Contents

v

Introduction

Introductions should introduce, but sometimes lead to engagements. That is our aim. We want to make Plato's *Republic* more easily read by modern readers, but do not want to do only that. For philosophy is like poetry, and cannot be learned second-hand. I can learn all sorts of facts about a poem, but unless I have entered into the poet's experience, if only in my imagination, it remains dead. Similarly, I shall not see the point of text-book analyses of philosophical doctrines unless I have felt the force of the arguments that led the philosopher to propose them, and have some sense of the objections he encountered and the way he sought to surmount them. That is why we still need to read Plato and Aristotle, as we do Homer and Sophocles, in a way that we do not, save as a historical exercise, read ancient textbooks of medicine or mechanical construction.

We need not only to be guided—Plato had no chapter headings or foot-notes—but to be involved. Many readers are infuriated by Plato: others are overwhelmed with admiration. Both responses are appropriate, but need to be explored further. Outrageous, unfashionable, politically incorrect though many of the things Plato says undoubtedly are, we should not just dismiss them as thoughts nowadays unthinkable, but think through them, recognising the force of the arguments that led Plato to enunciate them, and consider-ing the counter-arguments he might have marshalled to meet contemporary objections. And equally, deep and inspiring though some of his sentiments are, we need to remember that Aristotle, revering Plato greatly, revered truth even more, and came to reject many of Plato's platonic doctrines. Neither view is right; neither wholly wrong. But it is better to take either view than none at all. Plato believed that philosophy could only be properly carried out in the form of a dialogue, when there was a meeting of minds, and we are being truer to his precepts if we react to him than if we preserve a scholarly detachment. Indeed, there are not just two views of Plato, but as many as there are interested readers of the *Republic*, and each of us must make his own interpretation.

To do this, the reader must grapple with Plato's text. The first chapters are intended to help the reader to make sense of the text, either in transla-tion or the original Greek. In later chapters we deal more with themes that Plato raises than with the text itself, even at the cost of some anachronisms. We treat Plato as a contemporary, because his text is not just an ancient text, but one that never ceases to be relevant to contemporary concerns, and demands fresh discussion in every age. This book, therefore, is not intended as a new commentary on the *Republic*, written, as such a commentary must be, by specialists in ancient philosophy. There are already many commentaries, and many more articles elucidating particular passages in the *Republic*, some excellent ones by colleagues of ours, which we have passed over (and hereby apologize to their authors for not mentioning them), because our aim is different.

Readers will benefit from such commentaries, which will set Plato in the context of his own age, and avoid the anachronisms of this book. But the history of philosophy is different from philosophy itself, and our references to the Periodic Table, the African mole-rat, and modern theories of democracy and education, would be out of place in a scholarly commentary on a text from the fourth century BC, but, we believe, serve to illuminate the issues with which Plato was trying to grapple.

The interpretations we offer are, we believe, defensible, but it is not the purpose of the book to defend them up to the hilt. Many are taken from other scholars, but some we have developed ourselves where we think fresh insights are to be gained. Our views *are* controversial—that is inevitable, granted that our object is to relate Plato to contemporary issues, and to stimulate argument treating him as a contemporary. Readers will often disagree with them: our hope is that they will find them worth disagreeing with.

A Note on Translation

The most straightforward policy would have been to use English throughout and leave nothing in the original Greek. The trouble with this is that no translation can be entirely faithful. Modern English culture is different from ancient Greek culture, and some words used by Plato have no precise equivalent in English, and others make sense only against a background of assumptions or practices that no longer obtain. No English word adequately represents Plato's use of the words δικαιοσύνη (*dikaiosune*) and δίκαιος (*dikaios*); δικαιοσύνη is commonly translated 'justice', but that is often positively misleading; the question raised by Glaucon and Adeimantus in Book II is whether morality is worth it, or whether the amoral life is a better bet. Most translators adopt the best English word they can think of, and use it throughout. Words such as ψυχή (*psuche*), μίμησις (*mimesis*), διανοια (*dianoia*), are given standard translations, which are all right for those familiar with the original Greek, but can mislead others, because in some contexts the standard translation does not carry the sense of the original Greek. We follow the opposite policy. We try to find the English word that makes most sense in the context, but at the same time give the Greek word so that readers who know Greek can make up their own minds. Thus instead of the 'tripartite division of the soul' we shall talk of the threefold classification of facets of personality, ψυχή (*psuche*).

Publishers do not like Greek. They say—and they should know—that it puts off potential purchasers, much as equations do in popular science books. But since we translate the same Greek word differently on different occasions, giving the best rendering we can of its sense in the context, we go against the conventional wisdom, and give the Greek word. We also sometimes give the Greek where the interpretation of a passage is disputed.

We have, on the whole, avoided transliteration. Transliterated Greek is not easy to read and is error-prone. But we have given transliterated versions of key words like δίκαιος (*dikaios*), εὐδαιμονία (*eudaemonia*), μίμησις (*mimesis*), where the Greekless reader needs to know that the same Greek word is being used, though rendered by different English words in different contexts.

In his Theory of Forms Plato uses two words, εἶδος (*eidos*) and ἰδέα (*idea*), which are standardly translated as Form, but would often be better rendered as pattern, shape, species, feature, value. We shall use the stock translation, Form, with the capital letter indicating that it is a term of art. We have not used the stock translation, 'justice', for δικαιοσύνη or τὸ δικαίον, but have rendered it sometimes as 'righteousness', sometimes as 'morality', sometimes as 'integrity', or whatever best conveys the facet of its meaning that Plato is using in the passage under consideration. For δόξα (*doxa*) we use 'opinion', and for ἐπιστήμη 'understanding', and for νόησις (*noesis*) 'knowledge', as do most commentators. 'Knowledge' seems natural for γνῶσις too, and 'confidence' is usually adequate for πίστις (*pistis*) though sometimes 'settled conviction' or 'firm belief' is better. We found it difficult to translate εἰκασία (*eikasia*) in a way that would make Plato's argument plausible; no English word expresses Plato's range of meanings. 'Imagination' conveys the sense of visual imagery as opposed to reliable reality, but has too strong a sense of not being true. Although unreliable, appearances do not necessarily deceive. 'Guesstimate' is insufficiently pejorative. 'Conjecture' is often the best we can offer. Διάνοια (*dianoia*) was also difficult: 'derivation' captures the sense of deductive inference from premises, but presupposes our interpretation in terms of modern mathematical logic, an interpretation that many commentators would dispute.

Readers who do not know Greek should check our rendering against that in their translation. The best available translations are:

A.D. Lindsay, *The Republic of Plato*, J.M. Dent (Everyman), London, 1907.

H.P.D. Lee, *The Republic of Plato*, Harmondsworth (Penguin), 1955.

F.M. Cornford, *The Republic of Plato*, Oxford, 1941.

G.M.A. Grube, *Plato's Republic*, Indianapolis, 1974.

R.W. Sterling and W.C. Scott, *Plato: The Republic*, New York, 1985.

Plato's style is full, and sometimes readers will find a *précis* more helpful than a translation. Plato himself gives one of Books I to V in the *Timaeus* (17a-19b); A.E. Taylor, *Plato: The Man and his Work*, London, 1926, pp.262-298, combines *précis* with commentary.

References

References to Plato are given to the standard Stephanus pages, first a numeral then, if need be, a letter—a, b, c, d, or e—followed by another numeral; almost every edition and translation of Plato will show these in the margin. References to passages in the *Republic* are given in brackets in the text, preceded, unless it is otiose, by the number of the book in capital Roman numerals. References to other dialogues of Plato and to other works are given in footnotes. In almost all cases we give each reference in full, to save the reader (who may have not read all the previous pages) from having to look back to some earlier footnote. References to Aristotle are to the standard Bekker edition; the books common to the *Nicomachean* and the *Eudemian Ethics* are referred to as *Ethics* V, VI and VII.

Chapter 1
Questions Asked

An Evening's Argument

Shadow Boxing

Many would-be readers of the *Republic* give up. Not that it is very difficult to understand; but it seems all very trivial. After setting the scene in Cephalus' house, Socrates starts scoring rather unconvincing points over Cephalus and Polemarchus about homicidal maniacs, poisoners and bankers, and we feel a lot of sympathy with Thrasymachus when he finally bursts in and tries to get to grips with the basic problem of morality. That, in part, is the point: Plato wants to give Thrasymachus a fair wind, so that we can enter into his position and find it attractive, in spite of its crudity. But there are other points too. Plato, it was said, rewrote the first book of the *Republic* 37 times; he was hardly likely to have devoted the opening passages to purely pointless argumentation, simply in order to exasperate us into sympathizing with Thrasymachus. We should look beneath the surface, and try to discern an underlying theme.

The key is in the final sentence of Thrasymachus' outburst (336c7-d4). 'And don't tell me that morality, τὸ δικαίον (*to dikaion*), is the obligatory, τὸ δέον, or the advantageous, τὸ ὠφέλιμον, or the profitable, τὸ λυσιτελοῦν, or the expedient, τὸ κερδαλέον, or what is to one's interest, τὸ συμφέρον, but, whatever you say, say it clearly and precisely, σαφῶς καὶ ἀκριβῶς (*saphos kai akribos*).' Is this an important passage? Plato makes it clear that it is. There are many delicate allusions to the key words, ἀκριβῶς and σαφῶς in the next few pages.[1] He also shows what it is that he is trying to get across in the parody of Thrasymachus that Socrates puts forward in his protest at Thrasymachus' demand (337b1-c1). To demand that Socrates say what morality, τὸ δικαίον, is, not in terms of the obligatory, the advantageous, the expedient, or what is to one's interest, but clearly and accurately, is like demanding that he say what twelve is, but not as two times six, three times four, or any other numerical expression. The suggestion is that we cannot give a clear and precise account of morality, τὸ δικαίον, except in terms like obligatory, advantageous, or profitable, any more than we can give a non-numerical specification of twelve.

---

[1] 338d5, 340a1, 340e2, 340e8, 341b6, 342b7-8, 342d6, 342d9, 346b3, 346d2; see also 445b6.

1

What is common to terms like obligatory, advantageous, or profitable? Why are they not susceptible to a precise specification? All these words are 'gerundive' words: they indicate actions, other things being equal, which ought to be undertaken. If I am told that it is obligatory to stop at red traffic lights, I am being told that I must stop at red traffic lights; if I am told that it is advantageous to join a political party, I am being told that I should join a political party; if I am told that it is profitable to invest in mining, I am being advised to buy mining shares. In each case, of course, there may be further considerations which point the other way; but, in the absence of further considerations, the gerundive word indicates the course of action to be taken. Τὸ δίκαιον, however it is translated, is likewise a to-be-done word. Traditionally it is translated 'just', but often it means much more than what is meant by the English word 'just'. Sometimes it means 'right'. 'Righteous' and 'righteousness' sound old-fashioned to our ears, but sometimes capture what is meant by the δίκαιος and the virtue of δικαιοσύνη. 'Morality' is a more modern word: much of the *Republic* is concerned with working out what morality is, and in what circumstances men can live moral lives. But it is not a simple matter. Although Simonides, like many Old Testament prophets (*e.g.* Micah 6:8b, Ecclesiastes 12:13), offers a formula to guide us to the good life, each formula turns out, on examination, not to be as clear and precise as we could wish. Honesty (here the best translation of δικαιοσύνη) may be the best policy, but what is honesty? To tell the truth and give back what you have borrowed? As a general rule that seems fair enough, but there are difficulties in applying it in certain circumstances—when the homicidal maniac is around, we neither tell him where his intended victim is, nor return to him the hatchet we had previously borrowed. Equally nowadays, if a drug addict demands that we give him the money we owe him, we are not sure that that is what we ought to do. The words 'owe' and 'ought' are etymologically connected, as are the words 'debt', 'due' and 'duty', the latter all stemming from the Latin *debitum* and the French *du*. In most cases there is little room for argument whether we owe something: our debts can usually be clearly and precisely determined. Not so our duty: we have to take a whole range of factors into consideration in determining what we ought to do, what is due from us in the particular circumstances of the case—we ought not to give the drug addict the money we owe him, but ought to help him as much as we can to free himself from his addiction; a helping hand, not money, is what is due from us to someone no longer able to make autonomous decisions for himself.

The Greek word ὀφειλόμενον (*opheilomenon*) is ambiguous as between 'owed' and 'ought'. In 332a-c3 Socrates pushes Polemarchus from construing it, when used to define τὸ δίκαιον, in the former sense to understanding it in the latter. It is not simply paying one's debts, but giving people their due, that is, what is appropriate, προσῆκον—another gerundive word, like ὠφέλιμον, λυσιτελοῦν, κερδαλέον, and συμφέρον. Polemarchus thinks it is simply a matter of doing good to one's friends and harm to one's enemies, but Socrates first uses this specification to explore another possibility, that it is some sort of skill. Skills often cannot be reduced to simple recipes. There are many rules for writing good English prose, or Latin verses, but someone can follow all the rules and yet produce a wooden result. Knowing how to write cannot be exhaustively defined in terms of knowing that certain rules are to be obeyed. It could be that morality was similarly a skill, τέχνη (*tekhne*), a flair for doing the right thing. But that identification breaks down when we examine it more closely. Skills are specific: there are occasions when we are glad to avail ourselves of the *expertise* of a doctor or a pilot, but morality is not confined to special occasions; admittedly there are some professions where honesty is particularly important—banking for example—but paradox ensues if we try to make out that honesty is a special sort of *expertise*. Moreover, and more importantly, skills are abilities that enable one to achieve whatever ends one wishes—medical skill can be used to poison patients—whereas morality is concerned with what ends should be sought. Later, Aristotle at the beginning of Book V of the *Ethics* (1129a11-23) draws a sharp distinction between a disposition ἕξις (*hexis*), which is what δικαιοσύνη is, and an ability, δύναμις (*dunamis*), which, being indifferent as to ends, it cannot be.

After this digression (332c5-334b) Socrates returns to Polemarchus' gloss on 'appropriate', namely that it is appropriate to do good to friends, and harm to enemies. But who is my friend? Who is my enemy? Socrates draws a distinction between those who seem to be and those who really are. We know who our seeming friends and seeming enemies are; to that extent the injunction to do good to the one and do harm to the other is clear and precise—we have no doubt who are to be the objects of our benevolence and malevolence. But we could be mistaken in our assessments, and clearly it could not be right to harm those who were really our friends, though we did not know it. We should do good to our real friends—that is indisputable: but who our real friends are—that is difficult to say, and no simple formula will specify them clearly and precisely.

Socrates' example of Polydamas (338c4-d2) seems rather trivial, but is making the same point. Thrasymachus has defined τὸ δικαίον as τὸ τοῦ κρείττονος συμφέρον what is in the interest of the superior person: τὸ συμφέρον is one of the forbidden terms; equally, τοῦ κρείττονος, of the superior person is ambiguous, and might be an overall term of approbation, or might be a purely descriptive term. Socrates takes it as the latter, in which case there are clear and precise criteria for being κρείττων; physically, we can tell who is stronger than whom, and Polydamas comes out top. And by the same token, his συμφέρον, physically, is strengthening food—meat. So, if we are to take τὸ τοῦ κρείττονος συμφέρον in a clear and precise sense, it is meat. Thrasymachus protests, and explains that he had not meant τὸ τοῦ κρείττονος συμφέρον in a purely physical sense, but in a political one; but again he falls foul of the same point: if we take κρείττων to be the dominant political class, we may be able to identify it clearly and precisely, but it may be inept; and if we write in a requirement that the government be really superior, it is no longer clear precisely at any one time what it actually is.

In 335b2-336a10 Socrates makes use of various ambiguities to deny that it could ever be right to harm even one's genuine enemies. The conclusion is admirable, but the argumentation is full of holes. The Greek word βλάπτειν (*blaptein*) can mean 'frustrate', 'hinder', or 'hurt', but normally carries a stronger sense of harming and damaging. It could be right to frustrate or hinder or even hurt one's enemies, and the good horseman might, on occasion, hurt his horses to teach them a lesson. But the good horseman would never actually harm his horses, and the humane man would not want to make his enemies less human, even though they were genuine enemies. If morality, δικαιοσύνη, is the specifically human excellence, ἀρετή (*arete*), concerned with making humans as human as possible, then it would not be moral to inflict real harm on a human being. Besides the ambiguity in βλάπτειν there is an ambiguity in the range of concern: the humane man is not merely interacting with friends and enemies, but is considering them all as fellow-human-beings, and his humanity is not only the excellence he possesses *qua* human being, but also the peculiar characteristic of a humanitarian whose concern is with human beings in the same way as a horseman is concerned with horses. It is not surprising that this piece of word-play was too much for Thrasymachus, and provoked his outburst 'What absolute drivel possesses you, Socrates...'.

Cleitophon's Suggestion

After the political version of Thrasymachus' definition has been refuted, Cleitophon offers an emendation which would save Thrasymachus from refutation (340b). Cleitophon suggests that instead of saying that δικαιοσύνη was τὸ τοῦ κρείττονος συμφέρον (*to tou kreittonos sumpheron*), he should say that it was τὸ τοῦ κρείττονος συμφέρον δοκοῦν (*to tou kreittonos sumpheron dokoun*), that which the superior person took to be his interest.

Why was Cleitophon's emendation not taken up? It would have saved Thrasymachus' position, but at the cost of making it vacuous. How would we know what the seeming interest of the superior person was? We could not rely on what he himself said, because he might well claim to be guided by moral considerations. The whole point of Thrasymachus' position is that people are not to be believed when they claim to be acting on moral grounds. But if we cannot be told by the superior person what he takes to be his own interest, the only way of telling what it is will be to observe his actions. We shall know what his interest is from seeing what he does. But then it will be an empty tautology that he always acts in his own interest, since it is what he does that tells us what his interest is.[2]

Who was Thrasymachus?

It is with the entry of Thrasymachus into the discussion that the *Republic* comes alive for us. The argument with Cephalus and Polemarchus employs categories which are unfamiliar to us. Thrasymachus, however, holds a position which is permanently attractive and worthy of refutation. For this reason Plato's attempt to refute it in the *Republic* remains a classical essay in the justification of morality.

Thrasymachus was not a straw man. His views were widely prevalent at the time the dialogue is supposed to have taken place. Behind Thrasymachus stands Thucydides.[3] Thrasymachus' view is the view both of the protagonists, and of the historian, of the Peloponnesian War. The best-known passage is the Melian Dialogue at the end of Thucydides Book V. It is also taken for granted in the Mytilene debate in Book III, where Diodotus, who is advocating mercy, says (III.44.1): 'The argument is not about their wrongdoing, but about our self-interest.' That Plato had Thucydides in mind in shown clearly by 348c-d which turns on the meaning of the words εὐήθης (*euethes*) and εὐήθεια (*euetheia*). 'So that honesty is a virtue and dishonesty a vice.' 'As if I would say that,' answered Thrasymachus, 'when I maintain that dishonesty is the best policy, not honesty.' 'So you would say that honesty was a vice.' 'Not quite that; rather a naive good-naturedness.' 'And dishonesty an ill-naturedness?' 'No, just common sense.' We could translate the adjective εὐήθης as 'simple' or 'simple-minded' or 'well-meaning', which display a similar ambivalence. The word 'silly' underwent over a period of time the same change of meaning. When the carolist says 'Then to the stall the silly shepherds came' he is not to be taken as suggesting that in going to Bethlehem the shepherds were foolish, but that they were unsophisticated. Since then the word has gone the same way as εὐήθης did in Greek. We know the exact date when εὐήθης and εὐήθεια lost their good meanings and obtained a bad. It happened in 427 BC in Corcyra, when, according to Thucydides, the exigencies of revolution forced a change of meaning on many words, and in particular on the word εὐήθης. 'Thus every sort of evil doing was established throughout Greece by reason of the revolution, and the word εὐήθης,

---

[2] A further reason is given on p.10.

[3] Thus Oswyn Murray, commenting on Thucydides in John Boardman, Jasper Griffin, Oswyn Murray, eds., *The Oxford History of the Classical World*, Oxford University Press, 1986, p.196, remarks of the view of Thrasymachus in the *Republic* 'We know that this view of society was not a universal view in the fifth century, and very probably not a majority one; nevertheless it was clearly an influential one.'

which has a predominantly good sense, was laughed out of court' (Thucydides 3.83.1). This change of sense stuck, as in the *Republic* 336c1, 343c6, 400e, 425b7; Aristotle in his Table of Excellencies and Defects in the *Eudemian Ethics* has it as one of his defects (EE 2.3.4, 1221a13).[4]

Thucydides' account gives substance to Thrasymachus' explanation of what he means by saying τὸ δικαίον, 'right' or 'honesty', is τὸ τοῦ κρείττονος συμφέρον 338e-339a. In the Corcyrean Revolution words did change their accustomed meaning under the pressure of events (Thucydides 3.82.4) and were used in accordance with the interests of the dominant faction. It is because Thrasymachus' account is largely true that Plato felt unable to allow Cephalus or Polemarchus to give a simple answer to the question 'What is δικαιοσύνη, honesty?', and felt obliged to write the *Republic* instead. In stable societies, the criteria for the application of evaluative and gerundive words are generally agreed to be clear and fixed. The Greeks at the time the dialogue of the *Republic* is supposed to have taken place (perhaps during the Peace of Nikias) looked back, somewhat nostalgically, to a time when the traditional standards, τὰ πάτρια or τὰ νόμιμα were recognised and observed, and many hoped to recreate a society in which the rules for the words δικαίον, honest or right, εὐήθης, good-natured, and the rest would be applied σαφῶς καὶ ἀκριβῶς,[5] clearly and rigorously. If this had been possible, then Socrates would have had a short way with the sophists, being able to convict them of linguistic incompetence in not knowing the correct use of the Greek language.[6] But Plato saw that this was not possible, and that conventional wisdom as enshrined in language, even if unchallenged, is not necessarily right. Thrasymachus is raising a more fundamental problem than can be settled by an appeal to the correct use of words, and therefore it must be examined on its own merits.[7]

Thrasymachus' Position

What *is* Thrasymachus' position? It is useful to start from Cross and Woozley's clear but, in our view, finally mistaken discussion.[8] They suggest that there are four things that Thrasymachus might have been doing:

---

[4] In addition to 348cd, 343c5, d2, there are further uses of *euetheia* at 349b5, III 400e1-3, 401a7, b4, 409a8, 425b6 (silly) VII 529b3. The latter pejorative uses give some support to the view that these passages were written long after Book I.

[5] 336d4-5; see above pp.1-4.

[6] See further, ch.5, esp.p.60.

[7] See further, ch.5, p.62.

[8] R.C.Cross and A.D.Woozley, *Plato's Republic: A Philosophical Commentary*, London, 1966, pp.28-41.

1. *Naturalistic definition.* On this view Thrasymachus is giving a naturalistic definition of morality, so that 'x is δικαίον, (*dikaion*), right' means exactly the same as 'x serves the interests of the stronger'. 'That is, the apparently moral judgement "x is δικαίον, right" containing the apparently moral word 'right' is not really a moral judgement at all, making a favourable comment on x, for 'right' is not really a moral term, but a neutral factual term.' Cross and Woozley reject this interpretation on the ground that Thrasymachus does repeatedly say 'It is right to promote the interest of the stronger', which he could not intelligibly do if 'right' simply meant 'promoting the interest of the stronger'.

2. *Nihilist view.* Thrasymachus is saying that there is 'no such thing as morality', morality is an illusion. 'The strong man exploits the weak man's mistaken belief in morality, by persuading him that certain actions or policies of action are what ought to be pursued, when in fact all that is true is that they will, promote the strong man's interest.' Cross and Woozley ask what is the difference between the naturalistic definition view and the nihilist view, and reply 'On the naturalistic definition view, that there is something properly to be called morality and that some actions are or may be right, is not denied. What is denied is that any distinction is to be drawn between an action's being right and its serving the interest of the stronger. According to the Nihilist view, on the other hand, morality is an illusion—nothing at all corresponds to, or could correspond to, the word "morality"'. The nihilist interpretation is rejected for the same reason as the other. Thrasymachus does say 'It is right to...' thus implying that 'right' has a clear meaning.

3. *Incidental comment.* On this view Thrasymachus is not attempting to define morality or say what it really is at all. He is not claiming to explain what morality is, but is pointing out what he claims to be a fact about it, *viz.* that it serves the interest of the stronger. Cross and Woozley concede that this fits a lot of what Thrasymachus says and especially the fact that he is less interested in answering the question what morality is than in recommending the life of immorality if you can practise it successfully. This 'incidental comment' view, however, is rejected on the ground that Thrasymachus does repeatedly say what morality is, *viz.* that it is what serves the interest of the stronger.

4. *Essential analysis.* According to this view Thrasymachus 'does not think that morality is an illusion, and he does not think that there is no distinction in meaning between "x is right" and "x serves the interest of the stronger"'. In saying that morality is nothing but the interest of the stronger, he is maintaining that an action is right if and only if it serves the interest of the stronger: it is the fact of an act's serving the interest of the stronger that gives it the characteristic of being right. Cross and Woozley concede that it is a difficulty for this view that Thrasymachus

holds that morality is the other man's interest: because it cannot be the other man's good from the point of the stronger whose interest it is. But they take Thrasymachus to have overlooked this difficulty.

What Cross and Woozley actually show is that it is impossible to discover in Thrasymachus a view that is at the same time *entirely* consistent *and* at all plausible; but we can get closer to it than Cross and Woozley do. Basically Thrasymachus is a nihilist. The reason why he is impatient with all the blather between Socrates and Polemarchus is that they assume that there is *point* in their discussions as to whether, *e.g.* it is right to tell the truth and pay one's debts, or help friends and harm enemies, the point being to discover what is right in some objective sense. They assume that when they have discovered what is right they will have discovered an absolute standard which they are under some kind of rational obligation to observe. If this is what morality is taken to be, then there is no such thing as morality. And this is what Thrasymachus does maintain against Socrates and the common opinion.

In another sense, however, Thrasymachus believes that there is such a thing as morality and is prepared to give a naturalistic definition of it: morality is obedience to the laws. Since the content of the laws varies from one city to another, there are no sorts of action which are absolutely right; morality is relative to the laws of a particular society. The variations are attributable to the class-structure of these societies. Hence democracies make democratic laws, oligarchies oligarchic laws and so on. That is to say, the ruling class, the stronger, make the laws in their own interest. Hence, morality, law-abidingness, is the interest of the stronger, in the quite straightforward sense that the tendency of the ruled to act in accordance with the laws promotes the interest of the rulers, who have rigged the constitution in their own favour.

On this interpretation the assertion that the rulers make the law in their own interest is what Cross and Woozley call 'incidental comment'. It is a piece of sociological observation that this is so and not an attempt to define morality. The ruled, in obeying the laws and investing the notion of morality with an absoluteness and an imperativeness which it does not properly possess are, as Thrasymachus observes, εὐήθεις, guileless. There is a close analogy here with Marxist doctrine, according to which the law and the morality of a society reflect the class-structure of that society, *e.g.* bourgeois morality and law reflect the interests of the entrepreneurs and operate at the expense of the manual worker. The working man who believes in the essential morality of the so-called free institutions of a capitalist society is guileless. The point is neatly stated by Gibbon in his comment on the religions of the Roman Empire: 'The various modes of worship, which prevailed in the Roman world, were all considered by the people as equally true; by the philosopher, as equally false; and by the magistrate, as equally useful.'[9]

---

[9] Edward Gibbon, *The Decline and Fall of the Roman Empire*, ch.2.

Difficulties for this Interpretation

There are two problems for this interpretation of Thrasymachus. One is to account for Thrasymachus' insistence that ἀδικία immorality, or injustice, is better and stronger than δικαιοσύνη morality, or justice; that the answer to the question of 'how should one live?' is 'immorally', or unjustly.

This is not difficult to do. The immoral man rejects justice on the ground that it is another's good. Unlike the other cardinal virtues, courage, wisdom, self-control, which obviously benefit their possessor, justice benefits not him but other people. It is of the essence of justice that it inhibits people from pursuing their own advantage in deference to the rights of others; so the jingle:

> The rain it falls upon the just
> And also on the unjust fellah;
> But more upon the just because
> The unjust has the just's umbrella.

And so, as Thrasymachus points out, at the dissolution of a partnership it is always the case that the unjust man has more and the just man less. Hence one could characterize ἀδικία, immorality, or injustice, as the getting the better of the other man. Since the reasonable man will, of course, pursue his own interest, he will not wish to be moral and will regard those who are moral as deluded. Moreover, he has himself contributed to their being deluded; because as a member of a ruling class he has helped to engineer and to maintain the situation in which most people are misled into supposing that the laws represent some absolute standard of morality.

Cross and Woozley point out that Thrasymachus sometimes says that it is right to promote the interest of the stronger, in a way which strongly suggests that he does give 'right' a definitive evaluative force. *e.g.* 'Do you not say that it is right to obey the rulers?' (I 339b7) followed later by 'The ruled must do as the rulers require and this is morality' (339c10) and again 'Not only is it right according to your argument to promote the interest of the stronger, but also to promote the opposite, what is not his interest'(339d1-3).[10]

Here Thrasymachus seems to be letting Socrates assume that it is a permissible question to ask whether it is right to obey the laws and whether it is right to promote the interest of the stronger in a way that it could not be if δικαίου, right meant either 'in obedience to the laws' or 'in the interest of the stronger'. This objection is reinforced by the impression Thrasymachus gives throughout that it is *right and proper* that the stronger should prevail, that in some sense 'might is right'. This is what makes Cross and Woozley finally interpret Thrasymachus as maintaining that an act is right if and only if it serves the interest of the stronger.

---

[10] See further below, ch.6, p.74.

The truth would seem to be that, at this point, Thrasymachus has been betrayed into a slight, and entirely understandable inconsistency. What he really thinks—and is quite entitled to think in terms of his own theory—is that the ἄδικος is the best sort of man; he is the master of the art of living; he is the sort of man to become if you can. He is truly happy. This is where he differs from Socrates who believes that it is the δίκαιος righteous, man who is happy. But these evaluative and gerundive words—'best sort of man', 'master of the art of living', 'man to become'—are not to be understood in any moral sense. For Thrasymachus is an immoralist and believes that any reasonable person should repudiate morality as prejudicial to his interests.

His mistake is to allow himself to be beguiled by Socrates into expressing this conviction by the use of the *evaluative* word δικαίον, 'right'. He cannot use that word for this purpose because he has already given it a different non-evaluative sense. But so long as he avoids using the word δικαίον there is no reason why he should not express the view that the completely immoral man, who is also the stronger, *should* have his interests promoted.

His wanting to maintain that the immoral man is in all respects the superior of the moral man constitutes a further reason for rejecting Cleitophon's proposed amendment that 'morality is what the stronger *thinks* is to his advantage'.[11] On the face of it this would get Thrasymachus out of his difficulty and would accord with the facts; rulers do, after all, sometimes make mistakes and a purely sociological theory of morality would allow for this. But Thrasymachus' official theory is shot through with another which only gets made explicit later in the discussion, *viz.* that the ideal sort of person is the immoral man who recognises no obligation to obey the law and is out to get the better of other people. The main way he achieves this is by making laws and persuading or coercing other people to keep them. This is the sort of person to be: he is strong and clever and does not make mistakes. He is an artist in living.

The second objection to this proposed interpretation is that Thrasymachus does not initially say what on this view he ought to say, *viz.* 'morality is nothing else than obedience to the laws'; he says 'morality is nothing else than the interest of the stronger'. So that, if anything is his definition of morality, this must be it. The answer to this is that, notoriously, throughout Book I there is little care taken to distinguish between definitions and contingent truths, and that 'answer' is a much wider term than definition. When Thrasymachus says 'morality is nothing else than the interest of the stronger' this is shorthand for 'since morality is nothing else than obedience to the laws and, since the laws are made in the interest of the stronger, morality is (boils down to) nothing but the interest of the stronger'. The only point in the entire discussion at which he slips away from this contention is when he is

---

[11] See above, p.4.

led to say, incautiously, that it is right, δικαίον, to promote the interest of the stronger and that, as we have seen, was a mistaken way of expressing his belief that it is proper that the interest of the stronger should prevail or, as he finally puts it, immorality is better than morality. When (in Book II), Glaucon and Adeimantus undertake to reformulate his position and defend it against Socrates, it is this claim which they explicitly make, and which Socrates seeks to refute in the remainder of the *Republic*.

Three Further Arguments Against Thrasymachus

Before Glaucon and Adeimantus intervene, however, Plato makes Socrates deploy three further arguments against Thrasymachus which are all of considerable intrinsic interest. The first (I 349b-350c11) introduces the notion of virtue as a μέσον, or μέτριον, mean, which appears again in the *Philebus* and the *Politicus* and which has affinities with the traditional Greek identification of τὸ πέρας (*to peras*) with good and τὸ ἄπειρον (*to apeiron*) with bad.

Thrasymachus has claimed that immorality is a human ἀρετή excellence. The immoral man[12] is master of the art of living. Socrates seeks to show that this is impossible, logically impossible, if, as Thrasymachus claims, the immoral man has no other aim but self-aggrandisement, πλεονεξία (*pleonexia*). The argument is perfectly clear as soon as one is led to make the transition from πλέον ἔχειν (*pleon echein*) in the sense of 'get more than' to πλέον ἔχειν (*pleon echein*) in the sense of 'outdo' or 'overreach'. Socrates starts from the obvious point that when things are to be shared the immoral man gets more than the moral man (or less if it is unpleasant). He does this without regard to any consideration of what is the right amount for him to take. The moral man, by contrast, does not try to outdo (get more than) the moral man or to go beyond the right action.

Socrates employs the analogy of a musician tuning a lyre. He aims to get the right tension on the string and so would any other musician. Someone who was unmusical, by contrast, who did not know or did not care, what the right tension was, might seek to outdo the musician by putting greater tension on the string.

The musical metaphor is developed quite naturally by Aristotle when discussing the virtues in the *Nicomachean Ethics* (1138b21-25):

---

[12] Here and throughout this book we use 'man' to include 'woman'. Our reason is well expressed by Dr Kathleen V.Wilkes in her *Real People*, Oxford, 1988, p.27 n., who realises that her 'acceptance of this convention will annoy some; but, for my part, I am annoyed by the clumsiness of "he or she", "s/he", and their ilk. The use of "she" in place of "he" strikes me as misleading ...; and is, to my ear, distractingly precious and political. Anyone who thinks language helps determine sexual attitudes should contemplate Turkish'.

> In all the states of character we have mentioned, as in all other matters, the
> man who has the rule looks and tightens or relaxes his activity accordingly,
> and there is a standard which determines the mean states which we say are
> intermediate between excess and defect, being in accordance with the right
> rule.

The point of the argument against Thrasymachus is this. Thrasymachus represents the immoral man as having no σκοπός standard, by reference to which
he can determine what action is the right one πρὸς ὃν ἀποβλέπων ..ἐπιτείνει
καὶ ἀνίησιν always in unregulated competition with other people, moral and
immoral alike. He is not trying to achieve a standard, and competing with
others only in that endeavour; he has no standard and competes for competition's sake. If this is so, then he cannot be exhibiting any virtue or practising
an art of living.

This is a powerful argument against Thrasymachus, if he is actually committed to the rejection of any standards whatever, if, that is, he has to make
the transition he in fact makes, with encouragement from Socrates, from the
statement that the immoral man tries πλέον ἔχειν τοῦ δικαίου in the simple sense of 'get more than' to the statement that he tries πλέον ἔχειν τῆς
δικαίας πράξεως in the sense required by his argument. It is tempting to
argue—and perhaps Plato is trying to argue—that the notion of a perfectly
immoral man is logically incoherent because one could never tell when he had
finally succeeded in getting the better of others. However successful he was
in routing his opponents he might still fail at the next crisis; he can never
have a secure hold on πλεονεξία, if that is his object.

We are familiar with the contrast between the maintenance of standards
and unrestricted competition in the field of broadcasting. In Britain the BBC
is required by its charter to maintain certain standards of excellence, but it
is also involved in a struggle for ratings. Television companies subject to no
such requirement would be engaged in an unrestricted competition for viewers
in which the aim would be simply to achieve better ratings than their rivals.
They will ask themselves not 'Is this a good programme?' but 'Will it attract
more viewers than competing programmes?'

However, it is not clear that this argument succeeds. Perfection in an art
and success in it are distinguishable even when the art is the art of success.
The worst man (*i.e.* the best at being bad) may not win through factors
beyond his control, although by the standards appropriate to the art he thoroughly deserved to win. Thus we might study the career of a thoroughly
successful and utterly unscrupulous political schemer and still find it in some
respects defective when judged by the most machiavellian standards—'he
ought to have flattered that man not tried to bribe him', 'With that other
rival threats would have been more appropriate than false promises' and so
on. Similarly a TV programmer may be highly paid because of his skill in
putting together a mixture of programmes which attracts overall the largest

audience while finding his calculations upset on occasion by some quite gratuitous change in fashion. Herbert Butterfield's *International Conflicts in the Twentieth Century* opens with the following sentence: 'Political action may be assessed according to the brilliance of its conception or the degree of its success, but it also has to be measured against the principles of morality'. Thrasymachus can distinguish between success and brilliance of conception without concerning himself with principles of morality.

The second argument (I 351b6 ff.) calls attention to the need for 'morality among thieves'. A group of people cannot achieve any purpose unless they recognise some obligations to each other. This is an important argument which is bound to form part of any teleological justification of morality. The rules of morality are among the necessary conditions of any viable society; they are also among the necessary conditions of the individual's realisation of his own purposes. Hence a version of the argument finds a place in Cicero's *De Officiis*, in Hobbes' *Leviathan*, in Hume's *Treatise* and, more recently, in Hart's *Concept of Law* (OUP 1961) where it is treated under the heading 'The Minimum Content of Natural Law' (189 ff.). As Hart's heading suggests, it has its limitations, two in particular:

1. I may have an interest in the survival and welfare of any society of which I am a member, but do I have an interest in the survival or welfare of people everywhere, whatever society they belong to? Most historical societies have had a closed rather than an open morality.

Locke is aware of this limitation in chapter III of his *Essay*, entitled 'No innate practical principles':

> Justice and keeping of contracts is that which most men seem to agree in. This is a principle which is thought to extend itself to the dens of thieves and the confederacies of the greatest villains; and they who have gone furthest towards the putting off of humanity itself keep faith and rules of justice one with another...

> But it is impossible to conceive that he embraces justice as a practical principle who acts fairly with his fellow highwayman and at the same time plunders or kills the next honest man he meets with. Justice and faith are the common ties of society; and, therefore, even outlaws and robbers, who break with all the world besides, must keep faith and rules of equity among themselves or else they cannot hold together. But will anyone say that those who live by fraud and rapine have innate principles of truth and justice which they allow and assent to?

Locke is, of course, here campaigning against innate ideas, and his own position is not entirely clear, but he calls attention to the difficulty. Is morality, conceived as applying only to some limited group, fully morality? Perhaps Plato himself sees this: (I 352c4) δῆλον ὅτι ἐνῆν τις αὐτοῖς δικαιοσύνη, it is clear that there is some morality of a sort in them.

2. If this difficulty can be overcome and it can be shown that a universal morality is required for the stability of society and the fulfilment of human

purposes, there remains the question whether the determined immoralist can resist the conclusion that he personally should be moral. It is the contention of Glaucon and Adeimantus that he can.

The third argument (I 352e to the end) turns on the assumption that, like eyes and ears, a horse and a pruning knife, the soul has an ἔργον (*ergon*), a job or a function, for which it is the indispensable or best instrument. It is to superintend, to rule and to advise. Since morality is a virtue, or excellence, of the soul and immorality a vice, a moral soul will rule and superintend well and an immoral soul badly. So, Socrates concludes, a moral man will live well, but an immoral man badly, which is to say that the moral man will be εὐδαίμων (*eudaimon*) and the immoral man not.

This passage encapsulates the entire argument of the *Republic* and it remains to be seen whether in its complete form it is able to carry conviction.[13] In its present abbreviated form, it is open to a number of objections which have often been made:

1. Plato has generalised illegitimately from such things as pruning knives which are made for a purpose, by way of eyes and ears which can be seen biologically to be serving a purpose, to horses which are, indeed, used by men for a purpose but cannot be said to have one by nature. The soul as such may generate purposes but does not otherwise have one. If Plato wishes to maintain otherwise he needs to do more than rely on the analogies he employs in this passage.

2. Whether the virtue or excellence of the soul is morality or immorality is precisely the question at issue with Thrasymachus and he ought not to be allowed to concede this point.

3. The conclusion, that the moral man lives well and hence is εὐδαίμων is a pun which trades on an ambiguity of the Greek expression εὖ ζῆν, to live well. It does not follow that if someone lives well, *i.e.* morally, that he lives well in the sense of being happy.

That the argument as it stands is open to all three objections is undeniable. It remains to be seen whether the argument thus summarily and unconvincingly set out can, in the remainder of the *Republic*, in its full metaphysical development, be taken more seriously.

---

[13] See below, ch.8.

Chapter 2
Morality as Mental Health

Dissatisfaction

The first book of the *Republic* ends on a tentative note. Like many of the earlier dialogues, it raises questions rather than offering answers. We can imagine Book I of the *Republic* as a radio play, in which some typical characters express some typical opinions, which are then shown to be much more open to criticism than their proponents had realised. The actual arguments put in the mouth of Socrates are unconvincing. The best that can be said for them is that they make you think. The same can be said of many of Plato's early dialogues, the 'Socratic dialogues'. They show an opinionated individual, overly confident of his own opinions, being tripped up by Socrates, who does not himself express any views, but is content to be a gad-fly, forcing people to think for themselves, and not take their opinions second-hand from the conventional wisdom of their day. They are dramatic, with sharp delineation of character, easy to read, but negative in content. Although it is hard to fault any single dialogue, cumulatively they exasperate us, leaving us with a sense of not getting anywhere. They make us think, but they do not carry conviction. If we met Cephalus or Thrasymachus at a party, we should no longer be ready to accept their word for it that honesty was just giving back what one had borrowed, or that morality was a mug's game. But though they had been shown up, we should not be convinced that their positions were indefensible. Cleverer men might have done better. The local Marxist has been worsted in an argument in the village pub, but we are not sure that Marxism has really been refuted: when challenged to say exactly what we meant by some term, 'civilisation', say, we were at a loss, but we do not concede that we did not know what we meant when we used the word. Thrasymachus was made a fool of, but then he was a fool all along. A more skilful sophist could have made a better case for amoralism, and might be able to establish that morality is merely the ideology by means of which the dominant class keeps the rest of us in servile obedience to their wishes.

The reader is reasonably dissatisfied; even Socrates expresses dissatisfaction at the end of Book I. Questions have been asked which demand proper answers, not further questions. The rest of the *Republic* offers answers to this demand.

Structure of the *Republic*

Books II-X of the *Republic* are markedly different from Book I. Whereas we can imagine Book I as a radio play, the remaining books could only be broadcast as a series of lectures. Apart from the first two speeches by Glaucon and Adeimantus, there is no serious dialogue. It is just Socrates talking, with an occasional 'Of course', or 'How could it be otherwise?', to ease the flow of argument, and such drama as there is (432d, 580bc) seems somewhat contrived. Answers are offered, not only to the questions raised in Book I, but to many others as well. It seems natural to suppose—though many scholars controvert it—that Book I of the *Republic* was originally written as a separate book, possibly called Περὶ Δικαίου, *On Honesty*, and later incorporated into a more extensive treatise that attempted to work things out in a positive and comprehensive fashion.

If the *Republic* was not originally written all in one go, we can detect further stages in how it might have been composed. Book I raises the questions 'What is δικαιοσύνη?' and 'Is δικαιοσύνη worth it?'. In Book II (357-368) Glaucon and Adeimantus raise the question whether morality is worth it, or whether the amoral life is a better bet: they re-state Thrasymachus' amoralist thesis, and challenge Socrates to do better than he had in Book I. Socrates gives an answer at the end of Book IV (444c-445a). The moral man has an integrity of personality which is the psychological analogue to bodily health; and just as health is a good we all seek, so we should, if we are sensible, seek the psychological health that the moral life engenders and expresses. In order thus to justify morality, Plato needs to give—what he fails to do in Book I— some sort of account of what morality is. He draws an analogy between the individual and society which occupies the greater part of Books II, III and IV (368c-435a). It is a moot point whether the individual or the social aspect is dominant in his thinking,[1] but he evidently was very much concerned with the social side of the good life, and could have published his thoughts on the *Constitution of Society*, in which his earlier tentative probings are followed up by a positive account of the social context and psychological inwardness of the moral life.

At the end of Book IV (445c) Socrates starts to consider the less good constitutions of society and the individual psyche, but before he can develop his account, he is interrupted by Polemarchus and Adeimantus, who pick him up on some of his more outrageous suggestions on how the good society must be constituted, thereby starting a long digression which continues until the end of Book VII. Only in Book VIII is the main thread of argument resumed, and the increasingly bad constitutions delineated. The worst is the autistic autocrat, who occupies the first third of Book IX, leading up to a climax in 580, where Socrates suggests they should hire a herald to announce the verdict that the completely moral life in the completely moral society is far, far happier than the completely amoral life in the completely amoral society. This makes a natural conclusion to a second edition of the *Constitution*

---

[1] See below p.26.

of Society, consisting of *Republic* Books I-IV, VIII and IX. Glaucon's and Adeimantus' challenge to Socrates at the outset of Book II is answered more fully, showing not only that the moral life is worth it, but that the alternatives are emphatically not better bets.

Books V, VI and VII are ostensibly a digression, in which Socrates is called on to justify the guardians having to share women and children. But he rapidly moves on to the character and education of the φιλόσοφος, in which he raises fundamental questions of epistemology and metaphysics, which do not normally engage the attention of thinkers seeking to delineate the ideal society. It might be that Plato simply allowed himself to be diverted into discussing topics he found interesting although they were not really relevant to the *Constitution of Society*, but they are relevant. Plato needs his metaphysics to underwrite the objectivity of moral and political argument; and it is the mystical experience of the vision of the Form of the Good that inspires the guardians to their selfless dedication to intellectual search and public service. If, as Protagoras maintained, Man is the Measure of all things, the second version of the *Constitution of Society* would be open to the rejoinder that it offered only one option among many, and it was not an option that appealed to contemporary men. Only if it was grounded in some reality independent of the fleeting fashions of public opinion, could the objective superiority of the ideal society be secured against the dismissive sneers of contemporary opinion formers.

A similar consideration may be behind the arguments of the remainder of Book IX (580-588), where Plato sets out to show that the moral life is not only better than the alternatives but more pleasurable. The arguments are not very good, and we may wonder why Plato included them.[2] The serious-minded young men were already convinced, but there could be others who did not look beneath the surface of things, and were concerned only with the experience of the moment; rather than engage on an arduous study of mathematics and philosophy, they might opt for the immediate pleasures of wine, women and song, brushing off all reproaches with the words 'It is foolish, but it's fun'. To them it might be pertinent to point out that the fun was inherently fleeting, because it was in the nature of pleasure to be soon satiated rather than go on being satisfying, and that there were higher pleasures of a more exquisite kind. We can envisage Plato adding these afterthoughts as two appendices to the *Constitution of Society*. But appendices in the ancient world could not be described as such, and form an unsatisfying end to a dialogue. The last pages of Book IX (588-592), although slightly repetitive, constitute a summary and suitable finale to the whole work. But a further rejoinder on poetry seemed called for,[3] which again left an awkward

---

[2] But see further, ch.8, pp.110-111.

[3] See below ch.12, pp.156-157.

ending. The myth of Er provides a fitting epilogue. It relaxes the restriction imposed in Book II which excluded all considerations about what might befall us in the after life, and enables Plato to address the problem of evil, and the way men could be reasonably rewarded in the next world for what they had done in this. Having raised the question in Book I, ὄντινα τρόπον χρὴ ζῆν, what way to live, Plato can conclude with the words εὖ πράττωμεν, we may fare well.

The Case Against Morality

Plato takes great care to formulate precisely the challenge which Glaucon and Adeimantus put to Socrates at the beginning of Book II of the *Republic*. Glaucon accounts for morality as an an external constraint imposed on us by society, running counter to our own individual inclinations and interests. We would, if we could, be free of the shackles of morality, so as to be able to indulge our desires without fear of consequences. This shows that morality is not an intrinsic good, but a set of inhibitions inculcated by society for the benefit of others.

Protagoras, according to Plato's account,[4] explained our being constrained to be moral, as a social necessity; Plato articulates his account in terms of the Theory of Games. Each of us individually would do better if he could act immorally, but would fare worse—much worse—if he suffered from the immoral actions of other people. 'By nature, men say, to do wrong is good, to suffer it evil. Men therefore agree that it is more profitable that they should neither inflict wrong nor suffer it. Hence 'men began to establish laws and covenants with one another, νόμους τίθεσθαι καὶ συνθήκας, and they called what the law prescribed lawful and right'. Each trying to do the best for himself, suffers from the actions of others likewise motivated, with the result that we are all worse off than we need be if only we were, all of us, moral. This is the first appearance of the state of nature in political philosophy. In the most famous later development of it Thomas Hobbes sees its implications more clearly than Glaucon. Not only will such unrestricted war of man against man inflict particular evils on individuals but by preventing any joint action, it will impoverish the lives and frustrate the purposes of everyone.

> Whatsoever, therefore is consequent to a time of war where every man is enemy to every man: the same is consequent to the time wherein men live without other security that what their own strength and their own invention shall furnish them withal. In such condition there is no place for industry: because the fruit thereof is uncertain: and consequently no culture of the earth; no navigation, nor use of the commodities that may be imported by sea; no commodious building; no instruments of moving and removing such things as require much force; no knowledge of the face of the earth; no account of time; no arts; no letters; no society; and, which is worst of all,

---

[4] *Protagoras* 322ff.

continual fear and danger of violent death; and the life of man solitary, poor, nasty, brutish and short.[5]

We are, in modern parlance, trapped in a Prisoners' Dilemma.[6] In such a situation, morality makes collective sense, though a nonsense from each individual's point of view. To close the gap between individual and collective rationality, we may have to establish a system of social and legal sanctions, as Hobbes argued,though for many nice people brain-washing in early life is sufficient.

The Prisoners' Dilemma gives a plausible account of the origin of altruistic behaviour among men and other social animals; and hence a plausible counter-argument against those who hold that conscience witnesses to our having access to moral truth. There is, it would seem, a gap between collective and individual rationality which cannot itself be bridged rationally, but only by extrinsic social constraints. Glaucon illustrates his point with the fable of Gyges' ring, which conferred invisibility whenever its wearer wanted it, and enabled him to seize the throne of Lydia. The fable is corroborated by the grudging admiration society gives to those who get away with some piece of sharp practice. We admire such success, and secretly wish we were men enough to be able to sin and brazen it out if need be. Deep down inside each one of us is a Nietzschean Superman struggling to get out.

Glaucon gives a plausible naturalistic account. Adeimantus then deals with super-natural arguments for morality. Either the gods do not exist, or do not care, or if they do, they can be manipulated much as humans can. Humans can be deceived: gods can be bribed. Whereas the competent amoralist deceives his fellow men, thereby obtaining an undeserved reputation for being moral, the sophisticated sinner secures absolution by suitable sacrifices and appropriate rites. The gods cannot be deceived, as men can, but they may overlook or forget, and can be induced to forgive—that, according to some, is what they are for.

Adeimantus sums up the case against morality (II 366b3-367a4) and then challenges Socrates to show that morality is better than doing wrong irre-spective of public reputation or theological sanctions (II 357a5-e5). Socrates accepts the challenge (II 367e6-368c), but then embarks on a long digression on the ideal state, before finally answering it at the end of Book IV.

The exact form of the challenge is important. It rules out certain sorts of answers, and largely determines the answers Socrates finally gives. It rules out the Intuitionist answer that the claims of moral obligations are self-evident, neither needing nor admitting any further reason why they are mandatory. It

---

[5] *Leviathan*, I.13, §9; p.82 in Michael Oakeshott's ed. (Blackwell, 1946); p.84 in J.C.A.Gaskin's ed. (OUP, 1996).

[6] See Edna Ullmann-Margalit, *The Emergence of Norms*, Oxford, 1977, ch.2.

rules out also ordinary utilitarian and other consequentialist justifications. In particular, it rules out the standard rejoinder to the thoughtless youth who does not see why he should allow consideration for other people to stand in the way of his pursuit of his own interests. To the inconsiderate young it is an adequate answer to point out that if you are not nice to others, they will not be nice to you, but to the thoughtful questioner the real conclusion of that argument is, as Glaucon points out (II 361a), the eleventh commandment: τὸν ἁλισκόμενον φαῦλον ἡγητέον, thou shouldst not be found out. Glaucon has stipulated that all such worldly extrinsic considerations should be excluded (II 357-362c), and Adeimantus has added the requirement that other-worldly extrinsic considerations should be excluded too (II 362e-367e). Both are at pains not to deny that such justifications are valid, but the justification they are seeking is to be a non-consequentialist one.

It might seem that in ruling out appeals to the self-evidence of moral arguments and all consequentialist considerations, Glaucon and Adeimantus had ruled out every conceivable justification. But variants on these approaches escape their ban. The eleventh commandment is not the only reason a selfish man might have for being moral. Even if he escapes detection, he cannot be sure that he always will. I may not actually be punished, but the possibility remains; I shall have to live with the fear of punishment. In *Crime and Punishment* Dostoevsky presents a gripping account of how Raskolnikov commits the perfect crime, but is then led to confess it by the fear of being found out. However perfect my crime, I cannot be absolutely sure that the truth will not one day come out, and even if I reckon realistically that the probability is very low, and that the balance of expected advantage is overwhelmingly in favour of committing the crime, I should also reckon, knowing myself realistically, that I should not be able to suppress nagging doubts, and that the great benefits the crime would bring were not worth securing at the cost of my peace of mind. I should be deterred not by the fear of punishment but by the fear of the fear of punishment.

A critic might complain that the fear of the fear of punishment was an effect, albeit a psychological effect, as much as punishment itself, and the other rewards and reputation ruled out by Adeimantus. We need to follow Cross and Woozley and distinguish consequences from results.[7] Although he dismisses consequences, Plato does attend to the results of virtue, those things that follow necessarily or naturally from it. He wants to show that morality is an intrinsic good. And the Greek he uses makes 'intrinsic' mean the same as 'internal':

αὐτὸ δ'ἑκάτερον τῇ αὑτοῦ δυνάμει τί δρᾷ, τῇ τοῦ ἔχοντος ψυχῇ ἐνόν,
καὶ λανθάνον θεούς τε καὶ ἀνθρώπους, οὐ᾽δεὶς πώποτε οὔτ᾽ἐν ποιήσει

---

[7] R.C.Cross and A.D.Woozley, *Plato's Republic: A Philosophical Commentary*, London, 1966, pp.66-68.

οὔτ᾽ ἐν ἰδίοις λόγοις ἐπεξῆλθεν ἱκανῶς τῷ λόγῳ ὡς τὸ μὲν μέγιστον κακῶν ὅσα ἴσχει ψυχὴ ἐν αὐτῇ, δικαιοσύνη δὲ μέγιστον ἀγαθόν.

Nobody, either in poetry or in private discussion, has ever given adequate consideration to the effect of morality and selfishness on the personality in which they operate, even though concealed from gods and men, nor proved that the one is the greatest benefit, the other the greatest evil, for the personality that has them. (II 366e5-9).

The crucial phrase is τῇ τοῦ ἔχοντος ψυχῇ ἐνόν, (te_i tou echontos psuche_i enon), 'on the personality in which they operate'; the intrinsic merits and demerits—those that are concealed from gods and men—are the internal effects they have on the inner person.[8] The demand is for an internal, psychological justification of morality, to show that δικαιοσύνη is like τὸ φρονεῖν καὶ τὸ ὁρᾶν καὶ τὸ ὑγιαίνειν, thinking, seeing and being healthy (II 357c2-3). This Plato gives at the end of Book IV. It is a more profound justification than Dostoevsky's. Raskolnikov committed the perfect crime, but was not the perfect criminal. The perfectly selfish man should not suffer from psychological weakness. The possibility of the perfect criminal being found out is like the possibility of his being hit by a passing asteroid: not zero, but very, very small and therefore negligible. Plato argues for a psychological disturbance which is not merely contingent on our being only imperfectly wicked, but stems from the nature of the case. We can argue in more modern terms: in order to seem moral, and to be able to pass myself off as a moral man, I have got to know what morality is, and what it requires of me in every situation in which I may find myself. I must know that some of the things I do are wrong, in order to avoid doing, when they may be observed, other things that are wrong. I cannot be always able to do the right thing when required, unless I have a full understanding of what is the right thing to do. But if I do know what the right thing to do was, and also know that I did not do it, these two bits of knowledge are out of harmony with each other. So, if I am to be perfectly selfish, able always to seem to be moral, without really being so, and acting very wrongly when opportunity offers, I shall necessarily suffer from psychological dissonance between the norms I have to internalise in order to be able always to seem to be moral, and the realisation of what I have actually done on those occasions when I have overstepped the mark of accepted morality in order to gain for myself some great prize.

Thus Plato's first justification of morality is on grounds of psychological health: morality goes hand in hand with mental health, and selfishness with personality disorders.

---

[8] See further below, pp.24-28.

Identification with Society

Socrates, having accepted Adeimantus' challenge, immediately suggests that
the analogy between societies and individuals could help, and launches into a
discussion of the basic form of society, which then is developed in the remainder of Book II, Book III, and the beginning of Book IV (up to 427c), after
which δικαιοσύνη, (dikaiosune), justice, is identified as a feature of society.
Only then do we return to the individual, identify δικαιοσύνη (dikaiosune),
integrity, as a feature of individual men, and determine whether it is more
conducive to the good life to have it or not to have it. The exact status of
the analogy in Plato's argument will be considered in the next section, but
the shift of attention from the individual to society has a profound effect on
the implicit appeal of the Republic.

Plato argues for the most basic form of society from our need to cooperate
in order to satisfy our wants. As with the Prisoners' Dilemma, it is illuminating to analyse the problem in terms of the Theory of Games.[9] In many
cases we can secure short-term cooperation by bargaining on the basis of some
reciprocity; but often there is no obvious basis for a bargain, and both parties
are guided by conventions, which are purely conventional, νόμῳ (nomoi) not
φύσει (phusei). In the modern world the Highway Code is a familiar example,
but language itself is a much more fundamental example. No law of nature
lays down that 'men' should refer to specimens of homo sapiens in English,
while μὲν (men) should mean 'on the one hand' in Greek; but we are impelled to use the word according to the standard usages of English or Greek,
because we wish to be understood. 'Cooperation norms' are pervasive in our
social life, widely and whole-heartedly accepted because they are evidently
to everyone's advantage. Whereas in abstaining from stealing your goods, I
am conscious of some strain between my own unfettered self-interest and the
long-term advantages of social life, in passing the time of day, chatting you
up, or arranging an expedition for tomorrow, I have no inclination to cast
off the shackles of current linguistic usage in order to assert my autonomy of
action. So too with dancing, so too with etiquette, so too with a myriad of
unremarked customs that constitute our social life. We embrace them, and
regard them as a common possession, and as constituting a shared identity.
We are led from the first person singular to the first person plural without any
sense of sacrifice. In identifying with my society I enhance myself, rather than
diminish my individuality. Better be one of many Athenians, than Robinson
Crusoe, sole lord of his lonely isle.

The gap between collective and individual rationality, which we need to
traverse if we are to escape from the Prisoners' Dilemma, disappears if the
individual identifies with the community. I do not regret the time I spent on

---

[9] See Edna Ullmann-Margalit, The Emergence of Norms, Oxford, 1977, ch.3.

the football field, or the bruises I suffered, if we won. My identity is largely constituted by the communities I am proud to be a member of. My father's name is my name, my children's success is my success, I shout for the school or college team at matches, I take to heart national reverses and defeats, and, in time of war at any rate, I am prepared to make great sacrifices for my country. Plato does not make this point explicitly, but in developing an account of the ideal society, he is inviting us to identify with it; if we are caught up in enthusiasm for it, we shall no longer cherish an individual interest that might tempt us to break rules designed to further the interests of the community.

In Book I, Plato sees $\pi\lambda\epsilon o\nu\epsilon\xi\acute{\iota}\alpha$, getting the most for me, as the underlying cause of $\mathring{\alpha}\delta\iota\kappa\acute{\iota}\alpha$, wrongdoing. Selfishness, as ordinarily understood, we readily suppose to be the root of all evil. Plato sees the ideal society as the remedy for this kind of selfishness.[10] If we could all identify completely with the community we live in, then we should no longer quarrel over individual possessions, and could live together in amity and peace. The actual communities we actually live in are difficult to identify with completely. However strongly I feel myself to be English, there are many things England has done that I am ashamed of, and many occasions where England, in spite of my good advice, takes the wrong decision. The same for University, College, Church, and the many other communities I am a member of and partially identify with. If I am to identify with a community completely, it must be an ideal one. But if there were an ideal society, I could, so Plato believes, identify with it completely, so much so that I would no longer use the word $\mathring{\epsilon}\mu\acute{o}\nu$, 'mine', in a singular sense, but only as meaning 'ours' (V 463e5– 464d5). Underlying the explicit argument of the *Republic* that morality, $\delta\iota\kappa\alpha\iota o\sigma\acute{\upsilon}\nu\eta$, is the best policy, is an implicit appeal to overcome one's selfishness by identifying with the ideal society, thus transmuting the unlovely concern for self into selfless idealism in promoting the good of the community.

It is a powerful appeal. It has inspired many to devote themselves altruistically to the common good. But in our age we are aware, as Plato could not be, of the dangers of corporate aggrandisement. We know that it is not only individuals who can err and stray from the true path. Whole communities can run *amok*, and the more devoted their members, the more dangerous their armies. If the Germans had been self-indulgent, lackadaisical and cowardly, Nazism would have posed no threat to Europe.

---

10 The selfishness that Plato is against is the selfishness of ordinary life. Insofar as he gives prudential arguments in Book IV and Book IX for the moral life, morality can be seen as a kind of higher selfishness. Our concept of self has been much influenced by Christianity long after Plato's time. Here and in chapters 3 and 10 we are concerned with crude self-aggrandisment.

We also need to question Plato's implicit assumption that selflessness is the right antithesis to selfishness. Selflessness is not the same as unselfishness. The unselfish man is prepared to give up his own advantage for the benefit of others when their interests conflict, but does not abjure self-interest absolutely. We may admire the unconcern with self displayed by the selfless man, but may feel also somewhat uncomfortable in his proximity. True, he can be relied upon not to sacrifice our interests for the sake of his own; but will he have any compunction in sacrificing our interests for the sake of some higher good, as he sees it? And can we feel any affinity or close intimacy with someone who has schooled himself not to feel the inclinations or to have the ambitions that we experience as part of our human lot? In imposing selflessness instead of merely requiring a due degree of unselfishness, Plato may have maimed his guardians, precluding their being able to develop their personalities to the full.[11]

The Analogy between Individuals and Societies

The analogy is put forward in 368d2-7:

εἰ προσέταξέ τις γράμματα σμικρὰ πόρρωθεν ἀναγνῶναι μὴ πάνυ ὀξὺ βλέπουσιν, ἔπειτά τις ἐνενόησεν, ὅτι τὰ αὐτὰ γράμματα ἔστι που καὶ ἄλλοθι μείζω τε καὶ ἐν μείζονι, ἕρμαιον ἂν ἐφάνη οἶμαι ἐκεῖνα πρῶτον ἀναγνόντας οὕτως ἐπισκοπεῖν τὰ ἐλάττω, εἰ τὰ αὐτὰ ὄντα τυγχάνει. If someone told us to read some small letters at a distance, and we cannot see them very well, and someone else observed that the same notice is also written up somewhere else in much larger letters, it would indeed be a godsend, and we would read the larger ones first, and only then examine the smaller to see if they really were the same.

What is the status of the analogy? Is it merely a heuristic device? Or is it a premise on which a rigorous argument is being constructed? Plato does not make it very obvious which he intends. At a first reading it seems that he is placing great weight on the analogy, and that it should be understood in the second sense: but a more detailed examination of the text, combined with general considerations of the structure of the *Republic* leads us to adopt the former interpretation, and to say that the analogy, although important for Plato's thought, particularly his political thought, is not essential to the main argument of the *Republic*.

If we take the view that Plato meant the analogy between societies and individuals to be taken as a premise of an argument, then the way in which the argument is developed is entirely natural. We are given that societies and individuals are like each other: we discover that δικαιοσύνη, justice, in society is minding one's own business, τὸ τὰ αὑτοῦ πράττειν (*to ta hautou prattein*),

---

[11] See further, ch.10, p.134.

therefore an individual has δικαιοσύνη, integrity, if his component parts mind their own business too. But the status of the premise, when we think about it further, is dubious. If someone told us to read some small letters at a distance, and we cannot see them very well, and someone else observed that the same notice is also written up somewhere else in much larger letters, it would indeed be a godsend, and we would read the larger ones first, and only then examine the smaller to see if they really were the same (II 368d2-7). But how does the someone else know that the two notices are the same? If I see a large notice up saying Mammoth Sale Jan. 3-9, I shall be sadly mistaken if I assume that a smaller notice, saying Municipal Swimming Baths and Sports Gymnasium, is the same as the larger one. The mere fact that there are two notices is not enough to establish that they are the same: and the mere fact that there are both individuals and societies is not enough to show that they are similar in the relevant respects. There could be independent grounds for knowing that two notices were the same. They might both have the royal coat-of-arms on, and I might work in H.M. Stationery Office and know that the only royal proclamation recently issued was to announce the dissolution of parliament. Similarly, Plato might have some *a priori* reason for believing that societies and individuals were similar. But he does not produce it. And without some justification of the key premise, the whole argument falls to the ground. There only remains the possibility that the man knows that the two notices are the same because he has been able to read the smaller one, and so see that it is the same as the larger. But in that case the larger notice is otiose. All we need to do is to get him to read out the smaller. The only way we can know that δικαιοσύνη, justice, is the same in society and in the individual is to know what it is in society and what it is in the individual: and if we know what it is in the individual, there is no need to devote two books of the *Republic* to determining what it is in society, in order to discover what it is in the individual. Hence either the analogy is broken-backed or else it is unnecessary.

It follows that Plato cannot have meant the analogy to be regarded as a premise for a rigorous argument; and closer examination of what he actually says shows that he did not. Although the bystander had observed ὅτι τὰ αὐτὰ γράμματα ἔστι που καὶ ἄλλοθι (*hoti ta auta grammata esti pou kai allothi*), *that* the same letters were there and somewhere else (II 368d4-5), what the others, ourselves included, are being invited to do is to read the large notice first, and then see εἰ τὰ αὐτὰ ὄντα τυγχάνει (*ei ta auta onta tunchanei*) *whether* they really are the same. Plato himself has observed δικαιοσύνη, justice, in both society and the individual, and has seen that they are the same, but thinks that we shall find it easier first to consider it in the large in society, and then see whether it be the same in the individual. It is a reasonable procedure. So far as our visual experience goes, it is a help in making out a distant notice if one has an idea of what it is going to say. The local man can read the destination plate on the front of a bus long before the stranger, because he knows what it may say: he has to answer only the one question 'Is it, or is it not, a number 1 going to the Station', whereas the stranger has confusingly many questions he needs to answer. Similarly, biologists being taught to use the microscope, need to look at diagrams, not photographs, beforehand, because unless they know what to look for, they will not be able to see it.

Plato, having discovered the nature of individual personality by looking at the little letters directly, makes it easier for us to see them by portraying justice, in the large first. The analogy for him is not essential, and he does not first look at society and then read into the individual what he finds in society: rather, the other way round; Plato reads into society a structure which he first discerned in the individual. The threefold division is not a natural or convincing one when applied to society. If one was going to distinguish three classes, one would not normally pick on academics, policemen and the rest. Even if one picks out a ruling class and their supporters, one would hesitate to lump peasants, industrial workers and merchants together, all into one class. But, as we shall argue, Plato's threefold division of facets of personality is a good one, and it would be reasonable, having hit upon it, to suppose that the same held good in society, for, as Plato says,

Οἶσθ' οὖν, ἦν δ'ἐγώ, ὅτι καὶ ἀνθρώπων εἴδη τοσαῦτα ἀνάγκη τρόπων εἶναι, ὅσαπερ καὶ πολιτειῶν· ἢ οἴει ἐκ δρυός ποθεν ἢ ἐκ πέτρας τὰς πολιτείας γίγνεσθαι, ἀλλ᾽ οὐχὶ ἐκ τῶν ἠθῶν τῶν ἐν ταῖς πόλεσιν, ἃ ἂν ὥσπερ ῥέψαντα τἆλλα ἐφελκύσηται. You realise that there must be as many types of individual as there are of society. Or do you think that societies come out of a tree somewhere or out of a rock, and not from that behaviour of their members which predominates and sets the tone for everything else. (VIII 544d-e)

That is, although for the reader the analogy is to take us from society to the individual, for Plato himself the analogy goes the other way. Society is like the individual, not the individual like society. If the analogy is only an expository device, it must remain open that we shall be unable to read the small letters, even after having read the large ones. Plato explicitly allows for this possibility at the end of the analogy in Book IV (434d-435a) where he says:

ὃ οὖν ἡμῖν ἐκεῖ ἐφάνη, ἐπαναφέρωμεν εἰς τὸν ἕνα, κἂν μὲν ὁμολογῆται, καλῶς ἕξει· ἐὰν δέ τι ἄλλο ἐν τῇ ἑνὶ ἐμφαίνηται, πάλιν ἐπανιόντες ἐπὶ τὴν πόλιν βασανιοῦμεν, καὶ τάχ᾽ ἂν παρ᾽ ἄλληλα σκοποῦντες καὶ τρίβοντες, ὥσπερ ἐκ πυρείων ἐκλάμψαι ποιήσαιμεν τὴν δικαιοσύνην· καὶ φανερὰν γενομένην βεβαιωσόμεθα αὐτὴν παρ᾽ ἡμῖν αὐτοῖς. We must check our conclusions about society against the individual: if they agree, well and good, if anything different emerges as a feature of the individual, we must go back to society for a further check, and by examining

and rubbing them against one another make justice come, in the same way
as fire from rubbing sticks together.

Plato then goes on to examine the nature of individual personality, and dis-
cerns in it the same structure as in society. Whether we agree with him or
not depends on how convincing we find his arguments in Book IV after he
has finished the analogy with society. These must stand in their own right.
But provided they do, Plato is quite entitled to use the analogy as a heuristic
and expository device, and cannot be blamed for having done so.

Nevertheless his use of the analogy was unfortunate. It misled him in his
identification of δικαιοσύνη, justice, and caused him to convert the external
virtue of Book I and traditional Greek morality into the internal calm state
of mind he extols at the end of Book IV.

Τὸ δέ γε ἀληθές, τοιοῦτόν τι ἦν, ὡς ἔοικεν, ἡ δικαιοσύνη ἀλλ᾽ οὐ περὶ
τὴν ἔξω πρᾶξιν τῶν αὑτοῦ, ἀλλὰ περὶ τὴν ἐντός, It seems then that
really justice is not concerned with external behaviour, but with what goes
on inside, concerning the individual himself and his own affairs... (443c9-d1)

Plato is led to this conclusion because he gets the wires crossed between the
relationship of analogy which he supposes to hold between the individual
and society, and the relationship of membership which undoubtedly holds
between them. Individuals may or may not resemble societies, and *vice versa*,
but societies are certainly composed of individuals as members, and some of
the things we say about societies are in virtue of things already said about
their members. 'Britain is slack and self-indulgent' is a short-hand way of
saying that the citizens of Britain are slack and self-indulgent: and similarly
'Britain is a law-abiding country' is a short-hand way of saying that the
British are law-abiding. Plato identifies δικαιοσύνη, justice, in society as
τὸ τὰ αὑτοῦ πράττειν, minding one's own business (433a), and argues for
this identification by pointing out that the courts of justice aim to assign
to each individual the things that are his, and that if an individual fails to
perform his allotted task he is wronging society (IV 433e6-8, 434a-c). These
arguments are telling provided we give δικαιοσύνη its traditional, external,
sense. For then if the citizens are δίκαιοι, they will refrain from invading one
another's spheres of influence, both out of respect for their rights and out of
a general regard for the common good; and a πόλις, society, will be δίκαια,
just, if its πολῖται, citizens, are δίκαιοι, just, and so will show the features
described. But having established what δικαιοσύνη, justice, in the πόλις,
society, is, by virtue of its being *composed of δίκαιοι*, just, individuals, Plato
goes on to use the other relationship, not of membership but of resemblance,
and argues that an individual is δίκαιος, just, if he shows in himself the same
features as a δίκαια, just, society does in itself. According to this line of
argument, whether a society is δίκαια, just, law-abiding, or not is a matter
for its Home Office (or Ministry of the Interior, or Justice Department): to

say that there was an outbreak of ἀδικία, injustice, would mean that the citizens had stopped being δίκαιοι, and each was taking what belonged to someone else, or conversely was being deprived of what was his own, and was not fulfilling his *role* in society. And it would be the business of the Home Office (or Ministry of the Interior, or Justice Department) not the Foreign Office (or State Department), to put matters right. But there is another sense in which Britain could be said to be unjust that is concerned with foreign affairs. When the French talk of Perfidious Albion, they do not mean that each and every Briton is dishonest. They mean that Britain in its international relations with other countries is dishonest. It could be that every individual Briton was δίκαιος, honest, in his dealings with other men, but that Britain as a nation was dishonest in its dealings with other nations. In that case Britain could be said to be δίκαια, honest, in the Home Office sense—that is, its citizens were all individually honest—but not in the Foreign Office sense—it could not be trusted as a collective whole to be honest in its dealings with other nations. What Plato has done is to start with the individual and a fairly traditional, external sense of δικαιοσύνη, justice; and argue that δικαιοσύνη, justice in society is simply a question of whether the members of that society are individually δίκαιοι, just, so that it is an internal matter; and then argue that since individuals resemble societies, δικαιοσύνη, justice, must be an internal matter for the individual too. But this is to confuse the two different senses in which a society may be said to be δίκαια, just: the internal and the external.[12]

Two other factors predisposed Plato to ignore the external facet of δικαιοσύνη, justice. The first is the ambiguity, noted above, in the phrase τῇ τοῦ ἔχοντος ψυχῇ ἐνόν (te_i tou echontos psuche_i enon), 'on the personality in which they operate', (366e6) which suggests that an intrinsic justification of δικαιοσύνη, justice, must be one in terms of its internal results, and thus makes Plato the readier to see δικαιοσύνη, as integrity, an internal state of mind in order the better to prove that it is intrinsically good.

The second factor is Plato's political isolationism. He does not consider the problem of whether his ideal society should be δίκαια, honest, in its dealings with other societies, because he does not want it to have any dealings with them at all, since that would require some of the guardians to serve in the Foreign Office, and live abroad and contract corrupting ideas from

---

[12] For a more critical assessment of Plato's use of analogy, see Bernard Williams, 'The Analogy of City and Soul in Plato's *Republic*; E.N.Lee, A.P.D.Mourelatos and R.M.Rorty, eds., *Exegesis and Argument: Studies in Greek Philosophy Presented to Gregory Vlastos*, Assen, 1973, pp.196-208. Williams thesis was countered by Jonathan Lear, 'Inside and Outside the *Republic*', *Phronesis*, **37**, 1992, pp.184-215. Both articles are reprinted in R.Kraut, ed., *Plato's Republic: Critical Essays*, New York, 1997, as chs. 4 and 5, pp.49-59 and 61-94.

abroad, and some foreign diplomats to live in the ideal society and spread their un-ideal ideals among the citizens.

Mental Metaphors

Plato argues for his Theory of Personality, independently of the analogy with society, in *Republic* IV 436a8-441c8. He sets out first to establish that the personality is divided into parts, and then that the parts can be classified into three groups.

The claim that the personality is divided is fair, but runs into many terminological difficulties. The stock translation of ψυχή, soul, is unfortunate, because it is deeply embedded in our notion of soul that souls are indivisible. Moreover, the word 'soul' often has theological overtones. It is the right word to translate ψυχή, in the *Phaedo*, and again in Book X of the *Republic*, where Plato is discussing immortality, but when we are talking about psychology, the word we use is 'person', or occasionally, 'mind'. Again, to talk about parts can mislead, because it has materialistic overtones, and leads some people to think that Plato thought that if you open up the head you will find in it the λογιστικόν part, the θυμοειδές part and the ἐπιθυμητικόν part. Unfortunately Plato does sometimes countenance rather crude interpretations of his metaphors—*e.g.* Book IX, 588-589—and then objections must be made. It cannot be literally true that the workings of the human mind are to be explained by reason of the fact that each individual man is really a society of little men, organized together in a three-class society, and our various desires and decisions can be explained in terms of the balance of power between these three classes. For then how do we explain how these little men come to vote, to order, to obey as they do? Are they composed in turn of minute men? But in that case .... and so on, down an infinite regress. Alternatively, if the little men are not so composed, then, since in that case we can explain the little men without bringing in the πόλις, society, model, we could explain the big men also without bringing in that model, so why have it at all? That is, the πόλις model taken literally can only explain what it was meant to explain in terms of what it was meant to explain; so either it leads one down an infinite regress or it begs the question: either it is useless or it is unnecessary. In either case it is a bad model.

This criticism is fair. But it applies not only to Plato's, but to any account of the *psyche*. Plato's psychological terminology is a metaphorical one drawn from social intercourse. Modern psychological terminology is a metaphorical one too, but it is drawn from the language of physical science, the dominant thought-form of our time. The springs of action for modern man are motives and impulses, drives and inclinations; these are the motivating forces that make human beings tick; if they are impeded they will cause some friction, and often serious stresses and strains which will upset one's equilibrium. So much for Newton. Hydrostatics and hydrodynamics have not contributed so much, but occasionally the *psyche* is likened to a vessel containing liquid under pressure, and a tidal surge in the subconscious may burst out and overflow into the conscious. The most modern popular physical theory about the nature of the universe is that of electromagnetism, and high-grade people now have magnetic or electric personalities, and exercise mutual attractions and repulsions on one another—they are highly charged, their emotions are at a high potential and liable to be suddenly discharged, and it is possible to short-circuit these high-voltage systems. Chemistry is not so popular, though some hostesses claim to be good catalysts. When quantum mechanics catches on, resonance phenomena will come into fashion. Already, indeed, up-to-date people are on the contemporary wavelength.

This is only a *tu quoque*. But it illustrates that it is impossible to talk about the self without indulging in metaphor—not just ornamental metaphor which can be replaced by literal unvarnished truth, but essential metaphor which cannot be cashed into literal terms. This is because what we are talking about is private, unshareable, introspective experience, and the standards of literalness are, of necessity, public, shareable, and external. So we are faced with a dilemma.

Either we eschew metaphor, and refer only to behaviour that is overt and observable;

Or we continue to talk about ourselves and our experiences, but at the price of using metaphors and subject to perpetual difficulty in checking the truth of what a person says, or even being sure that you and he mean the same thing by those words—that you are taking him in the sense he means to convey. In brief, we can communicate with each other about our private experiences, but only by using metaphors which do in fact go home. We are right to be on our guard against pushing the metaphors too far, but cannot complain that they are metaphors, unless we are prepared to ban psychological discourse altogether.

The parallel with Freud is worth drawing, because not only is his message much the same, but he too describes the personality in very vivid terms, which are misleading as well as illuminating. He, too, splits the individual into many, but not so much into a well organized society as into a bear garden, in which *Libido*s and *Id*s try to bamboozle or seduce the *Ego*, and have to hide in the trees to avoid big, brutal *Super-Ego*, who goes marching round with the big stick. Plato anticipates Freud in the interpretation of dreams, and, in particular, the Oedipus complex (Book IX, 571c-572c).

Facets of Personality

Plato claims
1. that we have more than one motive for our actions
2. that motives can be classified into three groups.
   (a) ἐπιθυμητικόν, emotional,

(b) θυμοειδές, no natural translation; often rendered 'spirited';
'self-assertive' is better,

(c) λογιστικόν, rational.

Plato's first thesis now seems a truism. But it was not a truism in Plato's day, and is only accepted now because Plato's argument (IV 436-439) is valid. He formulates the Law of Non-contradiction (436b-437c)—the first time in the history of thought—and applies it in 439 to show that since we sometimes suffer from conflicting desires, it must be possible for one and the same man to have more than one desire at the same time. The data are unexceptionable; they are the facts of ordinary experience and common observation. That is, we know each from his own experience, from what other people tell him about theirs, and from observing them hesitating and havering, that people are often torn between two inclinations: our talk about motives is in fact little more than a verbal reformulation of this.

The reader should notice that in this appeal to ordinary experience there are two different sorts of experience being appealed to, or rather that there is one sort which Plato is ostensibly arguing about, and another which makes his arguments seem compelling and significant. The two cases are where we want two things which happen to be incompatible as a matter of fact, and where we want two things which are necessarily incompatible, incompatible as a matter of logic, inconsistent. Examples of the former are common enough: I want to go to the disco, but I want also to go to a Mozart opera, and I have not time for both. Often not shortage of time but shortage of money is the limiting factor: I want both to buy a second-hand computer, and to go to Prague during the summer vacation, and I do not have enough money for both. Such conflicts of desire are common enough—rather too common in fact to be called conflicts, because often we settle them quite easily, sometimes almost without noticing them. Would it not be better to say that it was not a tug of different motives pushing or pulling us in different directions, but rather there was only one motive, say pleasure, or that of maximising one's advantages, and we were only wondering which course would be the most effective means to that end? That retort, or some similar one, which would knock the bottom out of the argument for a division of motives, is what Plato is anticipating and guarding against in the obscure passage which contains the argument about correlatives, 437d-439b. It is a difficult argument to state, even with the resources of modern logic, and since Plato's main conclusion, that we have many different motives, is not seriously disputed now, we shall not discuss it further.

The second sort of incompatibility is more deep-seated: there are occasions where it is not just that the course of the world is so ordered to thwart all our desires being gratified, but that the trouble lies in us ourselves, we really do both want and not want the same thing. We want both to lead a life of ascetic purity and abstention from worldly pleasures, and to go on enjoying these same pleasures. This is the *amo et odi* phenomenon which crops up again and again with human beings; where any very deep feeling tends to go over to its opposite and all strong motives are mixed.[13] It is this latter feature, the inherent contrariness of desire, which makes Plato's account seem so important, so true and so tragic. It is like St Paul's account of the στάσις, conflict, in the inner man.[14] Many other philosophers have noticed it, and Kant's antimonies and Hegel's antitheses are, in part, a reflection of it.

These arguments establish that we are possessed of more than one motive, with the possibility of our suffering from a divided personality if they were not well balanced, or of our having a well integrated one if they are.

Threefold Classification

Plato's second claim (b) is that motives fall into three classes:

(a) ἐπιθυμητικόν, inclinations, or urges,

(b) θυμοειδές, self-assertion,

(c) λογιστικόν, reason.

Why does he divide them into these three classes? Consider the general question we can ask of a person's motives—'What were his motives?' 'What led him to do that?'. Sometimes we can give a simple answer: hunger, thirst, sexual desire, he wanted to be warm, he likes swimming, *etc.* Here we are ascribing to him some simple propensity, sometimes one which is common to us all, sometimes one which only a few possess. The things to note about these is that they are *simple*—there is something we want, which we try to get or do: that is all.

But we often have cases where we would not naturally put forward either of these types of ascriptions of motive. We answer not the question 'What were his motives?' but the question 'What were his reasons?'; we give his justification of his actions rather than a psychologist's account of his motives.

There are other motives which will not fit into these patterns at all: notably motives concerned with the self: assertiveness, wilfulness, a liking to

---

[13] This also is the reason for one frequently noticed difference between the sciences and the humanities, namely that in the sciences contradictories are as far away as possible from one another while in the humanities extremes coalesce and opposites meet (VIII 563b9 cf. *Phaedo* 70c4-72d9).

[14] See *Romans* 7:15-23; see also St Augustine: *Confessions* Book VIII, chapters IX/21-X/24; Butler's Sermon XI in L.A. Selby-Bigge, *British Moralists*, Oxford, 1897, I, §231 last sentence, p.231 top; R.Dalbiez, *Psychoanalytical Method and the Doctrine of Freud*, London, 1948, Vol. I, p.58. See also Butler's Sermon II, esp. §217 in Selby-Bigge's selections, for the general diversity of motives, and the necessity of harmonizing them and arranging them properly.

have one's own way, self-respect, keeping up with the Joneses, ambition, *kudos*, exhibitionism, prestige, face, vanity, a love of power and a love of glory. These are very common; and they will not fit in to the simple analysis. Little Bobby has just taken his sister's spade; it is no good trying to placate sister by giving her another one, nor to get Bobby to relent by promising him a better one—because he did not want it because it was a spade but because it was *hers*. Similarly reparation is a sufficient discharge of injury but not of insult—for that apology is required as well. The love of power is not just a love of the opportunities power gives of satisfying your cravings—the joy is in being able to make anyone do whatever *you* want.

Although we usually contrast reasons with motives, if we have to talk in the neutral third-personal way, as when we are putting forward a theory of personality, we assimilate them: we say 'He thought he ought to do it, and he is a very dutiful person'. Dutifulness, disinterestedness, high-mindedness, altruism, can, in a manner of speaking, be called motives: as when we say 'altruism got the better of selfishness, and ambition of greed.'

Plato then is saying that motives, in this extended sense, can be of three sorts: sometimes we play a passive part, we might as well not be persons but animals, borne along and impelled by animal passions: sometimes we are being active, keeping a tight grip on our natural lusts in the name of self-respect or honour, but being egotistical and proud. And sometimes we are neither, being neither carried away by our passions nor anxious merely to assert our egos, but just doing what we believe right and what we think it is best in the circumstances to do.

Plato is rather uncomfortable about the θυμοειδές, self-assertive, class. He defines it chiefly by exhaustion, showing that a simple dichotomy between λογιστικόν, reason, and ἐπιθυμητικόν, inclination, is inadequate. He does not say in Book IV that it is peculiarly associated with the self, but in Book VIII he associates the class with φιλονεικία, rivalry, and φιλοτιμία, ambition (548c5-7), and with being αὐθάδης, (etymologically from αὐτός, self, and ἥδεσθαι, to please), self-willed (548e4). More clearly still at the end of Book IX, where Plato recapitulates his theory of personality (with some significant alterations), αὐθάδεια, self-assertiveness, is characteristic of the lion-like part of the personality (588-592, esp. 590a9).

Tripartite classifications of this type have a certain plausibility: in the ancient world a version of Plato's became a commonplace. In Book IX he had argued that each type of motive is associated with a particular way of life bringing its own particular sort of pleasure; and the three ways of life, apolaustic, ambitious and academic/altruistic, were much discussed and evaluated in antiquity.[15] Some modern psychologists have adopted a similar

---

[15] See further below, ch.11, p.153.

classification. Sheldon and Stevens distinguish three personality types: Ecto-morphic, mesomorphic and endomorphic. Ectomorphic men are described as being tall, thin—almost scraggy—intellectual, academic; mesomorphic men are muscular, athletic, outgoing, confident, keen on getting their own way and ready to fight for it; endomorphic men are fat, passive—even sluggish except when food or sex are on the horizon—biddable, averse to physical or intel-lectual endeavour.[16] There are evidently many exceptions to this classifica-tion. There are many academics, who, far from being scraggy, are noticeably plump, like David Hume; and some muscular, mesomorphic men, are keen on wine, women and food. Most modern philosophers, however, have been too much impressed with the conflict between Reason and Pathological Inclina-tion to pursue the classification of motives any further. Plato's classification is an improvement on that, although it is still too crude for many purposes. The love of money, at least in modern society, is more bound up with the self than with bodily gratification. Many of our tastes are highly intellectual—is a liking for mathematical logic to be classified as ἐπιθυμητικόν, an inclina-tion, because it is a liking, or with λογιστικόν, something rational, because it is for logic? Moreover, there is a fundamental ambiguity in the status of λογιστικόν, it is not merely one type of motive, but the fundamental and constitutive type, and when Plato produces his second model in Book IX he represents it as being itself a man.

Plato has not given us a complete, satisfactory account of the human *psyche*. Neither has Freud. Neither has Jung, nor any of the psychologists of the twentieth century. But that was not his intention. He was trying to meet the challenge, posed by Adeimantus in Book II, to produce an intrinsic justification of morality. His theory of personality enables him to identify δικαιοσύνη as the state of mind in which each facet of the personality plays its proper part, especially with regard to leading and being led by the others. The nearest English rendering for what Plato has in mind here is integrity. Etymologically, it is derived from the Latin word *integer*, whole, as in the mathematical term integer for whole number (1, 2, 3, ... etc.). Wholeness is itself etymologically connected with health, and to make a man whole is to heal him. If a man has integrity, he has a wholeness of personality which is intrinsically desirable. Integrity is the best policy, since a well-integrated personality is the greatest good a man can have, and disintegration of the personality the worst evil that can befall any one. What would it profit one to have the whole world and lose one's psychological health? (IV 445a-b)

Plato's linking of moral behaviour with mental health is one which has found much favour in our own times. We often describe delinquents as malad-justed, and find it easy to believe that integrity of life is both a consequence and a cause of a well-integrated personality. Our generation is ready to be

---

[16] W.H.Sheldon and S.S.Stevens, *Varieties of Temperament*, New York, 1942.

convinced by an appeal to prudential considerations concerning psychological health. Don't be dishonest, says Plato or you will get a neurosis. The dissolute man is his own worst enemy. Honesty really is the best policy, because only honesty, and the moral life generally, will give one a quiet mind, mental stability and a well-balanced personality. Many of us would be happy with this quasi-Freudian justification of morality, and would be content if the *Republic* ended at 445b4. Plato, it would be felt, had achieved what he set out to do; he had achieved the difficult task of showing morality to be worthwhile, not on the grounds of penalties and rewards in an after-life, not for fear of the sanctions imposed by society, but intrinsically good, good in virtue of internal factors alone, as expedient as any other prudential maxim, but as categorically imperative as the care of one's own health.

Nevertheless the justification is not complete. For one thing it is not clear that the connexion between good behaviour and a quiet mind need be so close as Plato claims. He says that the well-integrated man will not indulge in various forms of anti-social behaviour (IV 442e-443a, 443e) and we may agree with him: but it is not clear why this should be so, and Thrasymachus might concede everything that Socrates says in praise of a well-integrated personality, but deny that one needed to be moral in any ordinary sense in order to achieve integrity. A single-minded pursuit of selfish interests might be, for all that Socrates has shown, just as conducive to a well-balanced personality and mental health as any practice of bourgeois honesty.

It may be that Plato felt nagging doubts such as these. The arguments of Books II-IV, though good, were not good enough. Even if he had shown that integrity was the best policy, further argument was needed to prove that there really was no alternative, and that any alternative principle of life, whether individual or social, had within itself the seeds of its own dissolution, and was on every count less to be desired than the life of integrity, lived within a well-integrated society.

And so Plato turns to consider the alternatives.

Chapter 3
The Return of the Self

Alternatives

The *Republic*, as we now have it, does not end at 445b5. Perhaps at one time it did. At this point Plato had completed the task he set himself in Book II in exactly the terms there laid down, and he may well have issued *Republic* I-IV as a complete work, and then in a later edition added on more either to meet criticisms, or because he himself felt that his arguments in Book IV were not as watertight as he would have liked. As we have the text now, after Socrates has elucidated the nature of integrity, δικαιοσύνη (*dikaiosune*), and identified it with psychological health, which it would be ridiculous—Γελοῖον γάρ ἦν δ᾿ἐγώ—not to regard as the greatest good, he goes on, 'but all the same—ἀλλ᾿ ὅμως—since we have come so far, we ought not to stop now in our attempt to see how matters lie as clearly as possible' (IV 445b5-7): he suggests we should look at less good arrangements to make sure they really are less good; and begins the theme of the deterioration of the constitution, both of society and of the individual personality. He is then immediately interrupted by Polemarchus and Adeimantus, and starts on a long digression comprising Books V, VI and VII. He resumes the discussion at the beginning of Book VIII, and continues through the first third of Book IX, describing the deterioration of the constitution, both of individuals and of societies, at the end of which it becomes clear that the alternative forms of organization of society and of the personality are much less desirable than the one Plato has sketched, leading to the verdict at 580b8-c4 that the best constitution is much better, both for individuals and for societies, than the alternatives.

> Let us hire a herald, or let me say it myself, that the son of Ariston adjudges meritocracy and the meritocrat to be not only the most moral but the happiest and in every way the best, and dictatorship and the dictatorial personality to be the most immoral, the most miserable and altogether the worst.

The Decline of the Constitution

In Books VIII and IX(i) four forms of constitution are considered:
   547c-550c τιμοκρατία, aristocracy
   550c-555b ὀλιγαρχία, plutocracy
   555b-562a δημοκρατία, permissiveness
   562a-580a τυραννίς, dictatorship

The reader should note that the Greek words do not have in the *Republic* the same sense as their derivatives in modern English. Many translators transliterate these Greek words into English, and then complain that what Plato is

36

talking about does not fit these English words. Greek does not have a word for meritocracy. Plato describes it here as βασιλικώτατον, most royal, and elsewhere as ἀριστοκρατία (*aristokratia*).[1] But 'royal' and 'aristocracy' in English have connotations of hereditary nobility: Plato, while acknowledging the importance of genetic inheritance, is adamant that selection must be on the basis of ability alone. His ideal society is a meritocracy. His ὀλιγαρχία is plutocracy. The Greek word πλουτοκρατία first appears in Xenophon,[2] and was probably made up by him. Plato, somewhat diffidently, makes up the words τιμοκρατία and τιμαρχία for the least bad of the suboptimal constitutions, which are governed by the ideal of honour τιμή. Although he was, indeed, a severe critic of Athenian democracy as a political institution, and draws on some elements of contemporary Athenian society for his picture of δημοκρατία, he is not concerned with democracy in either its ancient or its modern sense, but with permissiveness. And permissiveness, he suggests, leads finally to obsessive self-centredness, exemplified in the dictatorship of the autistic autocrat. Our word 'tyranny' comes closer to what Plato had in mind than the original Greek τυραννίς, since often, as critics of Plato like to point out, the Greek tyrants were benign—indeed sometimes populist leaders accomplishing the transition from a traditional aristocracy to a more democratic form of government. In modern English 'dictator' has the pejorative force required, although 'autocrat', and the adjective 'autistic' are closest to Plato's sense of obsessional self-centredness.

Plato discusses these four types of constitution in turn. In each case he follows the pattern of his πόλις analogy in Books II-IV, and describes first the organization of society and then the character of the typical individual. As with Books II-IV, there is dispute whether Plato's prime interest is in the social systems—his choice of names certainly suggests that—with the constitution of the individual *psyche* being explained by its social environment, or *vice versa*. Certainly Plato is deeply interested in society, and some of his insights are very shrewd. But it is the individual he is most of all concerned about. It is the autistic autocrat who exemplifies ἀδικία, wickedness, to the highest degree, and whose life is the most miserable. Although sometimes it does indeed seem that the argument about society is making the running, Plato's own words

> You realise that there must be as many types of individual as there are of society. Or do you think that societies come out of a tree somewhere or out of a rock, and not from that behaviour of their members which predominates and sets the tone for everything else. (VIII 544d-e)

are decisive here, even more so than for Books II-IV.[3]

---

[1] Book VIII, 544e7, 545c9, 547c6; see also *Politicus* 301a1.

[2] *Mem.* 4.6.12

[3] For Greek, see above, ch.2, p.26.

Plato's description is compelling, but in the way a novel is, rather than as an argument. He carries the same sort of conviction as Dostoevsky does, and we can read Books VIII and IX(i) as we do *The Possessed*. But Plato's account has been much criticized.[4] While acknowledging the literary brilliance of his depictions, critics complain that there is not much real argument, that the parallel between the individual and society is inexact, that the account of social decline is not borne out by the historical course of events in the development of the Greek city state, that the development is neither as inevitable nor as malign as Plato makes out. Why must we all rush headlong to our destruction? Is all our public and private life lived on the brink of a Gadarene precipice? Could not a dictator be a rationally self-controlled egoist?

The criticisms are misconceived—some arise from mistranslations, as we have noted. Admittedly, Greek city-states mostly had dictators before, not after, they became democracies, but it does not follow that Plato was offering an *a priori* scheme of historical change which fails to fit the facts. Plato is not offering a philosophy of history. His primary concern is with the individual, and in so far as he is discussing society, he is revealing certain sociological tendencies rather than propounding hard-and-fast historical laws. He is offering stereotypes. Actual societies and actual individuals may fail to instantiate any one of them perfectly, combining features from two or more. Empiricists, who believe that all our knowledge must be founded only on observation, object, and condemn Plato for his high-handed a-priori-ism; Aristotle assembled a large number of studies of the political arrangements of different city states, and his *Politics* is based much more on careful observation of what actually goes on. But important though empirical evidence is, insight is also important. Observations need to be interpreted, and interpretative schemata derive much of their value from the inner rationale of the systems they portray. Plato classifies individuals and societies by reference to the ideals that underlie them. In an actual example there may be no single one ideal that is always dominant, but in many cases we can identify one as generally predominant, and can understand how this shapes the other features there.

Plato believes that these different ideals have an inherent tendency to deteriorate. His classification is not only a logical one, in order of (de)merit, but, he fears, a chronological one, a degeneration that is likely actually to take place. The underlying theme is The Return of the Self. The ideal constitution is one in which each individual, ruled by reason, is selflessly devoted to the common good, and society is organized on the assumption that this is so. If this should begin to be no longer the case—and Plato is significantly shaky in his account of how and why this could come about—the self, no longer ruled by reason, will re-assert its ancient sway over individuals and the societies

---

[4] K.R.Popper, *The Open Society and its Enemies*, London, 1945; Julia Annas, *An Introduction to Plato's Republic*, Oxford, 1981, pp.295-305.

they govern. The different degrees of contamination by the non-rational self give the key to the order in which Plato places the different ideas of the good that motivate the individual and society in Books VIII and IX(i).

Power and Glory

In the ideal society the Guardians want only what is good for society as a whole, and are untouched, Plato hopes, by any tincture of self-concern. They are self-effacing civil servants, who exercise the power entrusted to them in a responsible fashion, and seek no other reward than the knowledge that they have done the job well. But I could want that knowledge to be shared. Having exercised power selflessly, I might wish for it to be known that I had done so. If mine is the power, mine is the responsibility for its use, and so mine should be the glory for its being used well. Although civil servants in Britain are trained to allow their minister to take all the glory for what they themselves have done, it is natural to yearn for some public recognition of good work, and to seek the *kudos* that is their deserved due.

Honour is assigned to selves. Someone, some particular person or persons, must be honoured if honour is to be conferred. The success of a collaborative enterprise may be attributed to everyone's having pulled his weight, but as soon as we pick out some individuals and mention them in dispatches, we are differentiating between one individual and another, and may cause some of those not mentioned to repine at their contribution being overlooked. Honour, glory, *kudos*, are assignable goods, which each individual could naturally want for himself, and could, therefore, compete for. He will be αὐθαδέστερος, more self-willed, not only φιλότιμος,, but φιλόνεικος, φιλόνικος, (*philoneikos, philonikos*), loving strife, seeking victory.

The man whose great aim in life is to secure *kudos* will be self-assertive, and a society whose members all seek honour will be a competitive one. In both the dominant aspect of motivation will be θυμοειδές. But self, though assertive, will not be supreme. If I want to be honoured, I want to be thought well of, and if I want to be thought well of, I want other people to think that what I have done was done well. There is a necessary connexion between honour and well-doing. Only under the description of having done deeds worthy of honour can I be honoured. Although people may be mistaken about what I have actually done and in their judgements about its worth, the necessary connexion in their thinking exerts a powerful pressure on my ambitions. If I am ambitious, my aims are constituted by values not of my own choosing: I shall succeed only if what I do is generally reckoned well worth doing. Though sometimes it might be possible to cheat, and always it is possible to have ideals that are different from the idols of the market-place, success is anchored to doing well. Ambition may be, as Plato avers, an infirmity: but, as Milton pleads, it is the last infirmity of a noble mind.

Plato's φιλότιμος, may have strayed from the path of absolute selflessness, but his self-concern is less bad than the other alternatives that Plato portrays.

The success that ambition seeks resides largely in the estimation of others. Of course, I may succeed in achieving some private aim; I may carve replicas of famous statues on cherry stones, or collect tickets of pre-war railway companies: but these are hobbies, and not the achievements an ambitious man yearns for. He wants to be recognised as having got somewhere that others would like to get to too; and not only to have got there but to continue to enjoy the plaudits of the public. Such success is inherently vulnerable. The good opinion of others is something I may lose, perhaps through my own fault, perhaps quite unfairly. However well I have done in the past, I may through some lapse forfeit public respect; and even if I have done nothing wrong, I may find the public fickle in its approbation—some new canon of correctness may emerge, and my past actions, however well justified at the time, may with hindsight be deemed unacceptable. History is constantly being rewritten, and my glorious deed may get reassessed or airbrushed out.

The Sovereignty of Wealth

Money is more secure than reputation. It cannot be blown away by a change in other men's minds. What I have I hold until such time as I choose to part with it. And money speaks. If I enjoy a good reputation, some people may be somewhat inclined to do some things I want them to do, but few are likely to put themselves out all that much or all that often, whereas if I can offer financial incentives, most people will be prepared to listen, and many will do my bidding whenever I pay them to, and as often as I want. We find convincing Plato's account of how the son of the φιλότιμος, seeing the fragility of the fame his father had been seeking, sets his sights on a less transient good. Wealth is a good. Like fame, it is assignable, but it is more securely possessed by him who has it. It is a more self-sufficient good, more independent of others. But by the same token, it is less closely connected with real values. Whereas the good opinion of others has to be earned by doing good, and is forfeited on the discovery of anything underhand, wealth is often acquired by shady dealing or through the capricious choices of others. There need be no merit in money, whereas an unmeritorious honour is a contradiction in terms.

Nevertheless, money is mostly earned. Although I may make money by ripping people off, or may just be given it, most money is earned by providing others with what they want. If wealth is my great goal in life, I shall have to discipline myself. I shall have to work for others, and curb my own expenditure. Industry and thrift will be my watchwords. A society dedicated to the pursuit of wealth will be correspondingly disciplined, efficient and eschewing extravagance. It may lack the finer flowers of civilisation, but will be noticeably un-bad.

But money is an unstable good, though less so than honour. Although it is not constituted by the changeable opinions of others, it is vulnerable to their actions, and is subject to an internal erosion with the passage of time. Money is not only an assignable good, but a necessarily privative one. The money I have is money you do not have. Honour, though often competed for, is not necessarily privative: it can be shared without being diminished thereby; you can shine in my reflected glory, and we both feel enhanced by public recognition of the contribution each made to great success. Money, being necessarily privative, is divisive. My great wealth is wealth that you and others do not possess, and may be envious of. Although I may have earned it in time past by serving the needs of others, perhaps even of you yourself, its very permanence makes that connexion less immediate to the onlooker, who only sees someone enjoying wealth which he would like to have in his stead. Hence the tension between the haves and the have-nots, and the perpetual possibility of forcible redistribution of wealth.

Money is an unstable good not only as between different sections of society, but over time. Why is money a good thing to have? Only because other people want it too, and are willing to do things in exchange for it. Take away the possibility of spending it, and it ceases to be seriously worth having—I might collect Confederate dollar bills as a hobby, but they could never make me rich. But if spendability is the point of money, thrift cannot be an all-life virtue. It may make sense to save now in order to be able to spend later, but the man who has sacrificed the best years of his life to making money, and then when he has made his pile, continues to go to the City every day, because he has allowed all his other activities and interests to atrophy, is an object of pity. His son will avoid that mistake, and having come into money will use it. The transition from money-grubbing to permissiveness is a consequence of the value of money being constituted by its enabling its possessor to do what he wants.

Free for All

Plato's account of δημοκρατία, has been much misunderstood. He was not in this passage primarily concerned with politics. Although elsewhere critical of many features of Athenian democracy,[5] his concern in Book VIII is with a pattern of society and the individual *psyche* in which there is no over-arching conception of the good, but each goes his own way doing whatever he feels like doing. It is a natural resort of the sceptical mind (although some liberal principles can be defended on quite other grounds), and has often been put forward as an ideal in both the ancient and the modern world. Ontologically it is cheap. We do not have to posit a world of Forms, or the

---

[5] See below, ch.9.

God, or objective values, or anything like that. All we need is the evident fact that people sometimes want to do things. With no shared idea of the Good, the object of society is to accommodate different people wanting to do different things, enabling each to go his own way with as little impingement on others as possible.

Plato believes such a recipe to be incoherent in principle and unfeasible in practice. It is based on a false picture of people as atoms with no common bond between them, and of the springs of action in the *psyche* as disparate inclinations which just happen to be uppermost at some particular time. The absence of a unifying theme, whether in society or in the individual personality leaves a void which, sooner or later, will be filled by some overmastering passion. We cannot, either collectively or individually, be nothingarians for long. If no vision of the Good is rationally acceptable, then some irrational enthusiasm will take over. We were asked ὅντινα τρόπον χρὴ ζῆν, 'how should one live?': if we answer 'do what you like', we have failed to answer, and the inquirer will go elsewhere with his question.

Plato claims that when we have purged our habitation of all commitment to objective values, a demoniac self-obsession will take its place. Others have said the same, but sceptical philosophers remain unconvinced: allowing the literary force of Plato's depiction, they protest that it does not have to be like that. And in one sense they are right. There are plenty of happy-go-lucky individuals who drift through life from one attachment to another without running *amok*; and relaxed pleasure-loving societies have survived over several generations without degenerating into dictatorships. Equally, the less bad exemplars did not have to decay. Sparta did not become a plutocracy in spite of many Spartans secretly amassing dishonourable wealth. But Plato, as we have argued earlier,[6] is not dealing with rigid historical inevitabilities. Rather, he is concerned first to show us what *could* happen, and then to suggest that it *would* so happen in default of some effective countervailing tendency. His modalities are internal tendencies, not external necessities. He is exploring the human *psyche* in its relation to values, and claiming that it needs values, and will always be ill at ease without them, and restless until it has found something really worthy of its respect. Others—Augustine, Pascal and Dostoevsky—have made similar claims. We may define philosophy so as to exclude discourse seeking to plumb the depths of the self,[7] and reckon that Augustine, Pascal and Dostoevsky are not proper philosophers, but only, poets or prophets, or perhaps, *philosophes*. But it is not clear that such a redefinition would be to the credit of philosophy. However we classify Plato's discussion in Books VIII and IX(i), its acknowledged imaginative power argues for its having something to teach us.

---

[6] pp.38f.

[7] See further below, chs.6 and 12.

The Depths of Degradation

In Book IV Plato rejects the view of the self as a rational maximiser, because the self it describes is a maimed one: I cannot flower except in society, and I cannot flourish unless I identify with my fellow men, and take their existence as a necessary concomitant of my being a self, and their views of me as largely constitutive of who I actually am. In Books VIII and IX(i) he is delving deeper, and is led to consider not only myself in relation to other selves, but ourselves generally in relation to the values we espouse. The final fate of the self-obsessed self is to be an autistic autocrat, surrounded by sycophants but with no friends, rationally afraid of his servants, believing that they would get rid of him if they could, because he knows that he himself would have no compunction in killing them if it suited him to do so. We need human company. And human company is not just a matter of there being human beings around—the autistic autocrat can have lots of eunuchs and concubines to minister to his physical needs, but they cannot be friends because they are not allowed to have wills of their own which they can make up differently from how he makes up his.

All this we can see. Most people would agree that the extreme of selfishness was self defeating; many would also concede that dictators can become obsessive, and that absolute power can make you mad. What is less clear is that this should be inherent in self-concern so long as it is rational. Having seen what happened to Stalin and Hitler, should not I settle for a lower content, abridging my power and being nice to people in order that they may be genuinely nice to me in return? But though many in a muddle-headed way adopt this position, it depends on their remaining muddle-headed and not being troubled by its incoherence. I cannot be genuinely nice to others in order that they should be nice to me in return: if it is just in order that they should act in ways I want, I am not being genuinely nice to them, but only manipulating them. And the same holds for them too. We can agree that a self that loves only itself is an unlovable self, and will not be able to love even itself for long, but then, if we are clear-sighted, we begin to see through other selves too, and wonder whether they could be worthy objects of our love. Neither I individually nor we collectively are self-sufficiently valuable. We need something other than ourselves, making for good, if we are to be whole, with a clear-sighted, single-minded commitment to a worthy object of worship.

Plato can meet this demand. In the metaphysical books of the *Republic*, Books V, VI and VII, he grounds values in the Form of the Good. If some such objective value exists, it is reasonable that the soul should yearn for it, and that the human *psyche* should have a natural need for commitment which subjectivism does not fulfil. Against that background the thoughts of Augustine, Pascal and Dostoevsky make sense.

Modern readers are surprised at Plato's devoting the central books of the *Republic* to metaphysics. We can now see why. Traditional morality was being challenged by philosophical sceptics, who denied the objectivity of morals. Man was the measure of all things, and if men thought δικαιοσύνη was the interest of the stronger, or that being moral was a mug's game, then that was it. Plato was convinced that morality, though possibly different from what it had been traditionally supposed to be, was objective. Our thinking something to be right did not make it so. You may be wrong in your moral opinions. So may I. So may we all. Just as we all thought at one time that the sun went round the earth, which was flat, our present moral opinions, although generally accepted now, may turn out to be misguided.[8] It is, in his view, a matter of great difficulty, requiring great intellectual ability and prolonged intellectual effort, to reach genuine knowledge, knowledge of moral truth. If such truth exists and knowledge of it is possible, then it is sensible to entrust the guidance of our society to guardians, who are best able to discern where the truth lies. But if no such truth exists, or if it cannot be discovered by rational thought, then there is no hope of our ever achieving a good society, not even if the intellectually *serieux* put themselves forward and exercise power, and those in power are committed intellectuals. For this reason at the end of Book V, Plato, having introduced the 'philosopher king', the intellectually committed holder of power, sets out to distinguish his knowledge of moral and political truth from the un-thought-out opinions of the fashionable opinion-formers.

Plato needed to have the argument of the metaphysical books both to defend himself against moral subjectivism generally, and in particular to ground the values of the ideal society. Moreover, Books V, VI and VII are not only about metaphysics. They also depict in further detail the ideal society, encouraging each one of us to identify with it, and subsuming our individual identities in the communal whole, to replace individual selfishness by a selfless devotion to the common good. It thus makes sense that Plato needed to have the argument of the metaphysical books before that of the decline of the constitution, to provide a better setting for the return of the self. But he might well have only come to realise this after he had written Books VIII and IX(i) as a foil to Book IV.

---

[8] We consider this question further in ch.4, pp.53-54.

Chapter 4
Knowledge and Opinion

Who are the φιλόσοφοι, (*philosophoi*)?

In V 473 with the breaking of the 'Third Wave' Socrates states the main thesis of the *Republic*, that there will be no respite from evil until philosophers become kings or kings philosophers. To modern ears this sounds strange. We picture elderly dons with white beards wearing crowns slightly askew, and holding sceptres, like pieces of chalk, awkward in their unaccustomed attire, and manifesting academic incompetence when faced with having to rule in the real world. But that is not what Plato had in mind. His view was that the good society would never come about, until the intellectually committed came into power, or those in power became intellectually committed.

Etymologically, a philosopher is a 'lover of all wisdom', but the need for a closer definition introduces a fundamental distinction between γνῶσις or ἐπιστήμη, knowledge, and δόξα, opinion. Plato contrasts the true φιλόσοφοι with the φιλοθεάμονες, but has some difficulty in characterizing the difference. The φιλοθεάμονες lovers of sights and sounds, are not, as we might otherwise have thought, simple and uneducated people who are easily taken in by the surface of things. They are often people of high intelligence and intellectual resourcefulness who are devotees of fashionable culture, readers, or contributors, so to speak, of the *Observer* or the *Spectator*. Plato seeks to distinguish them because the the serious-minded intellectual *knows*, whereas the journalist merely opinionates. Different views about matters of science, morals and politics, are not mere matters of opinion: they are capable of being true or false, correct or incorrect, right or wrong. The justification for entrusting all decision-making to meritocrats is that they will get the answers right, because they *know*.

Knowledge and Necessity

Plato characterizes knowledge in three ways: logical, epistemological, and ontological. In Book V 477e6-7 he has Glaucon say that knowledge is infallible, whereas opinion is not. Underlying Glaucon's claim is a genuinely different logical grammar of 'I know' and 'I think' and their second- and third-person parallels. When I am talking to you or about him, the use of the word 'think' (or 'believe' or 'opine') in the second- or third-person carries no further implication. But if I say '*I* think...', I am committed to holding to be true what I say I think. I cannot say 'I think there is a train to London at 10.22, but there is not one', or 'I think there is a train to London at 10.22, but that is not true', whereas it is perfectly intelligible for me to say 'You think there

45

is a train to London at 10.22, but there is not one', or 'He thinks there is a train to London at 10.22, but that is not true'. 'I think' does not merely introduce a biographical statement about someone who happens to be me, but is a 'performative' locution, committing me to a certain position.

'I know' is a performative too, but a much stronger one. It vouches for the reliable truth of what I say I know. 'I think' does not vouch. It is perfectly intelligible to say 'I think there is a train to London at 10.22, but there may not be one'; I am giving such guidance as I can, but hedging, and warning you not to rely on what I say but to make your own independent check. But I cannot say 'I know there is a train to London at 10.22, but there may not be one'. By using the words 'I know', I stake my credit on what I claim to know. It is like signing a cheque. I am in trouble if my cheque bounces, and equally if what I said I knew to be the case turns out not to be.

The same distinction holds if we conjugate 'know' and 'think' in other persons and other tenses. By saying 'He knows...', I endorse what he is said to know. In the past tense, even the first person, 'I thought...' is purely autobiographical, and not performative: 'I thought there was a train at 10.22, but there wasn't' is entirely intelligible: but not 'I knew there was a train at 10.22, but there wasn't', nor 'He knew there was a train at 10.22, but there wasn't'. If what we claimed to know turns out not to be so, we have to withdraw our claim retrospectively, and say '*I thought I knew* there was a train at 10.22, but I was wrong; there wasn't'.

Plato draws two conclusions: knowledge implies truth, and knowledge implies necessary (infallible, ἀναμάρτητος) truth. The former follows from the inconsistency of saying 'I/you/he/we know(s) that p, but p is not true', the latter from the inconsistency of saying 'I/you/he/we know(s) that p, but p may not be true'. Plato is sometimes accused of mistakenly arguing from the former to the latter. The former is a logical truth, arising from the grammar of the word 'know', and can, therefore be expressed as 'I/you/he/we know(s) that p' necessarily implies 'p is true'. It would be a mistake—a fairly common one in philosophy—to argue from this that 'I/you/he/we know(s) that p' implies 'p is necessarily true'. That would be to confuse, in the terminology of the scholastic philosophers, *necessitas consequentiae* with *necessitas consequentis*. But Plato has established his *necessitas consequentis*, that 'I/you/he/we know(s) that p' implies 'p is necessarily true' independently, from the grammatical fact that to say 'I/you/he/we know(s) that p, but p may not be true' would be inconsistent. We could recast this as 'I/you/he/we know(s) that p' necessarily implies 'p is necessarily true'.

The necessities involved in the concept of knowledge are necessities arising out of the way we use words. Plato, however, sees them as necessities in the nature of things. He also does not draw as sharp a distinction between truth and reality as we do (compare some of the locutions above, where we have replaced 'is true' by 'is so' or 'is the case'). He is therefore led to maintain that knowledge must be knowledge of reality, and of a reality that is necessarily (and not contingently or transiently) the case.

Knowledge as Understanding

If we know something, we can give an account of it (διδόναι λόγον); which is one reason why it has to be as it is. The φιλοθεάμονες, the 'lovers of sounds and sights' may, indeed, admire beautiful sounds and colours but are incapable of seeing or admiring the nature of real beauty. There is an important difference, though we may not be able to analyse it, between being able to recognise beautiful things and understanding what beauty is, as there is not between being able to recognise red objects and understanding what red is. In the first case it is natural to think in terms of penetration and insight, or to combine the two and talk of 'profound insight'. For example, if we ask what constitutes beauty in a building, we may be misled by inessentials. If used to stone buildings, we may think stone buildings beautiful, brick buildings not; or at a more reflective level we may still be unable to appreciate the virtues of a building because its style is unfamiliar or uncongenial. Thus, in Oxford, the nineteenth century condemned the classical facade of Queen's as spoiling the Gothic character of High Street and there are, even now, those who cannot see virtue in the Victorian Gothic of Keble. But if we examine paintings as well, it will become apparent that they all have something essential in common, *viz.* proportion or excellence of composition, which may be possessed by examples in very different materials and widely differing styles.

The notion that we can express beautiful proportions mathematically would be entirely congenial to Plato. Plato is impressed by the distinction between those who have a reflective understanding of beauty and those who identify beauty with a range of relatively superficial characteristics with which it may be contingently associated. In making this distinction he is encouraged by his fondness for visual metaphors to express it in terms of seeing objects of different sorts, seeing beauty itself rather than just 'the many beautifuls'.

A characteristic which makes something beautiful in one context may make it ugly in another. The colour purple may be beautiful as the colour of a dress, but ugly as the colour of the eyes of a statue (IV 420c). Polemarchus' mistake was to suppose that if an act of a certain kind was moral in one situation, it would necessarily be moral in a different situation, that if it was right to return a borrowed sword to a sane person, it would be right to hand it back to a madman (I 332-336).[1]

It follows that τὰ πολλὰ καλά, the many beautifuls, as picked out by the argument, represent a comparatively restricted class of evaluative and relational characteristics and yet the impression is given that Plato did not

---

[1] See above, ch.1, p.2.

intend to confine the objects of δόξα to this limited class, but took them to cover anything whatever that is subject to change and decay. If challenged to justify extending the objects of δόξα beyond those warranted by the argument, he would probably have claimed that they were all incapable of being objects of ἐπιστήμη in different, although comparable, ways.

To get a clearer view of Plato's distinction between ἐπιστήμη, knowledge, and δόξα, opinion, we shall need to look beyond the *Republic* itself. Light is cast on Plato's distinction between knowledge and opinion in the *Meno*. The main discussion about ὀρθὴ δόξα, correct opinion, occurs towards the end of the dialogue.[2] Socrates asserts that δόξα ἄρα ἀληθὴς πρὸς ὀρθότητα πράξεως οὐδὲν χείρων ἡγεμὼν φρονήσεος true opinion is no worse a guide to correct conduct than knowledge. Thus the man who has correct opinion about the way to Larissa will get there as safely as the one who knows the way because he has himself been there. What then is the difference between δόξα and ἐπιστήμη? It is the presence in the case of ἐπιστήμη of αἰτίας λογισμός, working out of causes. The person who knows gives a reason, an explanation. He is able διδόναι λόγον, to give an account.

The example of the road to Larissa does not bring this out very well. What distinguishes the man who has been to Larissa is his greater experience, not that he can give reasons. But perhaps this is taking the illustration too literally. The way to Larissa is not, after all, the sort of thing that, strictly speaking, Plato thought you could have knowledge about. It is, therefore, perhaps meant to be just an analogy. Having seen the way for yourself would be an image of the sort of intellectual vision that is needed for the attainment of αἰτίας λογισμός, the working out of causes.

The doctrine of the *Meno* that knowledge is distinguished from belief by the ability to provide a reason is very much closer to common sense than the further doctrine of the *Republic* that they are distinguished by having different objects. However, it could be the case that Plato in the *Meno* restricts severely what is to count as a reason. Thus Gould suggests that the slave who achieves ἀληθὴς δόξα, true belief, about a point of geometry is prevented from achieving ἐπιστήμη, understanding by the fact that his enlightenment is confined to the particular figure in front of him: 'The cause which stabilises knowledge of the particular example is the fact that the latter is a case of a general law (*i.e.* that the square on the hypotenuse of a right-angled triangle is equal to the sum of those on the other two sides)'.[3] In other words, the αἰτίας λογισμός is the same criterion as before; it consists in elevating the object of cognition from particulars to Forms, and, in addition, by some process not so far made clear, bringing the particular instance into relation with the Form as effect to cause.

---

[2] *Meno* 97 ff.

[3] John Gould, *The Development of Plato's Ethics*, Cambridge, 1955, p.139.

If this interpretation of the *Meno* is correct, coming to know what one has hitherto only believed, being able διδόναι λόγον, to give an account, involves coming to apprehend one kind of object instead of another.

The Ontology of Knowledge

Knowledge is also characterized ontologically by Plato. Knowledge is *of* reality. Reality is altogether knowable, he holds, τὸ μὲν παντελῶς ὂν παντελῶς γνωστόν (V 477a2), and conversely, the knowable is altogether real. We are more cautious about thus distinguishing knowledge from belief because

1. we do not normally think of belief as having an object at all;
2. although we can think of knowing as having an object this is only true of knowing in a special sense, and that not the sense which we contrast with believing.

Thus, as H. H. Price used to point out, there is 'know' in the sense of Old English 'ken' and 'wis'. 'D'ye ken John Peel' and 'I wist not that it was the High Priest'. It is 'know' in the sense of 'wis' that is contrasted with 'believe'; but it is 'know' in the sense of 'ken'—to be acquainted with—which takes a direct object. I can believe John Peel (what he says); and believe in him; but neither of these is parallel to my knowing John Peel. Why then does Plato introduce 'objects' of both ἐπιστήμη and δόξα?

One very striking feature of his treatment is his constant use of visual metaphors. This runs all through the central books of the *Republic*, culminating in the Cave. Different sorts of cognition are likened to different sorts of seeing or seeing different sorts of objects. Thus the φιλοθεάμονες, lovers of sights, are unable to see the nature of beauty itself, αὐτοῦ τοῦ καλοῦ τὴν φύσιν ἰδεῖν. Δόξα is said to be γνώσεως μέν σκοτωδέστερον, ἀγνοίας δὲ φανότερον, darker than knowledge, brighter than ignorance (V 478c14). They differ in σαφήνεια and ἀσάφεια, clarity and unclarity. If the metaphor is taken seriously it imposes a scheme of faculty and object. Knowledge will be seeing things clearly; ignorance will be failing to see them at all; and belief will be seeing them more or less unclearly.

But none of this implies that knowledge and opinion have different objects. Plato's attempt to show this by reference to what is implied by a δύναμις or 'faculty' is generally agreed by commentators to be based on a confusion. Socrates (V 478b10) says Ἀλλ᾽ ἕν γέ τι δοξάζει ὁ δοξάζων; 'does not the believer believe one thing?' 'What sort of thing', we ask? 'That Aristides is just?' Here the 'object' of belief would be a proposition expressed in a noun-clause. But a line or two before (478b7) Socrates asks οὐχ ὁ δοξάζων ἐπὶ τὶ φέρει τὴν δόξαν· ἢ οἷόν τε αὖ δοξάζειν μὲν, δοξάζειν δὲ μηδέν· 'does not the believer refer his belief to something?' *i.e.* is there not something which the believer believes what he believes about? In this case about Aristides. So now Aristides is the 'object' of belief. But then immediately we are back to a proposition ἢ οἷόν τε αὖ δοξάζειν μὲν, δοξάζειν δὲ μηδέν; 'Is it possible to believe, but to believe nothing?' It looks as if Plato is confused as between the sense in which a proposition, that Aristides is just, is 'the object of belief' and the sense in which Aristides may be. Similarly with knowledge: one may know that Aristides is just and one may know something about Aristides. But, unfortunately, one can also be said to know Aristides (to 'ken' Aristides as well as to 'wis' that Aristides is just). Plato, it seems, assimilates these different cases to one another and speaks of knowing a Form on the analogy of knowing Aristides; and of having a belief about a person or type of person, act or type of act, where this 'object' is thought of as an 'object of belief' in the same sense as Aristides is an 'object' of knowledge.

Between Knowledge and Ignorance

Plato's ontology of knowledge and belief has further difficulties. What is meant by saying of the objects of δόξα that they 'roll about between being and non-being' μεταξύ που κυλινδεῖται τοῦ τε μὴ ὄντος καὶ τοῦ ὄντος εἰλικρινῶς (V 479d4-5)? This appears to suggest that they belong to a realm of being intermediate between the Forms which are objects of ἐπιστήμη and τὸ μὴ ὄν which is the object of ἄγνοια, ignorance. This interpretation is, however, open to a criticism, well expressed by Murphy: 'It is vital to notice that to "fluctuate between being and not-being" does not mean to have an intermediate kind of degree of reality—in one relation the objects spoken of are real, in another not. Τὸ ὄν is entire or unqualified being: (παντελῶς or εἰλικρινῶς εἶναι): τὸ μὴ ὄν the equally entire absence of being. If then of x, whatever it may be, both ὄν and μὴ ὄν are truly asserted in different relations, x is being thought of as between the two (μεταξὺ) not in the sense in which grey is between white and black, but in that in which piebald is between them, as showing black in one patch, but white in another.'[4]

The trouble with this is that, if Murphy were right, δόξα would have to be piebald too, now ἐπιστήμη now ἄγνοια. But this runs against the whole tenor of the Republic, which makes the clearest possible contrast between δόξα and ἐπιστήμη. It is incompatible, too, with the symbolism of copy and original, dream and waking life, which dominates Plato's thought on this subject. A man who is dreaming is not sometimes awake and sometimes unconscious; a copy is not sometimes the original and sometimes nothing.

In the context of the rest of the Republic, it seems more plausible to say that what he is doing here, as he does more elaborately in the Line and the Cave, is assigning to different classes of objects different degrees of reality. The Forms are absolutely real, παντελῶς ὄντα, nothing is not real at all and τὰ πολλά, the many, have an intermediate status. This is brought out by his choice of metaphor. A copy is not 'the real thing' but neither is it nothing

---

[4] N.R.Murphy, *The Interpretation of Plato's Republic*, Oxford, 1951, p.116.

at all. The things one meets in dreams are not part of 'the real world' but neither are they entirely non-existent. When philosophers distinguish between what is real and what is not real or less real, they generally have in mind some criteria by which they make the distinction. Thus Locke in regarding primary qualities like shape, size and solidity as 'more real' than secondary qualities like colour, sound and smell, seems to have applied the criteria of measurability and causal efficacy. These were for him the important qualities of things; the qualities, in fact, that natural scientists are interested in, and in terms of which everything else in the physical world can be explained.

Plato did not, like Locke, think that you can explain things in terms of physics (as is shown by his complaints about Anaxagoras in the *Phaedo*). He thought that anything whatever was made intelligible only in so far as it was brought into relation to the world of Forms. The Forms are what is fundamental in his system: they are what everything else has to be explained in terms of: so only they are real. But he can, of course, tell the difference between real beds and illusory beds, just as you or I can. Of course the bed in my bedroom exists: but it isn't self-explanatory: to understand it you have to get acquainted with the Form of bed. So we have to ask, what were Plato's criteria of reality, which the Forms, he thought, possessed, but which the objects of δόξα to a greater or lesser extent lacked; what in fact is the nature of the unsatisfactoriness which he detected in the objects of δόξα? The virtue of the Forms, it is clear, is that they are are ἀεὶ κατὰ ταὐτὰ ὡσαύτως ὄντα (V 479e8). They are always necessarily what they are; they are, therefore, wholly intelligible. A particular action or type of action may be right or it may not be right, but righteousness, αὐτὸ τὸ δικαίον, remains unalterably and necessarily right. In no circumstances whatever could one say of it that it was not right.

But take a certain action (in the type sense), like returning something you have borrowed; this, as we have seen, will sometimes be right and sometimes not right. Even the particular right action, though, as an individual, it may be right, only happens to be right. No amount of study of right actions or types of action will enable you to understand them. That requires insight into the nature of righteousness itself. It follows that the different classes of things that Plato lumps together as τὰ πολλὰ are all unsatisfactory in that they lack the stability and self-consistency and intrinsic intelligibility of the Forms. Of course they exist, in the everyday sense of the word, but because of this unsatisfactoriness they are only partly real.

What are we to say, then, of τὸ μὴ ὂν, nothing, the object of ἄγνοια, ignorance? For Plato things are whatever they are in virtue of their participating in the Forms, *i.e.* perfectly definable, wholly intelligible characteristics. If one tries to conceive something without any characteristics at all, of which, therefore, nothing could be predicated, this would be at the furthest remove from the Forms and there could be no kind of cognitive attitude towards it.

Tὸ μὴ ὄν then, would be not that which does not exist, but that which has no character.

It has sometimes been argued that Plato by insisting so strongly that the objects of opinion 'roll about between being and non-being' has made it impossible for them ever to be the objects of knowledge, so that the possession of *ἐπιστήμη* would be of no practical use in the everyday world in which decisions have to be made. The entire scheme of the *Republic* would collapse if this were so. Plato clearly does think that the *φιλόσοφος*, the seeker of understanding, is superior to the *φιλόδοξος*, the opinion-former, in his capacity to deal with particular cases. His point is that, since particular cases owe their intelligibility, their being what they are, to their imitating or participating in the Forms, the only way properly to understand them is by coming to know the Forms. But then, of course, you do understand them and can handle them competently in the light of that knowledge. Does this make them objects of *δόξα*, opinion? No, because they are intelligible not in themselves, but only in relation to the Forms which alone are intrinsically intelligible.

The Corruption of the Intelligentsia

Having sharply distinguished *φιλόσοφοι* lovers of wisdom, committed intellectuals, who seek understanding, from *φιλόδοξοι* lovers of opinion, opinion-formers who follow fashion, Plato complicates matters by introducing the topic of the corruption of the naturally philosophical. The *φιλοθεάμονες* lovers of sights and sounds, are not, as we might otherwise have thought, simple and uneducated people who are easily taken in by the surface of things. They are often people of high intelligence and intellectual resourcefulness who are corrupted by the cultural influences to which they are subjected. They wilfully allow themselves to be seduced by the attractiveness of prevailing ideas.

As suggested earlier, to find a modern parallel, we should not look to social surveys to see what they reveal about the views most ordinary people hold, but rather to the organs of sophisticated opinion, such as, in Britain, the *Observer* and the *Spectator* (which will serve as translations of *φιλοθεάμων*). The views of the many, *τὰ τῶν πολλῶν δόγματα*, may be rendered 'the conventional wisdom' as the term was first defined by J. K. Galbraith in *The Affluent Society*: 'It will be convenient to have a name for the ideas which are esteemed at any time for their acceptability. I shall refer to these ideas henceforth as "the Conventional Wisdom" ' and later: 'A very large part of our social comment and nearly all that is well regarded is devoted at any time to articulating the conventional wisdom. To some extent this has been professionalised. Individuals, more notably the great television and radio commentators, make a profession of knowing and saying with elegance and unction what their audience will find most acceptable.' These are our modern sophists. There are certain ideas which are so far dominant at a particular time that it requires great independence of mind or some cultural handicap (like 'the bridle of Theages') not to be entirely uncritical of them. One of the most perceptive things about Plato's account is his awareness that it is the keenest and strongest intellects which are in the greatest danger of being corrupted. It is, for obvious reasons, difficult to see this process at work in one's own day, but if one goes back a generation or two, it stares one in the face. Marxism was such a dominant idea in the 20s and 30s of the twentieth century. The wilful and almost total blindness of the young intellectuals of that period to the true character of Stalin's regime in Russia is now beyond dispute, although the evidence was available to them at the time.

The comparison with the vogue of Marxism raises a question about Plato's attitude to common beliefs—the objects of δόξα. Marxism was never in the West the dominant outlook of the common man. The intellectuals who identified with it were not reflecting popular opinion but rather following philosophical fashion. If they were corrupted it was not by the influence of the masses but by the example of the intelligentsia. Plato certainly thought that the sophists had a malign influence and it was a shrewd way of criticizing them to claim that they were not, as they thought, original thinkers, but simply elaborating and amplifying the views of the many. But he was prepared to be critical of popular opinion too—as in his description of the plight of the released prisoner who returns to the Cave and finds himself 'with eyes still confused and before he has got properly used to the darkness that is around him compelled to contend in the lawcourts or elsewhere concerning the shadows of the just or the images which throw those shadows, or to dispute concerning the manner in which those images are conceived by men who have never seen real justice' (VII 517d5-e2). Yet, as commentators have often observed, the views of Cephalus who is represented as an ordinary man with no pretensions to intellectual sophistication, are treated with a degree of respect. There is, then, a tension in the *Republic* between regarding common opinion as acceptable so far as it goes though in need of more or less drastic correction, and dismissing it as entirely worthless. This tension is inherent in the metaphor of image and original which dominates Plato's thinking on this whole issue. To the extent that an image resembles the original it has a degree of likeness to it which makes it better than nothing. But to the extent that it falls short of the original it has to be condemned as unsatisfactory.

The latter view was supported by the example of Socrates. By his method of question and answer he had discovered that none of his contemporaries really knew what they claimed to know, and that none of them could give any good reasons for their beliefs. Every one of them, for all he could tell, might be wrong. And therefore he could not rely on their authority in deciding what he himself should believe. In the *Apology* Socrates recounts how he discovered that all established authorities of his time knew nothing, and how he was forced to rely on himself alone, and be guided not by the received opinions of his society but by the intimations of his own δαίμων, inner light. Plato in the *Republic* is convinced that real knowledge about right and wrong is possible, and from the fact that it is not to be obtained merely by collecting the opinions of the many or the wise, it seems to follow that there must be some independent access to a moral reality, open to each individual whereby he could discover what is right and true, even though all of his fellows are wrong in their opinions. Thus Plato construes knowledge as an objectified realm of the knowable which in turn he identifies with the Forms.

In Defence of Opinion

Although in the *Republic* it is the critical emphasis which dominates, and it is the objects of knowledge which are stressed as being most real, it is arguable that the objects of opinion have an indispensable part to play in the discovery of knowledge. As Annas points out, unlike Descartes, Plato does not start by doubting the truth of particular beliefs in a wholesale way.[5] The dialectical method itself, based upon the Socratic *elenchus* is a co-operative endeavour: it starts from the opinions actually held by the interlocutor and at each stage the hypothesis under discussion is tested by reference to beliefs which he is prepared to accept, although until this point he may not have attended to them or acknowledged them. In this respect Plato's use of the *elenchus* differs from Socrates'. He expects it to lead towards knowledge. Hence the most original moral insight introduced in Book I, that we should do good to enemies as well as friends, which runs quite counter to the popular view, is supported by the claim, which Polemarchus is prepared to accept, that we ought to make people better not worse. And when at the end of Book IV Socrates seeks to justify his definition of δικαιοσύνη, justice, in a somewhat summary fashion he does so by comparing it with τὰ φορτικὰ, common opinions.[6]

Thrasymachus does not represent the views of the ordinary man, but is a radical critic of them. His corruption does not consist in deference to common opinion but in a radical rejection of the elements of genuine morality that are to be found in it. To this extent, his position is hard to place in the hierarchical system of the Line. It is clearly not πίστις, settled conviction or firm belief, but nor is it εἰκασία, conjecture.[7] It involves a rejection of the whole metaphysical scheme of the Sun-Line-Cave sequence. Plato, in

---

[5]　Julia Annas, *An Introduction to Plato's Republic*, Oxford, 1981, pp.212-213.

[6]　See below, ch.7, p.100.

[7]　No English word expresses Plato's range of meanings. 'Imagination' conveys the sense of visual imagery as opposed to reliable reality, but has too strong a sense of not being true. Although unreliable, appearances do not necessarily deceive. 'Guesstimate' is insufficiently pejorative.

responding to his critique as reformulated by Glaucon and Adeimantus, does not simply oppose his own scheme to theirs, but builds upon what he and they have in common with popular opinion, the belief that men and women should seek their own good. The view of Thrasymachus that this implies an unregulated struggle to get the better of others is rejected as untenable in the light of a proper understanding of what is meant by 'good'.

Elizabeth Anscombe, in a radio talk highly critical of modern philosophers, nevertheless defended them against the charge of corrupting the young. To corrupt, she argued, is to make people worse than they otherwise would have been. Modern moral philosophers do not corrupt their students because they simply articulate the opinions they would derive in any case from the surrounding society. Professor Anscombe shared with Plato a conviction that moral philosophy is concerned with truth and that philosophy properly practised is capable of grasping that truth. Given that conviction, philosophers can be corrupted to the extent that they fail to adhere to that truth when they possess it or fail to use the rational methods best suited to discovering it, tempted presumably in each case by desire for some extraneous end, such as reputation, financial gain, or the excitement that comes from a constant search for variety.

Plato assumes that his guardians will possess the truth so that there is no need for further discovery, and that they will have acquired it by the method of dialectical enquiry as he understands it. Assisted by the example of mathematics, he assumes that the moral and metaphysical truths which have for him the primary explanatory role are necessary truths to be achieved by logical demonstration. These are the objects of knowledge; all other beliefs are matters of opinion only.

Knowledge and Opinion: Reason and Faith

Gregory Vlastos in his essay 'A Metaphysical Paradox'[8] while acknowledging and celebrating the vision of the Forms in which 'Plato finds happiness, beauty, knowledge, moral sustenance and regeneration, a mystical sense of kinship with eternal perfection' nevertheless laments 'his confidence that he could prove it'. But whether he thought he could prove it is doubtful. In the *Republic* certainly he seems to have thought he could not—hence his reliance upon the image of the Sun and what follows it (VI 506e). But he clearly thought that in principle it could be proved and that it needed to be proved. He is thoroughly rationalistic.

We have, therefore, to consider the possibility that in using imagery in the way he did Plato presented a rational case for his metaphysical scheme

---

[8] Gregory Vlastos, 'A Metaphysical Paradox' in Richard Kraut, ed., *Plato's Republic: Critical Essays*, New York, 1997, ch.11, pp.181 ff.

in the only way in which it could be done albeit not the way his mathematical model suggests. Vlastos' reaction is one which has become increasingly common in modern times among that minority of philosophers who respond sympathetically to the religious and metaphysical elements in Plato's thought in the face of what is currently accepted as proof. For whether one identified proof, as Plato did, with logical demonstration, or extended it to embrace inductive reasoning as found in the sciences, it was apparent that the sort of questions Plato was concerned to answer about the nature and purpose of the universe or the form and content of morality, and the relationship between the two, could not be answered by them. Whether knowledge was thought to consist solely of necessary truths or of scientific theories empirically verified, religion and metaphysics were relegated to the realm of opinion. Hume and Kant between them left no other option to those who still had religious or metaphysical yearnings but to rely on non-rational intuition or an existential leap of faith.

In fact, in so far as nowadays people think in terms of knowledge and opinion, they contrast the two in a way that retains only part of Plato's scheme. His conviction that the world is intelligible and has a straightforward structure which requires to be understood mathematically has been vindicated by the success of natural science. The realm of knowledge, it is assumed, is that of science, and common sense, thought of as incipient or vestigial science. Religion and morality, by contrast, lack this solid foundation and are essentially controversial, matters of opinion only. Plato's conviction that it was possible in principle to find a sure metaphysical foundation for morality is commonly regarded as chimerical. Either the need for an overarching framework for our moral beliefs is denied altogether, or any such framework is to be adopted simply as the object of an individual's act of faith.[9] Hence the opposition between knowledge and opinion has been replaced by that between reason and faith. That science is an exercise of reason is not in dispute, although views differ as to whether reason is exhausted by science. Faith is interpreted as a venture beyond the realm of the knowable and must lack the support of reason.

Vlastos points out that Plato's concern with these issues has had little attention in English-speaking commentaries in recent years. 'The job has to be done all over again from the bottom up, as it surely must be if we are to understand Plato.'[10] It is clear that there is no prospect of recreating the theory of Forms in the full range of applications that Plato gave it. Two features of the Platonic world-view, nevertheless, are worth arguing for. The first is this very conviction that the structure of the universe is intelligible and

---

[9] *cf.* Charles Taylor, *Sources of the Self*, Cambridge, 1989, pp.16-23.

[10] Gregory Vlastos, 'A Metaphysical Paradox' in Richard Kraut, ed., *Plato's Republic: Critical Essays*, New York, 1997, ch.11, p.189.

knowable. As we have seen, some elements of the Platonic dialectic are found in the hypothetical method of modern natural science with the qualification that the testing of them is by observation and not simply by appeals to logical consistency. Most scientists believe that scientific discoveries achieve or, at least, approximate to the truth of the matter, but this belief is no longer unchallenged. It is called in question by "post-modernist" thinkers who point out that science itself is a cultural product which, they claim, need not be universally accepted.

In resisting this sort of relativist critique scientists cannot rely on scientific method itself, for it is this which is being criticized. They find themselves in the position which Plato called διάνοια, 'derivation'[11] in which they have to rely on assumptions which, *qua* scientists, they are unable to justify. Hence scientists themselves, once again, have an interest in asking the metaphysical questions which Plato addressed. The second feature of Plato's scheme which is worth defending, is his insistence on the need to ask the questions, why is the universe as it is and why is it intelligible, and his offer of an answer in terms of a final good which at the same time provides an answer to that other fundamental question περὶ τοῦ ὄντινα τρόπον χρὴ ζῆν, how one is to live. Vlastos' response to the mystical vision, which undoubtedly inspired Plato, acknowledged a fundamental theme of the *Republic* which modern commentators have almost always neglected but in his project of 'doing the job all over again from the bottom up', he would be discarding altogether too much if he dispensed with Plato's attempt to substantiate it by metaphysical argument. We need to sustain the attempt, while revising his conception of metaphysical argument.

---

[11] There is no adequate translation. This is the least inadequate of those we considered.

Chapter 5
Theories of Forms[1]

A Theory of Adjectives

In the *Republic* Forms are introduced to justify the claim that the φιλόσοφος (*philosophos*) should rule. The φιλόσοφος, the serious-minded intellectual, differs from the journalist because he *knows*. Different opinions about matters of science, morals and politics, are not mere matters of opinion: they are capable of being true or false, correct or incorrect, right or wrong. The justification for entrusting all decision-making to meritocrats is that they will get the answers right. Forms are essential to the argument of the *Republic* because they underwrite moral arguments. They are what make knowledge possible, what enable us to know the difference between right and wrong, and what prove Thrasymachus wrong, if he maintains that δικαιοσύνη, morality, is simply the interest of the stronger.

Plato adduces several arguments for the existence of Forms. In Book V he starts with a theory of adjectives. We use adjectives, such as καλὸν (*kalon*), αἰσχρόν (*aischron*), δικαίον (*dikaion*), ἀδίκον (*adikon*), ἀγαθόν (*agathon*) and κακόν (*kakon*), *etc.*, and apply them to individual instances. Communication would break down if I applied adjectives just as I fancied. Contrary to Humpty-Dumpty's assertion, words cannot just mean what I want them to mean. I have to subject myself to some interpersonal discipline if language is to be intelligible at all. It is reasonable in some cases at least, to go further, and say that my application of adjectives to particular instances must be in accordance with features they actually possess. I call a daffodil yellow because it has the colour yellow. It is the colour of the daffodil that sets the standard for the correct application of colour words. Similarly the shape of a wheel makes it right to call it circular, wrong to call it square. If Thrasymachus calls the interest of the stronger δικαίον, he is just misusing language. It is like a colour-blind man calling a rose green, or a lettuce red; it may not be his fault that he cannot distinguish red from green, but he is wrong nonetheless.

It is an attractive theory. There are certainly features of the world in virtue of which some adjectives are applied correctly and others incorrectly. Some people seem to lack a moral sense, and it is tempting to regard them as being, so to speak, morally colour blind. But an argument from language cannot give Plato all he wants. It refutes extreme moral subjectivism, but

---

[1] 'Form' is a stock translation. See note on translation, pp.viii-ix.

not the more moderate thesis that moral standards are a function of society. Words cannot just mean what *I* want them to mean, but they can, and do, mean what *we* want them to mean. Meaning, we are told, is constituted by use, and use is simply a matter of what men do. We English-speakers have a word 'yellow' which we apply to daffodils, primroses, privet leaves, straw and candle flames: the ancient Greeks had no equivalent word, but used χλωρός for greenish yellow, and ξανθός for orange-ish yellow. Where to draw the line between orange and yellow, red and purple, green and blue, is largely a matter of linguistic convention, and although I individually can be convicted of error if I use words idiosyncratically, we collectively cannot. If we want them to mean something different, they do mean something different: εὐήθεια had meant something like 'good nature', and after the civil war in Corcyra came to mean 'stupidity'.[2]

But Plato does not accept Protagoras' claim that Man is the Measure of All Things, and is concerned to controvert not merely extreme subjectivity in morals, but all forms of relativism. The theory of Forms seeks not only to correct deviant usage by appeal to standard usage, but to correct standard usage by appeal to objective principles. It is an intelligible aim. We can understand the moral reformer who criticizes our accepted morality in the light of some deeper understanding of human nature and man's place in the general scheme of things. 'Ye have heard of old time..., but I say unto you...' is entirely intelligible. But is it more than a mere aim? or is it just his word against ours? Not if the moral reformer is like a scientist, who claims that, contrary to popular belief, the earth moves, or that apparently solid objects are really constituted of subatomic particles separated from one another by unoccupied space. If morality is only a matter of what everybody thinks, then the opinion-formers cannot be controverted; their opinion on what they think cannot be gainsaid. But if the φιλόσοφος knows what beauty is, he can maintain his judgement that some particular instance is beautiful in the face of almost universal dissent, so long as his knowledge is genuinely grounded in reality.

Can the theory of Forms, understood as a theory of adjectives, provide such a ground? It must be difficult, one would have thought, for Plato to argue, on that basis, that current linguistic usage is wrong. If Greeks no longer call a good-natured man εὐήθης, but use the word to describe a simpleton, then that is what the word now means. But this is too simple a theory of meaning. Words obtain their meaning not only from the situations in which they are used, but in relation to the other words they are compatible or incompatible with. Plato's example is the word 'equal'. In the *Phaedo* (74a9-75b8) he points out that although two sticks are never exactly equal, but only approximately so, we nevertheless have a concept of exact equality. Certainly

---

[2] See above, ch.1, pp.5-6.

this is what, at least in some situations, we would say. If we had a large number of sticks, each one of which seemed equal to the next, but the first was visibly longer than the last, we should conclude that some of the pairs of sticks were not exactly equal even though they seemed so. We have an *ideal* of equality, against which we are prepared to check and correct our perceptual judgements. The basis for this judgement lies in the logic of the word 'equal', which expresses a relation that is transitive and symmetric. This is part of what we understand by the word 'equal', and if there is a conflict between this and how we are inclined to apply the word in particular situations, it is the latter that gives way.[3] Similarly with circularity, radial symmetry counts for more than appearances. Protagoras had argued against the claim of the geometers that a tangent touches a circle in just one point: if we observe a wheel on a road, or a hoop on a pavement, or a top lying on a table, we see that they do not touch at just one point, but are evidently touching over some small, but finite, distance.[4] Plato was worried by this argument, but concluded that the fault lay in material objects such as wheels and hoops and tops, and all particular exemplifications of circles.[5] In modern English we might distinguish 'circular' from 'round', defining 'circular' in geometrical terms, and 'round' more observationally. In a similar way, we might come to have an understanding of τὸ κάλλος, beauty, distinguishing what is really beautiful from what is merely attractive; and similarly of τὸ δικαίον, integrity, distinguishing true integrity of spirit from merely conventional patterns of behaviour. A Socratic discussion could, by sensitive probing, bring out the implications of a concept, and enable us to formulate a definition of the ideal, on the basis of which we could correct current usage.

Plato's theory of adjectives could thus provide the φιλόσοφοι with a justification for his claim that they, unlike the other would-be leaders of the public, really knew what was right and good. But he came to realise that it none the less had other defects. Grammatically adjectives are monadic. That is to say ' is red' has just one blank needing to be filled. Plato started by assuming that all general terms were monadic predicates, ascribing qualities to individual items, but soon ran into difficulties with polyadic predicates, as when we say 'This is *equal to* that', or 'This is *double* that', or 'Simmias is *taller than* Socrates', or 'Socrates is *short*', or 'Bedford is *between* Oxford and Cambridge'. Modern logicians have no difficulty with relations, and see qualities as just a special case, as monadic relations, so to speak; but many philosophers have found difficulty in relations, Plato only gradually came to

---

[3] For a full and careful examination of Plato's argument, see David Bostock, *Plato's Phaedo*, Oxford, 1986, ch.IV, pp.60-115.

[4] Aristotle, *Metaphysics*, II, 2, 997b34-998a4.

[5] Plato, *Seventh Letter*, 343a.

see that not all adjectives ascribe simple monadic qualities. In the *Phaedo* (102b) and *Republic* (VII 523c-524e) he is worried by such words as 'big' and 'small', and in the *Hippias Major* (289a3-4) by the fact that what would pass as a beautiful ape would be reckoned an ugly human being. Adjectives do not always work on their own, but often obtain their force from their context, especially from the nouns they are qualifying. Socrates may have been short—that is, he was short *for a man*: but a youth who was short *for a man* might still be a tall boy. Although grammatically the words 'short' and 'tall' are simple, and the comparatives 'shorter' and 'taller' are derivative, logically it is the other way round: a short x is an x which is shorter than most xs, a tall x is an x which is taller than most xs. Even colour words are sometimes open to a similar analysis. Snow-flakes look white on the ground, but grey as they are seen against the clouds.[6] There is no great mystery here—only a minor matter of logical grammar—and in the *Philebus* (14d) he dismissed the problem that had worried him in the *Phaedo* and the *Republic* as childish.

A Theory of Nouns

Forms are introduced in the *Republic* as a theory of adjectives, but become a theory of nouns. In Book X we read of the ἰδέα κλίνης, (*idea klines*) Form of bed, and the ἰδέα τραπέζης, (*idea trapezes*), Form of table, of which particular beds and tables are copies. It was an easy transition to make, especially in Greek, which did not have inverted commas, and therefore found it difficult to distinguish τὸ κάλλος from τὸ καλὸν, beauty from 'beautiful', or δικαιοσύνη from δικαίον, righteousness from 'right'. More important still was Plato's concern for the philosophy of mathematics. In *Republic* VI (510d8) he makes mention of the triangle itself, τοῦ τετραγώνου αὐτοῦ, with clear reference back to the *Meno* (82b-85b) where he describes a method of doubling the square by drawing its diagonal. Shape words, such as τετραγωνός, square, and κύκλος, circle, can be used adjectivally to say that something is square-shaped or circular, but can also be used as nouns to refer to shapes; and, similarly, colour words, such as white, λευκός, can be used as adjectives to describe, say, a piece of paper, or as nouns to refer to the colour white. Plato was deeply impressed with geometry, and concentrated much of his thought on the science of shapes, where the transition from the quality of circularity, which different coins share, to the prototype circle, which different coins resemble, is very easy.

One of the words Plato uses for a Form, εἶδος (*eidos*), was rendered into Latin as *species*, and it is helpful to think of this theory of Forms as a theory of species. The world we live in is a world of natural kinds. There are different kinds of plant, different kinds of animal, and we learn to apply common nouns

---

[6] See further, E.H.Gombrich, *Art and Illusion*, London, 1960, ch.1, §§III,IV, pp.45-54.

to many different items, in much the same way as we do with adjectives. It is reasonable to infer that specimens of the same species have something in common, in much the same way as instances possessing a common feature do. The ἓν ἐπὶ πολλῶν 'one over many', argument applies in both cases. It goes too far to argue *unum nomen, unum nominatum*, that since we use the same one noun in each case, it must refer to one (abstract) entity: for although we use one noun in many different cases, we use it to refer to different things; the word 'dog' is used sometimes to refer to Fido, sometimes to Hector, sometimes to Gesi, sometimes to Psyche. But although the word is used to refer to different animals on different occasions, it is in virtue of their all being dogs that the word 'dog' can be used to refer to each of them.

Plato is on to something, but his first formulation of the theory of species runs into difficulties. His examples are artifacts—beds, tables—rather than natural kinds, and the idea of an ideal bed which all actual beds imperfectly resemble lacks plausibility. Like many other things we use—food, fuel, razors and mowing machines—beds are defined functionally, not by reference to some authoritative prototype. And we extend the use of the word by metaphor and simile, speaking of flower-beds and the sea-bed, without bothering to define the species *bed*, or consider what its essential features are. Usage is all. The essence of beddishness is just how we use the word 'bed'. In Locke's terminology, it is a nominal essence, without there being any real essence of beddishness to constitute a standard for correcting current usage. Moreover some common nouns refer to ignoble things, which can scarcely claim kinship, however remote, with the divine and immortal and eternal. For this reason Socrates, later in the *Parmenides* (130cd), is unwilling to concede the existence of Forms of Mud, Hair, and Dirt. Not every common noun can have an εἶδος a species, corresponding to it. Nevertheless, some do, notably the common nouns we use of vegetables and animals. That the world around us is articulated into natural kinds is a profound truth with implications not only for ontology—what there is—but for epistemology— the theory of knowledge. We are able to recognise items as specimens of particular species on the basis of few cues, because only some species exist, so that certain observable features are characteristic of some species, and are never found in others. Were it not so, birds could not distinguish at a distance predators from potential mates, and would either get eaten or fail to produce progeny. Biological species are objects of knowledge, and if we understand them aright, we can invoke them to correct current usage. When Jonah was swallowed by the whale, whales were thought to be fishes: now we know that they are mammals. Locke was unclear as to how we could come to know real essences, but if we do, we are in a position to correct current usage. And so we might hope that, by coming to know the εἶδος τῆς δικαιοσύνης, the real essence of righteousness, we should be in a position to correct current misconceptions about it.

The biological species of modern science are not exactly what Plato had in mind. Their boundaries are too indeterminate. Chemistry offers a better example. It is based on there being many substances of the same type. There are innumerable instances of a limited number of elemental types, Hydrogen, Oxygen, Carbon, Chlorine, *etc.* In the *Timaeus*, which Plato presents as a sequel to the *Republic*, he develops the theme of the universe being created by a Demiurge, a semi-divine Lord Nuffield, or Henry Ford, who mass-manufactures copies of a limited number of prototypes. We can adapt modern motoring usage further, and use the word 'model' to express this theory of Forms. The word 'model' is ambiguous. It can refer to an instance—'I have got a very good model of the Peugeot 305', where what I am referring to is a particular material object, with a particular registration number, a particular location in space, and a particular owner. Or it can refer to the type—'Volkswagen are launching a new model next year'. A model in the former sense is a model *of* some prototype or paradigm: a model in the latter sense is the prototype or paradigm *of which* other things are models. In the former sense each particular protium atom is a model of the paradigm given in the quantum theory of Protium, which, along with its isotopes Deuterium and Tritium, occupies the first place in the Periodic Table. In the latter, Protium, Deuterium and Tritium are prototypes, all variants on the same basic Hydrogen model, the first element in the Periodic Table: they are, so to speak, Hydrogen mark one, Hydrogen mark two, Hydrogen mark three. The first model, Hydrogen mark one, has been enormously successful, and has had one of the largest productions ever: the second, Hydrogen mark two, is a pretty specialised job, with a fairly short production run: the third, Hydrogen mark three, turned out to have some internal design defects, and to be liable to disintegrate; it is extremely rare, and there are very few models of this model around. A contemporary chemist views the material universe as composed of millions and millions of atoms, each one being an atom of some one of approximately ninety-two elemental types. As with the spectrum, we can locate elements in the Periodic Table, and say where Boron, or Silicon, or Sulphur comes, but cannot say where the Periodic Table itself is located. Aristotle criticized Plato for having his species quite separate from their specimens,[7] but Plato was right.

The Third Man

Plato did not distinguish his theory of species from his theory of features. Although they both offered a solution to the problem of universals, the problem of how one word could be applied to many instances, there were important differences between them, and these generated paradoxes Plato was unable to

---

[7] *Nicomachean Ethics*, I, 1097b31-35.

solve. The key difference was in the relation that obtained between a particular instance and the Form. When the same adjective is applicable to a number of different instances, it is because they all *share* a feature, all participate in the same quality, all have the same property in common. The Greek verb is μετέχειν (*metechein*), with the corresponding nouns μέθεξις (*methexis*) and μετοχή (*metoche*). When the same noun is applicable to a number of different instances, it is because they all *resemble* the paradigm, or are copies of it. The Greek verbs are μιμεῖσθαι (*mimeisthai*) and ἀφοιμοῦσθαι (*aphoimousthai*). Either relation can be used, but not both. For then there arises the question "In virtue of what common properties do we apply the word 'deuterium' both of the atoms found in particular specimens of heavy water and of the Hydrogen mark two that, together with Protium and Tritium, occupies the first place in the Periodic Table?". If we follow the previous line of argument we are led to posit the existence of a third paradigm of Deuterium to account for the same name being applied both to particular atoms and to the prototype in the Periodic Table. And then clearly we are embarked on an infinite regress. Plato discusses this in the *Parmenides* (132a-133a). His example is not of a third Deuterium, but of a Third Man, and it is referred to as such by Aristotle's *Metaphysics*[8] and all modern commentators. It is more difficult to disentangle it if we consider the abstract quality humanity and the species man (or *homo sapiens*) because these words are in constant use and have lost their sharp edges. Deuterium, because it is less familiar, is better. It is evident then that the difficulty arises from our use of the two metaphors together. If we keep to sharing, μετέχειν, then although particular atoms of deuterium are called deuterium because they all share certain properties, these properties which they all have in common—*e.g.* that of having mass 2 and of having only one proton in the nucleus—are properties, not atoms. So, too, in Plato's example, if all men are each described by the word 'man' by reason of their all possessing a common humanity, that common humanity itself is not a man, and the question of what justifies us in calling it, too, a man does not arise. The name of the common set of qualities in virtue of which each man is called 'man' is not itself 'man' but 'humanity'. The question "In virtue of what do we ascribe the same word 'man' both to individual men and to the abstract quality 'humanity'?" does not arise. Equally, the property of having atomic weight 2 is not itself an atom, and cannot find itself either in the world around us or in the Periodic Table. To accept the latter locution, we have to use, rather, the metaphor of copying, resembling, or being a model of. In that case we can ask "in virtue of what do we apply the word 'deuterium' both to particular atoms in specimens of heavy water and to Hydrogen mark 2 in the first place in the Periodic Table?". To this question there is a perfectly good answer. The particular atoms of deuterium

---

[8] *Metaphysics* A,990b12, Z,1039a2-3; also *Soph.El.*,178b36-179a10.

are called 'deuterium' because they resemble the prototype Deuterium in the Periodic Table 1: and the prototype Deuterium in the Periodic Table is called Deuterium because it, too, resembles the prototype Deuterium in the Periodic Table; *i.e.* it resembles itself. Resemblance is a reflexive relation. If we explain our use of language by reference to resemblance to an ideal type, then no third type is required to explain the use of language of that ideal type.

Some difficulty may be felt in the use of the other metaphors 'copy', 'model'. These carry with them in ordinary use an implication of non-identity, in the same way as, although I am my brother's brother, I am not my own brother. A copy in ordinary usage resembles, but is not identical with, the original, just as my brother is a son of the same parents as, but not identical with, myself. If we keep the requirement of non-identity, then certainly we have an infinite regress. But there is no reason to insist on it. With the word 'model' we have sometimes had occasion to allow that something can be a model of itself; with the word 'copy' publishers have to use the word for each book (token) that they publish. Plato's use of the words is metaphorical anyway. It is quite reasonable to construe them in a way that will obviate unnecessary problems. If we take resemblance, rather than non-identity, as the key to the copying metaphor, then we can accept, as an alternative account of how common nouns can be applied to different specimens, that each specimen is a copy of, is modelled on, an ideal prototype, in the way that each deuterium atom is an exact replica of the paradigm Deuterium atom which, along with Protium and Tritium, occupies the first place in the Periodic Table.

We may ask 'How did Plato come to swap metaphors in mid-stream, thereby landing himself in the Third Man problem?' The answer lies in his philosophy of mathematics. It is natural to say that the circle itself is circular, the square itself is square, whereas it is not natural to say that humanity is human. Equally with colours, the colour white can be said, without obvious strain, to be white, the colour red to be red. Self-predication becomes easy when practised on shapes and colours. Plato believed that in the science of shapes he could find the key to all knowledge. And shapes provided the ambiguous bridge that led him from the metaphor of sharing to that of copying, or resembling, and so gave rise to the Third Man paradox.

Two other reasons for Plato's confusing sharing in qualities with resembling paradigms may also be noted. First, it was much more difficult in Greek than it is in English to distinguish words from what they might be taken to refer to. In English the word 'just' is typographically distinct from the concept of justice. In Greek, which had no inverted commas, τὸ δικαίον could be understood as referring either to the word or to the quality. In the *Republic* it is used interchangeably with δικαιοσύνη. It is not at all natural to say in English that justice is just: it is not at all easy to deny in Greek that τὸ δικαίον ἐστί δικαίον. Hence in the *Protagoras* (330c-d) he is led to affirm that δικαιοσύνη is δικαίον (the neuter is significant here—we might have expected a feminine, agreeing with δικαιοσύνη): that Plato often uses the neuter with δικαιοσύνη—as in *Republic* IV—shows how closely it has been assimilated to δικαίον.

The second reason stems from Plato's concern for values. In the *Phaedo* (100c4-6) he argues εἴ τί ἐστιν ἄλλο καλὸν πλὴν αὐτὸ τὸ καλόν, οὐδὲ δι᾽ ἓν ἄλλο καλὸν εἶναι ἢ διότι μετέχει ἐκείνου τοῦ καλοῦ—if anything else is beautiful besides beauty itself, it is beautiful for no other reason than that it shares in that beauty. Similarly in *Republic* VI the Form of the Good is itself good. Values *are* valuable. The distinction between the timeless impersonal world of abstract entities, and the temporal personal world of human affairs which we readily evaluate, becomes much less clear when the abstract entities are themselves values, and self-predication becomes that much more acceptable. Nevertheless, it is self-predication which gives rise to the paradox of the Third Man. And Aristotle, in his criticism of the Forms in *Metaphysics* A, (ch.9, 991a20ff.) points to the use of the two metaphors, of resembling paradigms and sharing in properties, as generating nonsense:

τὸ δὲ λέγειν παραδείγματα αὐτὰ εἶναι καὶ μετέχειν αὐτῶν τᾶλλα κενολογεῖν ἐστὶ καὶ μεταφορὰς λέγειν ποιητικάς. To say that they (*i.e.* the Forms) are paradigms and that other things share in them is to talk nonsense and utter poetical metaphors.

The Logic of Nouns

There are other difficulties in a theory of Forms taken as a theory of nouns. Nouns have a different logic from adjectives. I can negate an adjective, and consider something's being not-white, non-Greek, non-English; in *Republic* V, when Plato first discusses Forms, he considers them in pairs, αἰσχρόν, shameful, as well as τὸ καλόν, fair; τὸ ἀδίκον, wrong, as well as δικαίον, right; κακόν, bad, as well as ἀγαθόν, good.[9] But there is no species of not-man, no place in the Periodic Table for non-Hydrogen. Similarly, adjectives but not nouns can be conjoined and disjoined. Aristotle distinguished substances, which can be referred to by nouns, from adjectives, which characterize what they are predicated of. Within the category of substance, he distinguished primary substances, such as those referred to by proper names, like 'Socrates', from secondary substances, referred to by common nouns. Species were only secondary substances; the names that referred to them—'man', 'horse'—could also be used to describe—'Socrates is a man', 'Bucephalus is a horse'. Plato did not develop a doctrine of substance. He came to be uneasy about species. In the *Parmenides* (130a-e) as well as rejecting Forms of Mud, Hair and Dirt, he is doubtful about Man, Fire and Water, although still confident of the Forms of Justice, Beauty, and Goodness, as well as the more abstract ones

---

[9] But Plato does not properly distinguish between contradictories and contraries.

of Likeness, Unity, Plurality, *etc.* Later still he distinguished the objects of mathematical thought—τὰ μαθηματικά—from the Forms, and thought of them as some subordinate category of entities. Aristotle in *Metaphysics*, M, chapters 4ff.,[10] discusses the many different versions put forward, but his many detailed criticisms are of the theory propounded in the Academy, not the tentative explorations of the *Republic*.[11]

Objects of Knowledge

The Forms are objects of knowledge. As we have seen,[12] Plato is assimilating *knowledge that* (I wist not that it was the High Priest) to *knowledge of* (D'ye ken John Peel). We often do so too. If I know the Periodic Table, I know that Hydrogen comes first, Helium second, *etc.* and *vice versa*. It is because the Forms can be known, that they can correct common opinion. They are objectively true, and therefore have the edge over what is merely subjectively believed. Even as a theory of adjectives, explaining how communication is possible, the Forms have many marks of objectivity. The language we use to talk about qualities and relations is impersonal, placeless and timeless. It makes no sense to talk about my yellow or your yellow; equally, they are not located in space.[13] If I ask where yellow is in the spectrum, you can tell me that it is between orange and green: but if I then ask where the spectrum is, you are at a loss to know how to answer my question. Similarly the chemical elements exist placelessly, tenselessly and impersonally—I can say where Oxygen is in the Periodic Table, but not where the Periodic Table itself is, nor that Oxygen used to be where Nitrogen now is, nor that it belongs to Imperial Chemical Industries Ltd—whereas particular atoms can be located in a particular place at a particular time, and in some cases—the calcium of my teeth—can belong to a particular person. The objects of knowledge are likewise placeless, tenseless and impersonal. We do not say that π *be* irrational in Oxford, and wonder whether it *be* in Cambridge too. When Voltaire said that he left space a plenum in Paris and found it a vacuum in London, the joke depended on the logical inappropriateness of ascribing a place to abstract entities. Nor do we say that Pythagoras' Theorem was true yesterday, or Newton's Second Law of Motion will not be true in 2005 AD; nor that the Second Law of Dynamics is true for Peter, but not for Paul. Recently philosophers have adopted J.J.C. Smart's suggestion of italicising the tenseless

---

[10] *Metaphysics*, 1178b7ff.

[11] For a scholarly discussion of Plato's views on the Forms, see J.Adam, *The Republic of Plato*, ii, Cambridge, 1902, pp.86-87.

[12] In ch.4, pp.49-50.

[13] Aristotle, *Physics*, 203a8-9.

use of the present tense,[14] so that we write two and two *is* four, or π *is* irrational. Even better, at least for reading aloud, is to replace the italicised *is* with an italicised infinitive—two and two *be* four, π *be* irrational. Plato's claim in the *Timaeus* (37e-38a) that 'was' and 'will be' cannot properly be used of the Forms can be seen in part as stipulating, in an entirely acceptable way, the use of the tenseless present for qualities, relations and other abstract entities. The requirements of impersonality, tenselessness and placelessness are connected. They contrast with the personal tensed discourse of the here and now. The first- and second-person singular of tensed discourse depend on who is speaking to whom and when. Words such as 'I', 'you', 'this', 'now' and 'here' are sometimes called 'indexicals' or 'token-reflexives', but Russell's term, 'egocentric particulars' is peculiarly illuminating, for they depend for their reference on who I am, whom I am addressing, what I am pointing to, when I am uttering, and where I am situated. Plato, as we have seen,[15] supposed that the opposite of selfishness was selflessness, and so was disposed to welcome a form of discourse that eschewed all egocentric particulars. He may have gone too far.[16] But certainly the impersonal, tenseless, placeless discourse he promulgated is the language of mathematics and science, and carries with it strong connotations of objectivity. Not only can we *talk* about the chemical elements, and discuss their properties, but if we understand their properties, we are well on the way to understanding the nature of things.

Necessity

The objects of knowledge are not only impersonal, placeless and timeless, but in some sense necessary. Plato is moved by two considerations: one stems from the logical grammar of the word 'know'. As we saw in the previous chapter,[17] I cannot properly say 'I know that *p*, but it is possible that not-*p*'. But that locution does not imply either that my knowledge must be infallible, or that only necessary truths can be known. Although I should not say 'I know that *p*', if there is a real possibility of my being wrong, I can properly say 'I know that *p*, although it is just conceivable that not-*p*', thereby vouching for *p*, while humbly acknowledging my own fallibility.

Plato's other argument follows from timelessness. Timeless Forms cannot change. The cannot be other than they *be*. But though timeless truths cannot change to being other than what they are, they can be *about* things that could be different, and indeed, about things that change. The chalk downs of southern England were laid down in the Cretaceous age, but that

---

[14] J.J.C.Smart, *Philosophy and Scientific Realism*, London, 1963, p.133.

[15] Ch.2, pp.23-24.

[16] See below, ch.10, pp.134ff.

[17] Ch.4, pp.46-47.

is not a necessary truth—they might have been a Jurassic formation. And though it is unalterably true that the battle of Hastings was won by William the Conqueror in 1066, it was a temporal event, and its outcome might have been different.

Plato's argument is invalid, but has been widely accepted. Logical Positivists used to deny that we could have genuine knowledge of ordinary empirical propositions: I could only have a probable belief, they said, that the sun would rise tomorrow, since it was not logically necessary that the sun would rise tomorrow. But invalid though his argument is, Plato is feeling towards an important truth. Purely contingent propositions, such as the time of the next train to London, may be knowable, but we do not feel that we have really comprehended them, until we not only know *that* they are true, but also *why*. Science, *scientia*, ἐπιστήμη, is more than an assemblage of assured truths; it requires also an understanding of why they are true, the rational necessity that makes them be true. There is some sense of hardness about scientific truth which makes it not only ineluctably true, but profoundly true. In this Plato was following Pythagoras. By understanding mathematics, the Pythagoreans supposed, they would understand the harmony of things and be able to construe justice in terms of a geometrical figure. Plato is very much of the same way of thinking, and one indication of the importance of mathematics is that it is immune to the changes and chances of the fleeting world of transient phenomena, and tells us about a reality that is necessarily (and not contingently or transiently) the case.

Plato carried his views into educational practice. At the end of his life he wrote a passage which reads very much like a modern, but Platonic, Minister of Education giving guidelines to the Higher Education Funding Council on the re-shaping of the republic of letters.[18]   Besides banning such banausic subjects as Architecture, Dietetics, and Wool Technology, he looks askance at the humanities[19] and most of the natural sciences, allowing only mathematics and mathematical physics as worthy of study by serious minded men.

We still are guided by his sentiments. Mathematicians think that mathematical physicists are less clever then they are themselves, and mathematical physicists look down on mere experimentalists, who in turn regard chemistry as a less good subject. Chemists believe that biology is only practical biochemistry, and among biologists, physiologists believe that they can one day supply the key to explaining the behaviour that ethologists observe. Anthropology is only a special case of primatology, and psychology is not really a science unless it is reduced to physiological mechanisms which can properly explain it. As for the arts subjects, history, literature and the like, hard-nosed

---

[18] *Epinomis* 975-979.

[19] An embarrassment to those reading *Literae Humaniores* in the University of Oxford for which Plato is one of the main authorities.

scientists agree in their heart of hearts that they are not really science, that is to say, not really knowledge, but only soft options, suitable only for girls, weaklings and aspiring after-dinner speakers.

These prejudices are illuminating, as are also the counter-prejudices of those in the despised disciplines. Although Plato was wrong to deny the name 'knowledge' to anything other than mathematical science, he was responding to some modal feature of scientific understanding. It is unclear exactly what it is. Rational necessity is not the logical necessity many philosophers have taken it to be. It may be different in different disciplines. If Plato was wrong, we are not yet in a position to put him right.

Conclusion

Plato's theory of Forms is difficult. Much of the difficulty arises from the fact that Plato's own thoughts do not form a single coherent doctrine. The theory of Forms was meant to solve a number of different problems, and a theory of adjectives did not serve also as a theory of knowledge. He was continually thinking, and therefore continually re-thinking, his ideas. Often he criticized in one dialogue what he had put forward in an earlier one. In the *Parmenides*, the *Sophist* and the *Philebus* he criticized arguments and doctrines he had advanced in the *Phaedo* and the *Republic*.[20] It is a mistake to try and produce a completely worked out theory of Forms. Instead, we should distinguish a number of themes which Plato was working at, which are not all compatible, and which he was refining and modifying as he came to see more fully their implications. It is helpful also to consider not the arguments which Plato gives for believing in Forms, but the positions he was trying to establish, and those that he was trying to controvert. He gives good arguments against subjectivism and nominalism. He introduced a discourse in which we can talk about abstract entities, such as qualities, relations, species. In the *Theaetetus* (182a8), which he wrote after the *Republic*, he invented the word ποιότης (*poiotes*), *qualitas* in Latin, our 'quality', and Aristotle took it over,[21] and invented the corresponding ποσότης (*posotes*), *quantitas*, our 'quantity'.[22] Part of what Plato is doing in his theory of Forms is arguing that abstract entities can be the objects of discourse, and laying down the rules for talking about them. Our language now is full of abstract nouns enabling us to talk about abstract entities. We talk not only about qualities and quantities, but about orderings, equivalence classes, real numbers and SI^3 groups, and our understanding of the world would be greatly diminished if such terms were not available. This constitutes a powerful argument against

---

[20] See above, this ch. pp.60-61.

[21] *Categories* 8, 18b25, and *Nicomachean Ethics* X, 3, 12, 1173a15.

[22] *Metaphysics*, Z, 1,2, 1028a19.

nominalism: things are not the only things to exist. Nor can a thorough-going scepticism be plausibly maintained. The sceptic may make out that beauty is in the eye of the beholder, but not every feature can be, or we should not be able to establish an objective language at all. Subjectivism and relativism are ruled out. Words cannot just mean what I want them to mean, and sometimes accepted usage can be corrected in the light of fuller knowledge. The language of science is replete with intimations of objectivity. It does not follow inevitably that morals must be objective, but it does show that the idea of objective moral discourse is possible, and, indeed, that the onus of proof is on those who would deny the objectivity of morals, not on those who maintain it.

In the Middle Ages, besides nominalists and conceptualists, there were two sorts of realist: those who, like Aristotle, allowed the existence of 'universals', but only inasmuch as they inhered '*in rebus*', and those who, like Plato, sep-arated universals from their particular instances, maintaining that universals existed independently of any particular instance, existing '*ante rem*'. The dispute is unresolved still. With artefacts and biological species, Aristotle's account seems more plausible. There are innumerable possible artefacts, in-numerable possible species, and it is only when some specific type is invented or has evolved, that we take notice of it. Chemists are more Platonist. No atoms with atomic number 85 or 87 have ever been discovered, but we still talk of Element 85 and Element 87. The Periodic Table so circumscribes the possibilities for atomic structure, that the available ones seem definite and describable, whether or not they are actually instantiated. Modern mathe-maticians are, for the most part Platonists. They deal in structures, and it is a matter of indifference whether a structure is instantiated or not, except that if it is instantiated, then clearly its specification cannot be inconsis-tent. It is a matter of importance that mathematical propositions are true or false, independently of our knowing whether they are true or false, and that structures, especially sets, exist or fail to exist, independently of our being able to construct them. The Platonist is entitled to use classical logic with the Principle of Bivalence, and to consider impredicative sets. But if inde-pendent existence is denied to abstract entities, then mathematics is much diminished—mutilated, some mathematicians would say. Plato's ontology was never properly worked out; but he gave good reasons for believing in entities we believe in still.

Nevertheless, it leaves awkward questions that sometimes cannot be answered—how long is Euler line?—though somewhat similar questions can. More seriously, he never gave an adequate account of the relations between the Forms themselves, or between the Forms and the experiences of every-day life. In Book VII (529-530) he insulates ἀστρονομία (*astronomia*) from possible refutation by empirical observation,[23] but if the Forms are entirely

---

[23] 'Astronomy' is not really the right translation: see below, ch.6, p.80.

separate from everyday life, they are open to Aristotle's criticism that they are irrelevant to everyday life and the way we should live it.[24]

Almost all Plato's metaphors are visual: but middle C, or the melody of Greensleeves, is as worthy a candidate for being a Form as the square on the diagonal. Even in mathematics algorithms and manipulations are important, but Plato discountenances all talk of *doing* things (*Republic* VII, 527a6-b8), and saw mathemtics as a contemplation of an essentially static reality, not as a way of grasping and manipulating concepts to make them more comprehensible. Epistemological Platonism is less plausible than ontological Platonism. In the *Republic* Plato says that the Forms are apprehended with the eye of the mind (VII 518). But often the visual metaphor will not work. Often we reach understanding not by focusing the eye of the mind, but by argument or empirical observation. Plato half realises this. It is the $\mu\acute{\epsilon}\theta o\delta o\varsigma$ $\delta\iota\alpha\lambda\epsilon\kappa\tau\iota\kappa\acute{\eta}$, the method of discussion, that leads us to grasp the principles of mathematics and the Form of the Good. And it is to his theory of argument that we must now turn.

---

[24] *Nicomachean Ethics*, I, 6, 13, 1096b31-35.

Chapter 6
Plato's Theory of Argument

The Search for Absolute Cogency

There is, as we have noted,[1] a marked break between *Republic* I and *Republic* II-X, in tone and style. Book I resembles many of the earlier dialogues: there really is some give and take in conversation. Its approach is tentative, its conclusions negative. The other books, however, are much more like the later dialogues, which are dialogues only in name. Instead of being tentative and negative, they are positive and constructive. Plato himself is aware of the change; he is becoming less happy with the dialogue form as a vehicle of his views. Formally speaking the *Republic* is not dialogue at all: it is a monologue, by Socrates, reporting a discussion he had had the day before. There is a single speaker, Socrates, who starts off Κατέβην χθὲς εἰς Πειραιᾶ 'I went down yesterday to Piraeus'. Similarly the *Phaedo*, although technically a conversation between Echecrates and Phaedo is really a report by Phaedo of a previous conversation between Socrates, Simmias and Cebes. In the *Parmenides*, later than the *Republic*, the structure is even more cumbersome, and the *Theaetetus* takes the form of two friends reading another dialogue in a book. Plato is consciously reconsidering his use of dialogue, and feeling some pressure to change to a more monologous form.

The practice of διαλεκτική, discussion, leads to a great clarification of concepts. One might ask: In what way does it add to our knowledge or understanding? In part it is just that it gives experience of thinking: talking, that is, thinking aloud, is the best way of obtaining skill in thinking exactly: we obtain more understanding—a greater ability to think exactly. We also obtain knowledge, knowledge about meanings; we are able to say what we mean by a word more precisely, with greater definition. Here what we are doing is drawing on our ability to use the concepts, that is, our ability to speak the language; and by the method of διαλεκτική, discussion, we are making explicit what we knew already implicitly; it is a πορεία, a progress, from knowing how to use words to knowing how words are used.

This method suffers from being formless. It is all right if an amiable young man will chat and agree whenever agreement is seriously needed: but there does not seem to be any rigour in this sort of discussion: it is too soft. Suppose there was a real argument; how are we to choose between the parties? We feel the force of Thrasymachus' complaint in *Republic* I (336c1):

---

[1] In ch.2, pp.15-16.

καὶ τί εὐθίζεσθε πρὸς ἀλλήλοις ὑποκατακλινόμενοι ὑμῖν αὐτοῖς;
what is the use of your always giving way to each other good-naturedly?

If we want to argue with all comers, even unreasonable sophists, we shall need a more compelling form of argument than mere friendly discussion. Plato was looking for really cogent considerations, which would work even against Thrasymachus. Inconsistency—self-contradiction—is a telling charge. Socrates uses it against Thrasymachus in *Republic* I (339b-e), where Thrasymachus, having said that τὸ δίκαιον, morality, is the interest of the stronger, agrees also that it is δίκαιον, moral, to obey the government, and that the government can make mistakes, whereupon Socrates derives a contradiction, and drives Thrasymachus to withdraw the third premise, and make out that the government, *qua* government, is infallible.[2]

We might ask why Thrasymachus should be averse to contradicting himself. The answer is that if he or any other sophist were prepared to contradict himself, he would show not that he was very hard-headed, but that he did not understand Greek; communication would break down with him, and all we could do with him would be to ἐᾶν χαίρειν, say good-bye. Plato has found a sure-fire method of argument, which will work against even Thrasymachus, but at a price. It is no longer a genuine discussion between two parties, each anxious to discover the truth, but essentially a monologue, in which the respondent contributes nothing beyond a bare commitment to speaking a language intelligibly. Arguments which will work against all comers, no matter how unreasonable, are essentially one-sided monologues, so far as their underlying logic is concerned.

In Book IV of the *Republic* Plato formulates the Law of Non-contradiction (436b-437a). In the *Phaedo*, written about the same time, he tries to formulate a theory of argument based on non-contradiction, which can be seen as an idealized formal account of Socrates' own procedure in trapping his opponents into having to allow absurd conclusions, thereby discrediting their original claim. He says (*Phaedo* 101d4-5):

οὐκ ἀποκρίναιο ἕως ἂν τὰ ἀπ᾽ ἐκείνης ὁρμηθέντα σκέψαιο εἴ σοι ἀλλήλοις συμφονεῖ ἢ διαφονεῖ. Do not give an opinion on a supposition until you have examined whether the consequences that follow from it are mutually consistent or not.

It is a negative criterion. We can refute an opponent's thesis by deriving an inconsistency from it, though the fact that its consequences are consistent with one another does not show that it is true. It is simply an indication of the badness of a contention. Its virtue is that it does not depend merely on a common standard of absurdity, where it is not necessary to be talking to a Glaucon who will say Ἄτοπον μεντ᾽ ἂν εἴη, 'That would be absurd,'

---

[2] See above, ch.1, p.9.

when required. If a contention is self-contradictory it can be dismissed as unsound. This is the first stage of logical awareness. If from a thesis mutually contradictory consequences can be deduced, then the thesis is necessarily false. It is a *reductio ad absurdum* properly so called. An argument like this is used in *Theaetatus* 171a.

The difficulty about this sort of argument is that it is solely destructive: we cannot establish a true assertion by means of it, only demolish a false. Some philosophers have hoped otherwise. Kant assumed that the principle of universalisability would eliminate all possible courses of action save one. Plato himself uses an argument by exhaustion in identifying δικαιοσύνη, justice (IV 433b-c). But such arguments are unconvincing. It is difficult to establish the premise that all the alternatives have been surveyed, and that there are no others left out of consideration. The only effective use of the Law of Non-contradiction on its own is to refute false theses, not to establish true ones.

Plato felt this. In *Republic* I, Plato makes Thrasymachus very critical of Socrates' method (337a4-7):

Ὦ Ἡράκλεις, ἔφη, αὕτη ʼκείνη ἡ εἰρονεία Σωκράτους, καὶ ταῦτʼ ἐγὼ ᾔδη τε καὶ τούτοις προύλεγον, ὅτι σὺ ἀποκρίνεσθαι μὲν οὐκ ἐθελήσοις, εἰρονεύσοιο δὲ καὶ πάντα μᾶλλον ποιήσ- οις ἢ ἀποκρινοῖο, εἴ τίς τί σε ἐρωτᾷ. Oh lord, this is Socrates' usual mock-modesty which I was telling them about, that you are never prepared to give an answer, but will play ignorant and do anything rather than give an answer, should any one ask you something.

At the end of Book I, Socrates confesses how very little he has been able to establish (354ab). Plato seems to accept himself the criticisms he puts into Thrasymachus' mouth, and to be coming himself to recognise that the Socratic method of the early dialogues is inadequate to the tasks the philosopher should set himself. It is too destructive, too negative, too tentative, unable to lead to definite conclusions or positive statements. In Book I Plato proved that no simple Socratic definition of δικαιοσύνη, honesty, is possible. Thus he is forced, if he is to give an adequate account of δικαιοσύνη, honesty, to go beyond the critical method of Socrates, and launch out into a radical reconstruction of society, and a large-scale metaphysical enterprise. *Republic* I is the last Socratic dialogue.

Deduction

Although the Law of Non-contradiction is essentially negative, it can be put to positive use. If the respondent will grant suitable premises, conclusions may follow with logical necessity. If it would be self-contradictory to affirm the premises and deny the conclusion, then we have a *deductive* argument, which can drag agreement even out of a Thrasymachus (I 350c12-d7). For example if I were to say:

All men are mortal,

Socrates is a man,

and   Socrates is not mortal,

I should be contradicting myself; and should be making myself unintelligible. I show that I do not understand the meaning of the words 'all', 'are', 'is', 'and', and 'not', if I utter the three propositions above. Hence, deductive arguments are arguments whose validity even sophists must acknowledge, on pain of not being able to say anything at all, if having conceded the premises of a deductive argument, they refuse to admit the conclusion.

Plato was discovering deduction while he was writing the *Republic*. In Book VI, where he is revising his views on mathematics, he complains about the habit of contemporary Greek mathematicians of using figures, instead of deductive proofs, in geometry (510b4-5, 510d55-511a1, 511a6,c1). In the *Phaedo* (92d) he makes Simmias say that he regards as quacks those who fashion proofs for themselves from probabilities. Again, in his intellectual autobiography (*Phaedo* 96-100) he tells us how he gave up the search for efficient causes and turned to look for formal causes instead: that is, he abandoned the search for causal explanations in favour of deductive logical ones.[3]   And so, when he comes to think about argument, he is ready to conclude that arguments, if they are to be both irresistible and positive, must be deductive.

In the *Phaedo* Plato tries to formulate a theory of argument. He says (*Phaedo* 100a):

ἀλλ᾿ οὖν δὴ ταύτῃ γε ὥρμησα, καὶ ὑποθέμενος ἑκάστοτε λόγον ὃν ἂν κρίνω ἐρρωμενέστατον εἶναι, ἃ μὲν ἄν μοι δοκῇ τούτῳ συμφωνεῖν τίθημι ὡς ἀληθῆ ὄντα, καὶ περὶ αἰτίας καὶ περὶ τῶν ἄλλων ἁπάντων, ἃ δᾶν μή, ὡς οὐκ ἀληθῆ. My procedure was on each occasion to suppose true whatever proposition I reckoned to be best established, and then whatever else (whether about causes or any other thing) agreed with it I took to be true, and whatever did not as false

and then, in *Phaedo* 101de, after the passage cited in the previous section:

ἐπειδὴ δὲ ἐκείνης αὐτῆς δέοι σε διδόναι λόγον, ὡσαύτως ἂν διδοίης, ἄλλην αὖ ὑπόθεσιν ὑποθέμενος ἥτις τῶν ἄνωθεν βελτίστη φαίνοιτο, ἕως ἐπί τι ἱκανὸν ἔλθοις If you have to give a justification for it, do so by positing some other supposition, whichever seems the best established of those under which it could be subsumed, and so on until you come to an adequate one.

In contrast to the preceding passage, Plato here is offering a way we can establish our own thesis, by getting our opponent to accept a premise from

---

[3] *Phaedo* 96-100.

which it can be deduced. It is positive, and became the paradigm of cogent argument. Argument should proceed *more geometrico*, in the geometric manner, in a way that would brook no denial.

Deductive argument is sometimes used by Socrates; but the phrase ἐπί τι ἱκανὸν (*epi ti hikanon*), some adequate premise, presents difficulties—can we assure ourselves of the adequacy of our premises? Plato is unclear on this point. In his earlier dialogues, his method was informal, and he found adequate suppositions by trial and error. It seems that he was relying on a comparable informal method in his search for the ultimate first principle of the Form of the Good.[4] But such a procedure would not be Thrasymachus-proof. He would not willingly concede any premise that might be of use to his opponents. How is argument to procede in the face of unreasonable unwillingness to concede anything?

Mathematicians secure the premises they need by supposing that certain facts are given—the data of the problem. Greek mathematics at the time of Plato consisted of a number of somewhat separate problems and their solutions, each problem being phrased so as to have the requisite premises included among the data. But not all argument is with mathematicians implicitly conceding the premises needed in stating the problem. If our opponent is going to be unreasonable about the arguments he will allow, he will be equally unreasonable about the premises he will admit; if he is going to cavil at 'He is a man, so he is mortal' and will only concede the inference that he is mortal from the premise 'He is a man' granted the further premise 'All men are mortal', then he will equally cavil at admitting that further premise. So we then will have to establish that all men are mortal first, before going on to our original argument. But how are we to establish that? By deduction? Then from further premises, more general than those he has already refused to accept. But will he not refuse those also? With a sufficiently unreasonable man, we shall have an infinite regress, like the Indian rope trick, looking for an adequate premise from which all else will follow.

In Books VI and VII of the *Republic* Plato is trying to formulate a theory of philosophical argument to surmount the difficulties of a purely deductive account. In the course of doing so, he changed his mind about the nature of mathematical argument. It is largely because of this that his account at the end of Book VI and in Book VII of the *Republic* is difficult to follow.

Plato's Philosophies of Mathematics

Even as he was articulating his philosophy of mathematics, Plato was having to alter it.

In the *Meno* he had pointed out that mathematical theorems are true *a priori*. He got a slave boy and by a series of questions elicited from him a

---

[4] See below, ch.7, p.101.

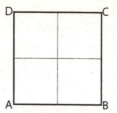

Figure 6.1. How can we draw a square twice the size of ABCD (four square feet—each foot square marked faintly in figure)?

method of constructing a line $\sqrt{2}$ as long as a given one of two feet (AB in the figures), using a special case of Pythagoras' theorem.[5]

The boy was asked to construct a square twice the size of ABCD, which was two foot square, *i.e.* four square feet. The boy tried first AIKL (sixteen faint squares) and then AQSR (nine faint squares). In each case Socrates could lead him to see that he was wrong merely by asking him questions, *i.e.* without telling him any *a posteriori* truth.

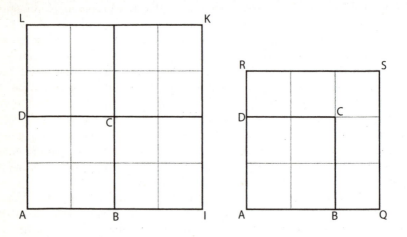

Figure 6.2 First stage: rejection of false answers (*Meno* 82-83).

Again he drew a 4 x 4 square ATYX. He then constructed the diagonals DB, BU, UW, WD. Since each diagonal cut each of the squares ABCD, BTUC, CUYW, and DCWX in half, the square DBUW was half the big square ATYX, and so twice the original square ABCD, as desired.

---

[5] *Meno* 82-85; the letters are as in A.D. Lindsay, *Five Dialogues*, Everyman ed., London, 1910, pp.102-108.

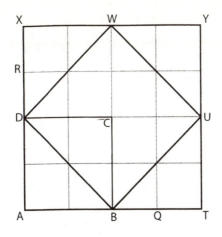

Figure 6.3 Second stage: pointing out the true answer (*Meno* 84-85).

Plato used this as an argument for ἀνάμνεσις (*anamnesis*), recollection: the argument does not hold, but the point made about the nature of mathematics is a sound one. Mathematical truths are not dependent on sense experience in the way that most truths—factual truths—are. If we want to know the truth about a matter of fact—the date of the battle of Marathon or the melting point of sulphur—we must either use one of the senses, sight, touch, hearing, taste or smell, directly, or accept someone's statement about it on trust. In mathematics this is not so. We *can* know mathematical truths without using any senses, and without taking anybody's word on trust. This is what happens when a person 'sees' a theorem on his own. Of course often we do not get very far on our own, and have to have hints, or have things pointed out to us. This is what Socrates did for the boy. It is often objected that Socrates used unfair methods, since his questions are all leading questions. That is to miss the point. They *were* leading questions, and *did* lead the boy to see what he otherwise would not have seen: but at no time did Socrates *tell* him anything, and he always could have answered No to Socrates' leading questions, had not the force of reason been too strong for him.

The *Meno* argument shows that in an important way mathematics does not depend on the evidence of the senses. In Kant's terminology it is *a priori*. Plato attached immense importance to *a priori* truth. We can know *a priori* truths in advance of, and independently of, experience; they seem to be harder, more basic, more fundamental than *a posteriori* truths based on experience. Our experience could have been otherwise,[6] and truths based on

---

[6] Aristotle, *Ethics*, VI, 1139b21, 1140b35-1141a1.

it are only contingent: but *a priori* truths are necessary, and immune from the changes and chances of fleeting actuality: they represent the underlying realities of things, the necessary framework in which alone experience can be experienced, and to which it must always, everywhere, inevitably conform. *A priori* truth is necessary, universal and timeless: *a posteriori* truth is contingent, particular and changing. So *a priori* truth is good: empirical, or *a posteriori*, truth is less good.

That Plato regards empirical truth as less good is shown most clearly in his discussion of ἀστρονομία (*astronomia*) (VII 529a-530c), where Socrates rebukes Glaucon for thinking that observation of celestial objects is a proper way of discovering the truth about the universe. The proper approach is that of mathematics—'Natural Philosophy' as it is called in Cambridge—in which problems about planetary motion are set and solved entirely within the framework of deductive derivation, operating in this case with the axioms of Newtonian mechanics. Actual astronomical examples may be given, but only as examples, further problems to be solved. They are exercises in Ramsey's *Introduction to the Theory of Newtonian Attraction*,[7] not empirical confirmation of astronomical theories. We should translate ἀστρονομία (*astronomia*) as 'Dynamics', or 'Rational Mechanics', rather than 'Astronomy'. Empiricists object. Protagoras, as we have seen,[8] argued against the geometers that a wheel does not touch a straight line at only a single point, but along a finite length. Plato conceded that this was true of diagrams drawn by geometers, or tops turned on a lathe, but attributed that to the imperfection of the sensible world, and held that the circle in itself, αὐτός ὁ κύκλος (*autos ho kuklos*), was quite separate from the visible world, and conformed perfectly to geometrical specification of what a circle really was.[9] The ideal shapes of geometry, like the Forms generally, preserve themselves from empirical refutation by being entirely separate from the world of contingent transient things. Although geometers often in practice use visible diagrams and frame arguments about them, what they are really talking about are their ideal exemplars, *the* square and *its* diagonal (VI 510d7-8). Mathematics, thus understood as the supreme example of an *a priori* discipline, comes in the upper part of the Line (VI 511d2-5), being intelligible, νοητόν (*noeton*), not merely observable, ὁρατόν (*horaton*) (VI 509d8).

But there are difficulties. One difficulty, which has been much commented on, is the ontological status of the ideal mathematical shapes. In the Line Plato speaks of *the* square as if it were a Form, but in later dialogues distinguishes the Forms,[10] which are necessarily unique, from τὰ μαθηματικά,

---

[7] Cambridge, 1981.

[8] Ch.5, p.80.

[9] Plato, *Seventh Letter*, 343a.

[10] *Philebus* 56d4-e3; Aristotle, *Metaphysics* A, 991b28-31.

mathematical objects, which may be more than one, as the squares in the *Meno* diagram. It is difficult to read awareness of this problem into any passages in the *Republic*. He was still in process of thinking out his position, and had not yet faced this difficulty.[11]

Other difficulties, however, Plato did face, and was led in consequence to revise his opinion about the nature of mathematical proof, changing from an εἶδος, *Gestalt*, theory to a formal, deductive one. In the *Meno* the solution to the problem jumps out at us, as soon we see the relevant diagonals. We *see* them. Only, Plato argued, since they are not visible lines drawn on a diagram, we see them not with our ordinary eyes, but with the 'eye of the mind'. Mathematical knowledge comes from our being able to discern the underlying patterns interconnecting the different concepts with which we are dealing. There is much truth in this account. It was endorsed by the Cambridge mathematician, G.A. Hardy, in an article in *Mind*[12] and has recently been illustrated with telling examples by Roger Penrose.[13] Nevertheless, the claim that we simply 'see' mathematical truths to be true has several disadvantages:

1. In spite of talk about the eye of the mind, we naturally construe our seeing to be of only some particular figure. We may be able to 'see' that what holds good of it, holds good of any, but there are difficulties in giving a satisfactory account of that.

2. It fits only a particular context of discussion. If I am arguing with you, who know all about the nine-point circle, I can go on from there to the Euler line: but with someone else I must start further back.

3. It depends on 'seeing'. Once I can get the person I am talking to, to have a certain *Gestalt*, well and good. But it is difficult to theorize about getting people to have experiences. It is perilously like ῥητορική, rhetoric, a psychological technique for effective presentation rather than a logical argument. Altogether, the account is too *simpliste* to accommodate the various ways in which we acquire mathematical knowledge, and, in particular, fails to deal with Thrasymachus, who refuses to 'see' things that run counter to his preconceptions.

For this last reason alone, Plato had to formalise. To bring out the deductive nature of mathematical inference, he had to replace 'seeing' features of figures by inferring conclusions from premises. He therefore sought to assimilate

---

[11] See further, A.E.Taylor, 'Forms and Numbers: A Study in Platonic Metaphysics', *Mind*, **35**, 1926, pp.419-440, and **36**, 1927, pp.12-33.

[12] *Mind*, 1929, p.18.

[13] 'On Understanding Understanding', *International Studies in the Philosophy of Science*, vol.11, no.1, March, 1997, pp.11-15. The example is due to Dan Isaacson, Fellow of Wolfson College, Oxford. See also M.D.Resnik, 'Mathematical Knowledge and Pattern-Cognition', *Canadian Journal of Philosophy*, **5**, 1975, p.32.

mathematical reasoning to deductive reasoning. This is why the account he gives in the Line is confusing; it is a conflation of two different views:

1. *Gestalt* (VI 510b6-9, 510d5-e)
2. Deductive (VI 510b4-6, 51Oc)

In working out the latter, he is led to outline the ideal of the axiomatic method.

The Axiomatic Method

Deductive argument can work only if premises are provided. The premises required for one proof are propositions which are themselves susceptible of proof. If an unreasonable interlocutor refuses to grant a premise required for a proof *more geometrico*, then we may set out to establish this premise first, and hence the theorem we originally sought to prove. Thus, in the face of sceptical opposition, we systematize, making each theorem follow deductively from other results already established. Plato's Academy set about formalizing geometry and much of arithmetic, which had been begun by Hippocrates a generation earlier; it was carried on by Eudoxus, who came from Cnidus to join the Academy, and the final result has come down to us in *The Elements* of Euclid, in which everything is proved in an orderly and logical sequence, and each theorem follows from theorems previously proved.

Axiomatization meets the three difficulties raised at the end of the previous section:

1. It gives *definitions* and operates with these. A three-sided figure *etc.*
2. It states what the disputant is to grant. These are the *data*.
3. It requires us to *deduce* instead of to 'see'.

Geometrical theorems can then be proved as conclusions of deductive arguments from premises. The premises may be of three kinds:

1. Definitions. *e.g.* trapezium = quadrilateral with two sides parallel.
2. Special *data* of the problem: *e.g.* given $AB = BC$, prove $AD = DC$.
3. Truths about the figure, which have been already proved.

In the unformalised procedure we could use any truths about the figure that our disputant would concede. We should be merely going from what he would allow to what he hitherto had not conceded. Now, however, we must add the qualification that the premise has been already adequately established both in order to avoid arguing in a circle, and because we are exhibiting our argument formally, and have to be ready to take on any comer, not a particular man who might concede this particular point.

The difficulty is that we have got to start somewhere. We can prove theorems from previous theorems, but how do you prove them? From yet earlier theorems, but then, what about those? Obviously, since deduction can yield true conclusions only if there are given true premises, there must be some ultimate premise (or premises) whose truth cannot be deductively established. So that if deduction is the only form of inference, our chain of argument is left suspended from the air.

As a temporary makeshift, we can decide to start somewhere: have a set of axioms, postulates, suppositions—ὑποθέσεις (*hupotheseis*)—and go on from there, deducing what we can. For *mathematical* purposes this is entirely satisfactory. We have various sets of axioms, and we see what we can get out of them. Euclidean, Riemannian, Hyperbolic, Projective, Geometries all can be developed axiomatically from slightly different sets of axioms. But the *philosopher* cannot be content with that. We obviously have not set our ἐπιστήμη, knowledge, on sound foundations if it all depends upon a series of suppositions whose truth we just assume. If we are to achieve real knowledge, we need to have some premise which is not just postulated. Only an ἀνυπόθετος ἀρχή, unpostulated first principle, can provide an adequate premise from which genuine knowledge may be established by deductive inference.

The Price of Postulating

Mathematicians are scornful of philosophers' discontent. They find questions about foundations upsetting. They are content to grant one another the axioms they need, and then discover what follows from them, assuming, but not having to prove, that they are true. But there is a further difficulty about the axiomatic method, concerning meaning rather than truth, which turns on a subtle distinction between implicit and explicit definitions. Ordinarily, if we give definitions at all, we give explicit ones. We give necessary and sufficient conditions for the use of a word which uniquely identify the occasions for its correct use, *e.g.* 'A puppy is a young dog'; or 'A planet is a body which moves round the sun'. When we develop a subject axiomatically, however, we do not give explicit definitions of the primitive terms. Thus in Projective Geometry we do not say what a point or a line is. All we do is to postulate certain axioms in which the words 'point' and 'line' occur at certain places: everything follows from the axioms, because our system is a formal one, and therefore it does not matter what the words 'point' and 'line' mean in ordinary parlance outside the system. We could replace them by any other distinct words, say 'Tweedledum' and 'Tweedledee', and since everything we say about points and lines in the system follows strictly from the axioms, if the axioms now say about Tweedledums and Tweedledees what they previously said about points and lines, the theorems which previously held for points and lines will now hold equally good of Tweedledums and Tweedledees. One example is that of a dining club with the following rules:

1. Periodical lunches were to be given by the club, and they were to be attended only by members of the club.
2. Every member of the club was to meet every other member at least once, but not more than once, at one of the club's lunches.

3. The lists of members selected by the Secretary to attend any two lunches were never to be entirely different, at least one member was to be present at both.

4. The President, the Treasurer, and the Secretary were to be the only members present at the first lunch, and at all subsequent lunches there were to be at least three members present.

These rules exactly parallel the axioms for a certain finite projective geometry; if a member of the club be a 'point' and a club-lunch be a 'line', and if by definition a 'point' is 'on a line' when the member in question is present at the lunch in question, then the following axioms of incidence are verified:

(a) two distinct points are on at least one line;

(b) two distinct points are on not more than one line;

(c) there is at least one point which is on both of two distinct lines.

Formally there is no difference between the rules of the lunch club and the axioms of Projective Geometry. The Axiomatic Method works with Abstract Uninterpreted Calculi, in which the primitive terms are only implicitly defined, and which can be interpreted onto any entities which satisfy the axioms.

One might hope to get round this difficulty by adding a few more axioms to exclude the unwanted interpretations. Points are very different from people, lines from lunches. It should be easy to exclude the unwanted lunch-club interpretation. So we can; but we cannot exclude all unwanted interpretations. However many extra axioms we add, there are still interpretations which satisfy them, but which are not the one intended. Skolem proved this for any set of axioms in first-order logic seeking to characterize the positive integers: $1, 2, 3, 4, \ldots$. They are not the only things to satisfy such a set of axioms: The non-negative integers do so equally well; $0, 1, 2, 3, \ldots$. So do the negative integers: $-1, -2, -3, -4, \ldots$. Likewise also the fractions: $\frac{1}{1}, \frac{1}{2}, \frac{1}{3}, \frac{1}{4}, \ldots$ Any set of first-order axioms which specifies an abstract system containing an infinite set of entities, such as the natural numbers, fails to particularise enough to identify any one set of entities to the exclusion of others significantly different. Even with an infinite set of axioms this is so: any set of axioms, finite or infinite, which are satisfied by the natural numbers will also be satisfied by something other than the set of natural numbers.[14] Russell's gibe 'the method of "postulating" what we want has many advantages; they are the same as the advantages of theft over honest toil'[15] is only half the truth. For what is appropriated by postulation, turns out to be counterfeit coin, not only illicitly gained, but of no significant value.

---

[14] T.Skolem *Fundamenta Mathematicae*, **23**, 1934, pp.150-161; or see Alonzo Church, *Introduction to Mathematical Logic*, Princeton, 1956. §55, exercise 55.18, p.336.

[15] *Introduction to Mathematical Philosophy*, London, 1919, ch.VII, p.71.

The fundamental weakness of the axiomatic method is that it deals in implicit definitions only, so that we never succeed in giving an account of the particular things we were trying to define. Thus if mathematics consists of the Axiomatic Method alone, it is merely a study of Abstract Systems, of which we can say with Plato (VI 510c2-d3):

οἶμαι γὰρ σε εἰδέναι ὅτι οἱ περὶ τὰς γεωμετρίας τε καὶ λογισμοὺς καὶ τὰ τοιαῦτα πραγματευόμενοι, ὑποθέμενοι τά τε περιττὸν καὶ τὸ ἄρτιον καὶ τὰ σχήματα καὶ γωνιῶν τριττὰ καὶ ἄλλα τούτων ἀδελφὰ καθ᾽ ἑκάστην μέθοδον, ταῦτα μὲν ὡς εἰδότες, ποιησάμενοι ὑποθέσεις αὐτά, οὐδένα λόγον οὔτε αὑτοῖς οὔτε ἄλλοις ἔτι ἀξιοῦσι περὶ αὐτῶν διδόναι ὡς παντὶ φανερῶν, ἐκ τούτων δ᾽ ἀρχόμενοι τὰ λοιπὰ ἤδη διεξιόντες τελευτῶσιν ὁμολογουμένως ἐπὶ τοῦτο οὗ ἂν ἐπὶ σκέψιν ὁρμήσωσι. You know, of course, how students of subjects like geometry and arithmetic begin by positing odd and even numbers, or the various figures and the three kinds of angle, and other such data in each subject. These data they take as known; and, having adopted them as assumptions, they do not feel called upon to give any account of them to themselves or to anyone else, but treat them as self-evident. Then, starting from these assumptions, they go on until they arrive, by a series of consistent steps, at all the conclusions they set out to investigate. (tr. F.M.Cornford, p.220) and (VII 533b6-c5):

αἱ δὲ λοιπαί, ἃς τοῦ ὄντος τι ἔφαμεν ἐπιλαμβάνεσθαι, γεωμετρίας τε καὶ τὰς ταύτῃ ἑπομένας, ὁρῶμεν ὡς ὀνει- ρώττουσι μὲν περὶ τὸ ὂν, ὕπαρ δὲ ᾽δύνατον αὐταῖς ἰδεῖν, ἕως ἂν ὑποθέσεσι χρώμεναι ταύτας ἀκινήτους ἐῶσι, μὴ δυνάμεναι λόγον διδόναι αὐτῶν. ᾧ γὰρ ἀρχὴ μὲν ὃ μὴ οἶδε, τελευτὴ δὲ καὶ τὰ μεταξὺ ἐξ οὗ μὴ οἶδεν συμπλέκται, τίς μηχανὴ τὴν τοιαύτην ὁμολογιαν ποτὲ ἐπιστημην γενεσθαι; Geometry and allied studies do to some extent apprehend reality; but cannot yield anything clearer than a dream-like vision of reality, so long as they leave the postulates they use unshaken and cannot give any rationale of them. If your premise is something you do not know, and your conclusion and the intermediate steps are a tissue of things you do not know, what mechanism can this mere formal consistency become a real science? (tr. Cornford, p.248)

Plato has been criticized for not being clear what he means by ὑποθέσεις (*hupotheseis*). In 510c, quoted above, the examples are all of *concepts*. But in 533d, also quoted above, it must be axioms he has in mind, since they are to be coordinate with conclusions, theorems, propositions. But now we see that axioms and the implicit definition of primitive terms or concepts go hand in hand. Plato is not so much at fault as prescient, offering a telling critique of Hilbert's formalist programme for mathematics in the 1920s and 1930s.

The Search for First Principles

Plato was right in his criticism of the geometers. Axioms cannot be just postulated. They need to be established as true. They could be established as
true, if we could deduce them from more basic principles, themselves given
as true. The search for such principles, though clearly an intellectual endeavour, would not be itself deductive. It is something for διαλεκτική to
do. Διαλεκτική is in part foundational research. It was carried on in the
Academy. Book VII of the *Republic* should be seen not so much as a syllabus for aspiring guardians, as a prospectus or research programme for the
Academy. Theaetetus did solid geometry, Eudoxus not only systematized
plane geometry, but went far in working out how to cope with surds, such
as the square root of 2, which to Plato's mind, was a major stumbling block
in the way of giving an adequate account of mathematics. Eudoxus' way of
handling irrational numbers came very close to Dedekind's explicit definition
of them, and was not surpassed for two thousand years. Granted the arithmetic of the real numbers, we can, as Descartes did, do algebraic geometry,
defining a point in terms of its coordinates, a curve as an equation (and, in
particular, a straight line as a linear equation), a point being on a curve as
the coordinates of the point satisfying the equation, and so on. The axioms
of Euclidean geometry then come out as theorems of the arithmetic of real
numbers. This is what τὰς ὑποθέσεις ἀναιρουσα (*tas hupotheseis anairousa*),
(535c8), 'eliminating the postulates' means. We no longer have to 'hypothesize', postulate, the primitive terms and primitive propositions of traditional
geometry, but can define them and derive them within a more basic theory.
Nor need we stop there. Dedekind and Cantor picked up where Eudoxus had
left off, and gave satisfactory accounts of real numbers, Dedekind in terms of
a certain sort of set—a 'Dedekind cut'—of rational numbers, Cantor in terms
of nested intervals of rational numbers. Once we can define irrational numbers in terms of rational numbers, we can go on to define rational numbers in
terms of whole numbers, and whole numbers in terms of the natural numbers.
Peano showed that the natural numbers satisfied five postulates, and Frege
was able to give explicit definitions of Peano's three primitive terms, 'number',
'successor', 'nought',[16] and Whitehead and Russell, in their *Principia Mathematica* attempted to carry through a complete building up of mathematics,
step by step, on a purely logical basis.[17] Their programme—'logicism'—was

---

[16] There has been much controversy whether the natural numbers were $\{1, 2, 3, \ldots\}$ or
$\{0, 1, 2, 3, \ldots\}$. According to A.E.Taylor (*Plato: the Man and his Work*, London, 1926,
ch.XIX, pp.505ff.), Plato was feeling his way to nought's being the first natural number.

[17] Gottlob Frege, *Groundwork of Arithmetic*, tr.J.L. Austin, Oxford, 1950. A.N.White-
head and B.Russell, *Principia Mathematica*, 2nd ed., Cambridge, 1925-27.

not completely successful. But the logicist programme, insofar as it is successful, is the perfect exemplification of 'treating assumptions, not as first principles, but really as hypotheses in the literal sense, from which one may work back until he reaches the unpostulated premise, the first principle of everything; and having grasped that, come back, holding on to what follows from it, and thus come down to a conclusion...'.(VI 511b5)

Plato needed not only to discover first principles, but to validate them. That cannot be by deduction alone. We may be able to reduce their number: Whitehead and Russell postulated five axioms for propositional calculus, but one of those was later shown to be deducible from the others; and now there are alternative axiomatizations which make do with only one. But still there must be at least one ἀνυπόθετος ἀρχή, unpostulated first principle. It cannot be deduced from any other premises. And though a proposition may be derived from no premises, it can be only because it is itself the negation of a self-contradiction; in which case it is an empty tautology, stating nothing significant, since to deny such a proposition is to flout the rules of language, and to make oneself unintelligible. Many philosophers have pursued the will o' the wisp of absolute certainty secured by absolutely valid deductive inference from absolutely incontrovertible premises. But absolute validity can be had only at the price of absolute vacuity. The very first principle cannot be validated by διάνοια (*dianoia*), derivation.

In his later life Plato gave a lecture on The One. Various accounts have come down to us—it seems that he never himself published a text. The First Principle, ἀνυπόθετος ἀρχή, was the Form of the Good, ἡ ἰδεα τοῦ ἀγαθοῦ, which was beyond being, and excelling it in dignity and power ἐπέκεινα τῆς οὐσίας πρεσβείᾳ καὶ δυνάμει ὑπερέχοντος. It was the final goal of all enquiry, οἷ αφικομένῳ ὥσπερ ὁδοῦ ἀνάπαυλα ἂν εἴη καὶ τέλος τῆς πορείας, and it is from Plato's attempts to lead us to the Form of the Good that we may glean what understanding we can of his method of argument.

Chapter 7
The Search for the Good

The Sun, Line and Cave

The allegory of the Cave is the best known and most memorable of Plato's imaginative creations. Metaphysically, it expresses the contrast between appearance and reality: morally, it portrays a conversion process whereby we free ourselves from the tyranny of other people's opinions, and come ourselves to know what is really right and wrong. Modern scientists explain the colours of the rainbow, the texture of metals, the sounds of musical instruments, in terms of vibrations of the electromagnetic fields, the quantum-mechanical properties of electrons, the motions of molecules in the air, which are accessible to the scientific understanding rather than perceived by the senses. Unlike Plato, modern scientists have a more economical—meaner, even—picture of reality; it is an austere reality that lacks colours, sounds and smells, and can be characterized in exclusively mathematical terms. In Plato's Cave, by contrast, the appearances were monochrome shadows, and the real world outside possessed the full panoply of colour. And whereas modern scientists know scientific reality only through appearances, the prisoners released from Plato's Cave would apprehend reality directly as it was in itself. Conversion, too, was different for Plato. It was achieved by the convert himself through strenuous intellectual effort, and resulted in an intellectual understanding of an impersonal reality, rather than being a response to an external call to a personal loyalty.

The interpretation of Plato's allegory depends on its context in the sequence Sun-Line-Cave, of which it is the culmination. It has engendered enormous controversy. It is not just an intriguing exegetical puzzle: the entire interpretation of the *Republic* hangs on it. Julia Annas remarks in a recent essay, 'Sun, Line and Cave are philosophically frustrating. They point us in too many directions at once', and she warns against the attempt 'to harmonize them in a consistent philosophical interpretation'.[1] What follows is an attempt to do just that.

First let us clarify our terminology. Sun, Line and Cave are sometimes called 'similes', but this is misleading. The Sun is indeed a simile. The Form of the Good is compared to the sun and the respects in which they are similar are clearly specified. As the sun is the source of growth and light, so is the Form of the Good the source of reality and truth. As the sun gives visibility

---

[1] Julia Annas, 'Understanding and the Good: Sun, Line and Cave' in R.Kraut, ed., *Plato's Republic: Critical Essays*, Rowman & Littlefield, Lanham, 1997, p.149.

to the objects of sense, so the Form of the Good gives intelligibility to the objects of thought. As the sun gives the power of sight to the eye, so the Form of the Good gives the power of knowing to the mind. The Line is not a simile. Nothing is being compared to a line. It is simply a diagram to exhibit the relationship between the various objects of cognition and, it would seem also, the corresponding powers of cognition. The Cave is an allegory or parable designed to illustrate the passage of the soul from the normal human condition of ignorance and confusion to the knowledge of the Good.

It is natural at a first reading to assume that the stages through which the released prisoner in the Cave has to pass on the way to final illumination are those outlined diagrammatically in the Line, in particular that the interior of the Cave represents the visible realm over which the sun rules and the world outside the Cave stands for the intelligible world which is the domain of the Good. Plato does, after all, say that the Cave is to be applied to what has gone before (VII 517a8-517b4):

> Now this simile, my dear Glaucon, must be applied in all its parts to what we said before. The sphere revealed by sight being contrasted with the prison dwelling and the light of the fire therein with the power of the sun.

Difficulties with the Traditional Interpretation

However, there are some difficulties with the traditional interpretation. They are summed up with typical clarity and incisiveness by Richard Robinson in his *Plato's Earlier Dialectic*.[2] Robinson says that the traditional interpretation is based upon the premise 'that Plato in 517b-c tells us that the Line is in exact correspondence with the Cave' but that this premise is false, for three reasons:

1. Whatever Plato may say about them, they are not, as a matter of fact, in precise correspondence.
2. Plato quite explicitly in two places asserts a relation between them which is other than exact correspondence.
3. He is not referring to the Line at all in 517b-c.

As regards the first reason he argues that the Cave is about progression from point to point; the Line is not. He concedes that it might have been the case that the motions described in the Cave were between the points indicated in the Line, but claims that we could, if we wished, discover as many as nine stages in the Cave: 1) looking at shadows; 2) turning from the shadows; 3) looking towards the fire; 4) looking at the fire itself; 5) being dragged out of the Cave; and then 6) looking at shadows; 7) looking at reflections; 8) looking at real things; 9) looking at the heavens at night, before, eventually, looking at the sun.[3]

---

[2] R.Robinson, *Plato's Earlier Dialectic*, Cornell University Press, 1941, chapter 11.

[3] p.195.

But perhaps the Cave allows us, if it does not invite us, to divide this more or less continuous progression into three changes between four states. On the contrary, Robinson maintains, it positively forbids it.

> For, if there were precise correlation, the state of the unreleased prisoner would have to be εἰκασία (*eikasia*), conjecture, and the next state πίστις (*pistis*), but πίστις, which means conviction or confidence and refers at least primarily to our ordinary attitude to 'the animals about us and all that grows and everything that is made' bears no resemblance to the prisoner's condition immediately after his release; for the latter is expressly described as bewilderment and as the belief that his present objects are less real than his previous objects. In view of this observation we must say that Plato's Cave is not parallel to his Line even if he himself asserts that it is![4]

Here Robinson goes on to his second claim. Plato asserts in two places a relation between them other than exact correspondence. 'He unmistakably says that in the Cave the viewing of the sun and stars and actual animals is dialectic' (*i.e.* the highest stage in the Line) 'and that the viewing of shadows and reflections in the real world, and of the puppets in the Cave, and everything down to his very moment of unchaining, is "the work of the sciences we have gone through"'.[5] So either the prisoner's original state corresponds to both the lower states in the Line, or one of the lower states in the Line has nothing corresponding to it at all in the Cave.

The passage to which Robinson is referring here occurs after the exposition of the mathematical curriculum, but there is also another passage just before that exposition:

> Then would you like us to ask now how such men will come into existence and how they will be brought up to light, as some are said to have gone up to the gods from Hades? Of course. This is not the turn of a shell, it seems, but the conversion of a soul from a night-like day to a true one, an ascent of reality which we shall say is true philosophy; so we must examine which of the sciences has such a power. (VII 521c5-d1)

These passages imply, says Robinson, that the mathematical curriculum covers everything from the moment of conversion to some moment outside the Cave in the real world.

So to Robinson's third charge: VII 517b-c does not refer to the Line at all: προσαπτέον ἅπασαν τοῖς ἔμπροσθεν λεγομένοις 'it must be applied in all its parts to what we said before' could refer to anything in the previous six books of the *Republic*. The rest of the paragraph, he says, states three correlations and a statement of doctrine without any metaphor. The statement of doctrine is that the Form of the Good is seen to be the cause of all that is good and

---

[4] pp.196-197.

[5] p.201.

right. This is entirely about the Good and the Line does not mention the Good. Of the correlations, the third asserts that we are to refer the prisoner's progress and view of upper things to the ascent of the soul to the intelligible realm. But nothing, says Robinson, is said about the Line which mentions no such ascent. The second compares the light of the fire to the power of the sun. But again the sun is not mentioned in the Line. The first correlation which compares the Cave to the 'domain that appears through sight' does indeed appear in the Line, but even more prominently in the Sun.[6]

At this point Robinson allows a possible objection: 'It may be objected to the preceding argument that it assumes the Sun and the Line to be distinct and co-ordinate similes, whereas Plato intends the Line to be a further elaboration of the Sun (VI 509c)'.[7] He answers this objection by claiming that there is a 'considerable difference of subject and temper' between the two: 'No one could possibly guess from the Sun what Plato was going to say in the Line about the differences between mathematics and dialectic, or that he was going to discuss these differences at all. There is therefore a real and important sense in which the Line is not a continuation of the Sun, but a new doctrine'.[8]

Robinson, therefore, concludes that the Cave, 'a passionate appeal to us either to become philosophers ourselves, if we can, or, if we cannot, to let philosophers rule over us' is not parallel to the Line nor does Plato anywhere say that it is. This is his central case. It is reinforced by two further considerations:

1. If the Cave corresponds to the Line, the unreleased prisoners are in a state of εἰκασία, conjecture; but they are like ourselves: Ἄτοπον, ἔφη, λέγεις, εἰκόνα καὶ δεσμώτας ἀτόπους. Ὁμοίους ἡμῖν, ἦν δ᾽ ἐγώ 'It is a strange picture', he said, 'and strange prisoners.' 'Like ourselves', I said (VII 515a4-5). But εἰκασία, conjecture, in the Line is a state of mind which either mistakes shadows for physical objects or conjectures the nature of physical objects from shadows and ordinarily we do neither of these things.

2. The lower main section of the Line, though the term δόξα, opinion, is twice used in connection with it, mentions only objects of perception. It has nothing to say about opinions regarding justice *etc.*, which is what the puppets in the Cave represent. The Line is concerned with ὁρατόν, the Cave with δοξαστὸν.

---

[6] p.200.

[7] *ibid.*

[8] p.158.

The Traditional View Reconstructed

Robinson's entire argument is a remarkable *tour de force* set out with impressive clarity and incisiveness. It suffers, however, from two serious defects. The first is that he is insufficiently sensitive to the differences in style and function between the Line and the Cave. The Line is a schematic diagram designed to display formal relationships with the minimum of substantial content. The Cave is an allegory or parable conforming to the canons of such compositions. It is a dramatic representation of the human condition and provides an imaginative picture of the entire argument of the *Republic*. The second is that he looks throughout for exact correspondences and, when he does not find them, concludes that there is no correspondence at all. But Plato has told us that he is not speaking accurately (VI 504b), so we should be looking, not for exact correspondence, but for as much correspondence as the satisfactory elaboration of his theme requires. We should not be worried by demonstrations that there is not exact correspondence so long as there is enough correspondence and we can explain why there is not more.

Robinson would have us believe that everything in the Cave from the release of the prisoners to the escape into the upper world falls within the province of διάνοια, derivation, so that if we were to assert correspondence with the Line, we should have to make the entire lower main section of the Line correspond to the lowest stage in the Cave, in which the prisoners are still bound. Either that or there is no correspondence at all. But surely neither of these alternatives is possible. It is admitted that the Cave refers to the Sun. The Sun distinguishes between the visible and the intelligible worlds, the one ruled over by the sun, the other by the Form of the Good. We are told that in the Cave the sun stands for the Good and the fire for the sun. How then can we resist the conclusion that the Cave represents the visible world and the world outside it the intelligible? The entire theme of the *Republic* is the insufficiency of δόξα, opinion, the necessity of ἐπιστήμη, understanding. The distinction between them is constantly described in terms of the contrast between copy and original, dreaming and waking existence. This theme is dramatized in a striking image which contrasts a cave in which men watch shadows cast by the flickering light of a fire with the everyday sunlit world; yet we are asked to accept that this dominant distinction between the world of belief and the world of knowledge is marked in the allegory not by this dramatic contrast but by an episode which takes place within the Cave. Such an interpretation is aesthetically impossible.

Still, if the traditional interpretation is to stand, we need to meet Robinson's detailed criticisms:

1. That, whatever Plato may say, Line and Cave do not correspond.
   a) The Cave is about progression from point to point, the Line is not. Robinson provides the answer himself: the movements indicated in the Cave are between the stages marked in the Line.

b) Robinson says that, nevertheless, this will not do because there are found to be far too many stages in the Cave. Let us look at them. There is no difficulty inside the Cave where there are two states of mind represented, that of the bound prisoners and that of the released prisoner, compelled to look at the puppets and the fire beyond them. These, then, can represent εἰκασία, conjecture, and πίστις, confidence. The complications come when the released prisoner gets outside the Cave and looks at shadows and reflections of real objects, then in turn at heavenly bodies reflected, at real objects, at heavenly bodies themselves at night, and finally at the sun. There seem to be far more stages represented here than there ought to be if the whole corresponds to the διάνοια, derivation, and νόησις, knowledge, of the Line.

This is the point at which Robinson is misled by his preoccupation with exact correspondence and his insensitivity to the demands of parable. Parables are stories which are told in order to illustrate certain truths. For them to do this effectively two requirements need to be met: the story should point unambiguously to the realities outside the story which it is designed to illustrate; and it should carry conviction as a story with its own internal consistency. Now if the stages through which the released prisoner must pass are to be those of the Line, the Cave must succeed in illustrating those stages. But it is also designed to illuminate the experience of an individual as he passes through these stages and, as later, he tries to communicate it to others. We should forget, then, for a moment the demands of exact correspondence with the abstract scheme of the Line and imagine ourselves trying, as Plato is trying, to portray the experiences of a man coming out of a cave for the first time into the world outside never having seen anything brighter than a bonfire. Dazzled by the light of day he looks at shadows and reflections before he manages to look at real things, at the earth before the heavenly bodies, at the heavenly bodies themselves at night and in reflections before he dare look at the sun itself.

Let us suppose now that Plato had clearly in mind all the time the two stages of the upper Line. Would he have told the story any differently? To be sure, for the sake of commentators, he could have seen to it that there were only two clearly differentiated stages once the prisoner was out of the Cave. He comes out into the open and—what shall we say?—looks first at shadows and reflections and then at physical objects. There is no possibility of confusion here, but the story as a story lacks all conviction. We can see that the bewildered man could have staved off the final illumination for longer than that in order to protect his eyes. What about night, what about the moon and stars? Plato preserves the verisimilitude of his narrative and puts all the detail in. But the moral is clear enough: in the outside world, as in the Cave, the released prisoner looks at shadows and reflections before he looks at the reality itself.

That the interpretation is correct is shown by Plato's own summary later in VII 532b8 ff.: 'Then', I said, 'the release of the prisoner from bondage, the turning round from the shadows to the images and the light and that stage in the world above when they are still unable to look at animals and plants and the light of the sun, but can look at the divine reflections in water and the shadows of real things: this is accomplished by all that pursuit of those arts which we have mentioned'. Here he distinguishes just two stages in the upper world.

However, this very passage is cited by Robinson in support of his interpretation. For 'the arts we have mentioned' are the mathematical sciences and they are the province of διάνοια, derivation. It must follow that the pattern of correspondence after all breaks down, and the released prisoner is in a state of διάνοια, derivation, from the moment of his conversion.

The argument succeeds, however, only if throughout the mathematical curriculum—πᾶσα αὕτη ἡ πραγματεία τῶν τεχνῶν ἃς διήλθομεν—the student is in a state of διάνοια, derivation, but there are indications elsewhere in the text that this is not so. A person is in a state of διάνοια, derivation, when he reasons about the objects of mathematics, whatever they are, the circle as such and the triangle as such, with the aid of visible diagrams, although he does not suppose himself to be reasoning only about the diagrams. When someone is being taught geometry this is the state of mind he will eventually achieve. But it is not the state of mind with which he starts. He starts, as the slave in the *Meno* starts, by supposing that he is reasoning about this particular circle or triangle and he cannot yet grasp the concept of a circle or triangle which is not a particular circle or triangle. His cognitive state is still πίστις, confidence, and he is still in the Cave.

But the passage ascribes the conversion of the prisoners from εἰκασία, conjecture, also to the mathematical sciences and this is, admittedly, more difficult. Do we have to say that Plato is here simply exaggerating in his desire to maximize the role of mathematics? This does not seem implausible, but the difficulty is, perhaps, not otherwise insuperable. In Book X, 602c-d, there is a discussion of visual illusions and their correction by measurement: 'Measuring, counting and weighing were invented to help us out of these difficulties and to ensure that we should not be guided by apparent differences of size, quantity and heaviness, but by proper calculations of number, measurement and weight, which can only be performed by the element of reason in man's mind'.[9] This is reinforced by VII 522c7: πᾶσα τέχνη τε καὶ ἐπιστήμη ἀναγκάζεται αὐτῶν μέτοχος γίγνεσθαι· 'every art and science has to be involved with them', where αὐτῶν, 'them', refers to ἀριθμός, (arithmos), number, and λογισμός, calculation.

---

[9] See further below, ch.12, pp.158-160.

The third argument against correspondence is that the state of mind of the newly released prisoner would have to be πίστις, confidence, but πίστις, confidence, refers primarily to our ordinary attitude to the animals and things about us and is a state of confidence. It cannot be compared to the bewilderment of the released prisoner. This is a genuine difficulty and is related to a similar problem about εἰκασία, conjecture. The problem is two-fold:

1. How can the bewildered state of the released prisoner be compared to our normal confident acceptance of the physical world?
2. How can Plato be supposed to have thought that most of us spend our lives taking shadows for physical objects (or conjecturing the nature of physical objects from shadows) and are only persuaded with difficulty to recognise physical objects for what they are?

The second of these will be considered later. The first is easily answered. Plato represents the prisoner as bewildered by every improvement in his state of mind. Once he has got used to seeing the puppets he is confident of their reality and initially thinks them more real than the objects he encounters outside the Cave.

It remains to consider Robinson's third main argument for non-correspondence of Line and Cave. This is that the crucial statement in VII 517b, 'this simile, my dear Glaucon, must be applied in its entirety to what we said before', does not refer to the Line at all, but solely to the Sun. Robinson anticipates the answer to this himself when he says 'it might be objected that the Line is simply a continuation and elaboration of the Sun'. A careful look at the text confirms that this is precisely how Plato in fact introduces the Line. Glaucon urges Socrates to explain the image of the Sun, τὴν περὶ τὸν ἥλιον ὁμοιότητα (VI 509c5-6), and Socrates embarks upon the Line in answer to this request. Nevertheless Robinson is right in insisting that the Line introduces new material and is different 'in tone and temper' from the Sun. As we have already argued, the Sun is a powerful symbol and the Line is simply a diagram. The Line is an abstract specification of what has been symbolically suggested in the Sun.

This is an important consideration and provides the clue to what has been thought to be the most troubling difficulty about the relationship between Line and Cave. This concerns εἰκασία, conjecture. The prisoners in the Cave are 'like ourselves', but it is absurd to suppose that we spend our entire lives in a state of εἰκασία, conjecture, whether this is understood as taking shadows for originals or conjecturing the nature of originals from shadows. As Annas puts it, 'the lowest stage, εἰκασία, conjecture, seems not to correspond to anything significant in our lives'.[10] The difficulty is reinforced,

---

[10] Julia Annas, 'Understanding and the Good: Sun, Line and Cave' in R.Kraut, ed., *Plato' Republic: Critical Essays*, Lanham, 1997, p.150.

in Robinson's opinion, by the fact that the shadows and images in the Cave represent opinions about δικαιοσύνη, morality, *etc.*, whereas the Line mentions only objects of perception. The Line is concerned with ὁρατά, objects of sight, the Cave with δοξαστά objects of opinion.

This switch from ὁρατά to δοξαστά which is thought to be problematic, is in fact the clue to the solution. The Line deals with ὁρατά partly because it is working out the parallelisms of the Sun, in which intelligence is compared and contrasted with sight, and partly because the relation between mathematical knowledge and other inferior cognitive states is most conveniently exhibited by reference to the diagrams which mathematicians use.

But the Cave is subject to no such constraints and is concerned primarily with the central theme of the *Republic*, *viz.* δικαιοσύνη, morality, and the states of mind there represented are possible attitudes to morality. What is said about objects of sight, ὁρατά, in the Line is applied generally to objects of opinion, δοξαστά, in the Cave.

Once this is recognized, the difficulties about εἰκασία, conjecture, dissolve. Although it is absurd to suppose that Plato thought that most of us spend our lives in a state of εἰκασία, conjecture, about the objects of perception, with the exception of some who achieve πίστις, confidence, about them, it is not at all surprising that he took us to be in a state of εἰκασία, conjecture, about morality. We can freely admit that perceptually the state of mind of the lower section of the Line is comparatively rarely encountered, having been included for purposes of illustration only. Plato holds that our understanding of morality corresponds to that of someone who is taken in by visual illusions. That the Line can be taken to cover δοξαστά is shown by VI 511d2-5:

> διάνοιαν δὲ καλεῖν μοι δοκεῖς τὴν τῶν γεωμετρικῶν τε καὶ τὴν τῶν τοιούτων ἕξιν α᾽λλ᾽ οὐ νοῦν, ὡς μεταξύ τι δόξης τε καὶ νοῦ τὴν διάνοιαν οὖσαν.

This faculty in geometricians and such people you seem to call understanding and not intelligence on the ground that understanding lies somewhere between belief and intelligence.

Even more conclusive is VII 533e7-534a2 where after discussing the mathematical sciences Plato reverts to the Line:

> Ἀρκέσει οὖν, ἦν δ᾽ ἐγώ, ὥσπερ τὸ πρότερον, τὴν μέν πρώτην μοῖραν ἐπιστήμην καλεῖν, δευτέραν δὲ διάνοιαν, τρίτην δὲ πίστιν καὶ εἰκασάν τεταρτην: καὶ συναμφότερα μὲν ταῦτα δόξαν, συμαμφότερα δ᾽ἐκεῖνα νόησιν.

It is enough, then, I said, to call the first segment understanding (*episteme*), as we agreed earlier, the second derivation (*dianoia*), the third confidence (*pistis*) and the fourth conjecture (*eikasia*); both the former being knowledge (*noesis*), and both the latter opinion (*doxa*).

Plato's Use of Allegory

There are two questions which spring to mind after this consideration of the allegory of the Cave. What, in his own terms, did Plato think he was doing in writing it; and what is the philosophical scholar doing in arguing for one interpretation against another?

At the least Plato is illustrating a coherent set of beliefs which he does not claim to be able to establish by rigorous proof. That they are not just imaginative constructions is shown by the fact that they can be stated non-figuratively: 'Men in their present condition are unable to grasp the real nature of things. They are unacquainted with true justice but in the law courts and elsewhere are content to dispute about matters which are as remote from justice as shadows from originals. One can conceive, however, of someone being freed from this condition by a process of rigorous thought which, assisted by mathematical reasoning, enables him to contemplate abstract entities without reliance upon sensible particulars. This enables him to attain to an understanding of morality itself and, finally, of the ultimate good. When he grasps this he realises that it is the cause of everything he has previously experienced and also of its being known for what it is. Equipped with this insight he can undertake the task of enlightening his fellows.' It is quite easy to draft this paraphrase, and the fact that it is reasonably accurate (and one can tell whether it is or not) shows that the parable itself is intelligible and capable of being true or false.

Why then did Plato, with his distrust of μίμησις, (*mimesis*), artistic representation,[11] use the parable to convey his message? To begin with, the plain statement might give the false impression that Plato himself understood fully the truths he was stating and could justify them rigorously. The parable, though enormously more impressive than the paraphrase, is also more modest. Then the story, as told in the allegory, is far more vivid than the paraphrase. It enables the reader to share the experience of the released prisoner as he makes his journey and his changing attitudes to what he experiences. He struggles against enlightenment, and the process of learning is long and toilsome.

Does it advance the argument? It is persuasive in so far as it engages with the reader's initial sense of dissatisfaction with the human condition, and his longing for enlightenment. This is why it fails to impress modern critics like Annas for whom 'the ascent out of the Cave offers no personal interest or fulfilment'.[12] Nonetheless, for some people it is undoubtedly persuasive. But is it rational persuasion? The answer to that question must wait until later.[13]

---

[11] See below, ch.12, p.158.

[12] *op.cit.* p.158

[13] p.107.

The second question is one that is not often asked, but is worth asking because it may throw some light on the first. The dispute with Robinson, like all such scholarly arguments, has been conducted on two assumptions:

1. that there is a truth of the matter which both parties hope to discover and may in due course claim to have discovered;
2. that the dispute is a rational one, in which some arguments are better than others.

There are some philosophers and even more literary critics who would reject both these assumptions, but most serious scholars accept them in practice.

In certain respects such disputes exemplify Plato's account of dialectic fairly straightforwardly. Both parties seek hypotheses which will explain the data, being what Plato actually wrote taken in its natural sense. When individual passages have been treated in this way 'higher hypotheses' are canvassed which are intended to explain a set of such passages. The process culminates in an interpretation of the whole text which, it is claimed, makes the best sense of it all, e.g. the whole Sun-Line-Cave sequence. Evidence from Plato's other works may also be relevant and from writers like Aristotle who knew Plato well. At each stage these hypotheses are open to criticism, and will be criticized by opponents for being incompatible with the plain sense of certain parts of the text. Either the Greek will not bear the meaning suggested or it can do so only in a forced sense. This bears some analogy to Plato's rejecting a hypothesis because it generates contradictions. Such considerations are rarely decisive, however, for two reasons:

1. Plato himself may not be entirely consistent;
2. it may be possible to mitigate the force of the objection by suggesting some plausible reason why Plato should have been led into this real or apparent inconsistency.

The Cave Interpreted

If the sequence of Sun, Line and Cave together form a coherent picture, it remains to ask what is the nature of the intellectual and spiritual progress that they are a picture of.

The predicament of the unreleased prisoners is that of εἰκασία, conjecture, which must represent the state of mind of ordinary unenlightened humanity. By an odd historical turn Plato's talk of being taken in by images, which until recently was an exegetical puzzle, has become a journalistic commonplace. Politics are in thrall to 'image-makers' and the *Independent* can claim that 'politicians have created a hall of mirrors in which even those mid-market newspapers rapidly losing readers become the arbiters of policy and ministerial destiny'. The vogue for 'docu-soaps' has created a situation in which 'To tens of millions of Americans, *Apocalypse Now* or *JFK* or *Nixon* are more real than the original events they purport to depict'.[14] Some have suggested that television as such provides the modern analogue for Plato's apparatus of puppets and their shadows.

There is for us, then, no difficulty, *pace* Annas, in making sense of εἰκασία, conjecture. Πίστις, confidence or belief, is equally straightforward: it is unreflective judgement about particular cases or equally unreflective adherence to rules for which no justification is offered. Because they lack the grounding which an explanatory account of them would provide, they are inherently unstable, but in the process of education described in the Cave they are presumably correct as far as they go. Adam usefully points out that 'the arts of carpentry, ship-building, house-building, *etc.*, *etc.*, as well as popular *arithmetike, metrike, etc.*,' are placed in the second lowest category of the *Philebus* (566e-7d) and suggests they would be objects of πίστις, confidence, in the *Republic*.[15] (We take it that we should not be worried that these practical crafts and the corresponding moral perceptions are found in ordinary life so that to that extent we are not all of us all the time in the state of εἰκασία, conjecture. Plato exaggerates the degree of our normal deprivation for the sake of dramatic effect.)

A delightful illustration of the difference between εἰκασία, conjecture, and πίστις, confidence, is provided by a Japanese screen to be seen in a museum in Lisbon. The picture on it represents a Japanese artist's impression of Portuguese sailors manning the yard-arms of a man-of-war. The whole gives a lively idea of activity but the human figures, though realistic in themselves, seem to be placed entirely at random. The artist, being ignorant of seamanship, had no knowledge of the function of the items of rigging and did not know what the sailors were doing up there.

The steep and rugged ascent up out of the Cave represents the process of instruction in the mathematical sciences which begins in the Cave with the mastery of crafts and ends outside the Cave with the student in a condition of διάνοια, derivation, in which he can justify his judgements by showing how they can be derived from a set of axioms. These assumptions themselves he does not, *qua* mathematician, justify.

None of this is problematic. But the question does arise whether there is a parallel procedure for progress in moral thinking and, if there is, and the Cave is concerned primarily with morality, why should the strictly mathematical curriculum be thought necessary at all? The answer must be that Plato wanted thinking about morality to be as rigorous as possible and the paradigm of logical rigour was to be found in mathematics. In much the same way a contemporary teacher of philosophy may decide to introduce his students to

---

[14] *Independent,* 25 May 1996, or *The Times,* 22 September 1998.

[15] J.Adam, *The Republic of Plato,* Cambridge, 1902, ii, p.159.

logic before venturing upon moral philosophy, which may otherwise seem to be a soft option dangerously close to common-sense.

But, in that case, what would it be like to be in a state of διάνοια, derivation, in respect of morality? What is needed here is a conception of morality which goes beyond the sound intuitive judgements of ordinarily decent people but falls short of the thorough understanding of philosophers who can provide a complete justification of morality, by showing how justice and the other virtues are ultimately good.

Plato does not in the *Republic* offer such a justification: ἄλλη γὰρ μακροτέρα καὶ πλείων ὁδός, the road which leads to that is longer and more toilsome (IV 435d3 and VI 504b2). He gives an outline of it in the central books which he does not fill in. But the point at which this warning is given suggests that Socrates and his interlocutors have, before it, reached the stage of διάνοια, derivation, in defining δικαιοσύνη justice, as τὸ τὰ αὑτοῦ πράττειν καὶ μή πολυπραγμονεῖν 'to mind one's own business and not to be meddlesome'(IV 433a8). Plato is content to adopt this principle as a basis for planning his ideal city with only a perfunctory attempt to test it by comparing it with common opinions, τὰ φορτικά.[16] A similar attitude is taken to the 'Law of Non-contradiction' appealed to in IV 436b7ff. Socrates is content to treat it as a hypothesis by assuming which he can proceed to demonstrate that the soul is tripartite. Here again he dismisses a few counter-examples and is then ready to 'proceed on the assumption that what we had said is right' because 'we don't want to be compelled to examine in detail all the difficulties of this kind and to waste our time establishing their falsehood' (IV 437a4-9).

This dependence on assumptions which are not questioned within the limits of the discipline itself is characteristic of today's sciences. Biology depends upon the Darwinian theory of natural selection, neurology on the assumption that mental events are to be understood as physical changes in the brain, and so on. It is not, as a rule, the job of scientists themselves to criticize these assumptions, but they are constantly tempted to venture into metaphysics and give them a status which their scientific usefulness does not entitle them to. Biologists often seek to give an exhaustive account of human behaviour in terms of the 'selfish gene', neurologists readily talk of the brain 'making choices'. Sometimes the assumptions are characteristic of particular schools of thought within the science in question and are to that extent controversial. But they are commonly held tenaciously without being submitted to philosophical critique. There are, indeed, plenty of thinkers who endeavour to unify the varied assumptions of the sciences in terms of an overall theory of metaphysical materialism, but they do this as philosophers, not as scientists.

---

[16] See above, ch.4, p.54.

It is argued by philosophical theists that explanation can be carried further than it is carried by the sciences, and that it culminates in a unified conception which answers the two fundamental questions: why the world is as it is, and how we should live our lives. This is the burden of the upper section of the Line and the corresponding part of the Cave. All this is the business of philosophy.

It is an undertaking which evokes little sympathy from modern critics who, for the most part, have been taught to distrust metaphysics. We shall argue that Plato's approach is both more intelligible and more defensible than is generally allowed.

The Nature of Dialectic

But first there is a further question of interpretation. What is the procedure of dialectic which leads the philosopher to apprehend the Form of the Good and how can he have thought it achieved its end? Plato gives no clear answer. In his attempts to clarify his own thoughts about the nature of argument he repeatedly changed his mind. He was able to articulate some account of what he was doing, but always there were further forms of argument which lay outside his formulations.

Διαλεκτική, dialectic, as we saw in the previous chapter,[17] was a development of the Socratic *elenchus*. As Plato thought about it, he tried to give an account of it, which we have in *Phaedo* (100a-101e), and tried to make it more formal and more stringent. He was feeling his way towards the ideal of deductive argument and the axiomatic method, but sensed that these by themselves could not exhaust the whole of argument, and that the μέθοδος διαλεκτική, dialectical method, must comprise something else. Robinson explains Plato's account of διαλεκτική in *Phaedo* (100a)[18] as a version of what is now known as the hypothetical-deductive approach. 'The whole method as so far described comes to this: in order to reach a desired conclusion,

1. hypothesize whichever hypothesis seems strongest to you of those that seem likely to lead to the conclusion;
2. draw the consequences of this hypothesis;
3. see whether they give rise to any contradiction; if they do, begin from the beginning again with another hypothesis, but so long as they do not,
4. posit as true that which the hypothesis entails, and as false that of which the hypothesis entails the contradictory'.[19]

Should doubt be cast on the hypothesis, Plato recommends a further stage, as follows: 'And when you had to discuss the hypothesis itself, you would do so in the same way, hypothesizing another hypothesis which seemed best of those above until you came to something adequate τι ἱκανὸν (ti hikanon)'.[20]

---

[17] See ch.6, pp.75ff.

[18] Quoted above, ch.6, pp.74,76.

[19] R.Robinson, *Plato's Earlier Dialectic,* Cornell University Press, 1941, p.140.

[20] *Phaedo* 101de, quoted above, ch.6, p.76.

In the *Phaedo* itself the theory of Forms is hypothesized in this way and the immortality of soul is proved by means of it. It resembles Popper's account of scientific method: 'Theories of some level of universality are proposed and deductively tested; after that, theories of a higher level of universality are proposed and in their turn tested with the help of the previous levels of universality and so on',[21] though there is the important qualification that Popper's hypotheses are tested by observation, Plato's by the logical consistency of their implications. Both agree, however, that this method can never achieve finality.[22]

This exegesis fits the *Phaedo*, but cannot accommodate Plato's belief in the *Republic* that the method could culminate in assured knowledge of the Form of the Good. Moreover, in the *Phaedo* the dialectical method appears to be offered as a second best, δεύτερος πλοῦς to the sort of explanation that Socrates really wanted. This is set out in the famous passage in which he confesses his early disillusionment with Anaxagoras: 'For I could not imagine that when he spoke of Mind, νοῦς, as the disposer of <things>, he would give any other account of their being as they are, except that this was best; and I thought that when he had explained to me in detail the cause of each and the cause of all, he would go on to explain to me what was best for each and what was best for all' (*Phaedo* 98c ff.).

The dialectical method sketched in the *Phaedo* has two obvious drawbacks if relied upon as a method of achieving certainty. How could one ever know that all possible objections had been exhausted; and how would one know where to stop in the 'upward path'?

In the *Republic*, however, Plato thought that the dialectical method could constitute, as it were, a coping stone upon the other disciplines. It is difficult to see how this might be: Robinson suggests that the obvious way of doing this is by an appeal to intuition. 'Intuition' is used by philosophers as a negative concept: they know what it is not, but find it difficult to say what it is. Plato's διαλεκτική is defined negatively: it is what is left over, when the other intellectual powers have been distinguished. It is not, as we have seen,[23] deductive inference, which will work against all comers, even recalcitrant sophists. It is not conjecture (VI 509e1-510a3). It is not reasoned prediction based on inductive inference (VI 510a5-6; VII 516e8-d2). Plato is

---

[21] Karl Popper, *Logic of Scientific Discovery*, London, 1959, p.276.

[22] 'Science is not a system of certain or well-established statements; nor is it a system which steadily advances towards a state of finality. Our science is not knowledge (*episteme*). It can never claim to have attained truth.' *Op.cit.*, p.278. Plato does not maintain, either, that dialectic can achieve finality. At best it arrives at 'something adequate' (*Phaedo* 101e1).

[23] Ch.6.

not alone in having difficulty in characterizing his fundamental principles of reasoning. Aristotle is able to give a good account of our reasoning about means, but is awkward and confused in Book VI of the *Ethics* when he tries to give an account of practical reasoning generally, and the way we reach right judgements about ends. We can give formal accounts of the right way to argue about clearly delimited topics in specific circumstances, but are liable to be negative and vague when we come to talk about the right way of thinking about the most general topics in uncharted areas of thought.

Διαλεκτικὴ, dialectic, is some rational apprehension of truth which takes all factors into consideration—ὁ μὲν γὰρ συνοπτικὸς διαλεκτός (VII 537c7)—and can be achieved only by the favoured few, who have undergone a profound re-orientation of mind, and devoted years of study and contemplation to comprehending the Principle of All Things. At some point in the upward path a hypothesis would be entertained which would be indubitably true. Once it was discovered mathematics and, presumably, all other knowledge could be deduced.

No doubt the discovery of such an intuited principle would formally solve Plato's problem, but it is difficult to see what sort of principle would conform to what he tells us about the role of the Form of the Good. One is led to ask whether he may not have had in mind a somewhat different conception of metaphysical reasoning. Admittedly he is able to describe it only by the use of imagery, and counsels against the dangers of that; but it may be worth examining his imagery more closely, together with the occasional comments he makes upon it.

The impression one gets from the *Republic* is that by assiduously practising dialectic upon a wide range of subjects we should get a reasonably good provisional understanding of them, which would not be confirmed and finally clarified until the Form of the Good had itself been grasped. Yet it seems that the work done on the outlying topics would all the time be leading one in the direction of the Good.

Dialectic studies the Form of the Good as the greatest study, τὸ μέγιστον μάθημα, but it studies other things as well which somehow contribute to that end. If the Form of the Good is the key to the whole intelligible world, it might seem the obvious procedure to tackle that first in the expectation that the rest would follow. Yet Plato plainly regards it as the final study as well as the greatest—the sun is the last thing the released prisoner looks at. There would have to be a lot of dialectical spadework before there was any hope of getting to grips with the Good at all. This suggests that the procedure is a cumulative one. Perhaps the metaphor of the keystone is appropriate. Until the keystone is in place the arch is precarious and incomplete: yet almost all the work has to be done on the arch before the keystone can be moved into place.

An Architectural Analogy

A more complete architectural analogy might be drawn from the attempt to piece together the fragments of a building, e.g. a ruined cathedral. Each time you encounter a fragment you ask yourself what it is ('dialectic endeavours systematically to apprehend concerning each reality what it is'). You try out the most plausible hypothesis you can think of : 'it is part of a capital'. (Notice that asking what it is involves asking what position it occupies in the total design: what it is for.) You reject this hypothesis because, if it were part of a capital, certain consequences would follow which are not found in the present case: e.g. it would be flat top and bottom. So you drop this hypothesis and try out another and another until you find one that works, at least for the time being, i.e. you cannot find anything against it. So you mark your lump of stone '?part of carved boss on rib vaulting?' and put it on one side. To begin with the entire exercise is highly conjectural, but, as you proceed, you get more and more fragments provisionally accounted for. If someone challenges the label you have put on one of them you can, to some extent, give an account of it, διδόναι λόγον. You can explain what it is in terms of the position you believe it to have occupied in the building and you can point out how it differs from other pieces which you think had other functions. What you do not do is to regard the matter as self-evident. You do not say 'anyone can see that this is part of a capital'.

To begin with you have only a hazy idea of what sort of building it is that you are trying to reconstruct. The idea of a plan, possibly of a religious building of some sort, is obscurely present to your mind from the start, but it would be useless to speculate about the precise nature of the plan until you have worked your way through and labelled provisionally a large number of fragments. At some stage you begin to hazard 'higher' hypotheses: that we have here an arcade of arches, a ribbed vault, and so on. There comes a point, however, at which it becomes worthwhile to direct your attention to the question, what is the plan of the building, although you have all the time to persevere with the work on the fragments. Then quite suddenly you 'see' the entire plan, you grasp the concept underlying the design. As soon as this has happened you start on the downward path. You can confidently run over the fragments you have already labelled, confirming or revising your diagnosis as the case may be. And you can piece together the remainder with much less trouble and complete confidence. The Form of the Good would correspond to the total design which the architect planned in that way because he thought it was best, proceeding in the way that Socrates thought that Mind in Anaxagoras would have proceeded.

It is, of course, extremely risky to interpret Plato's meaning by analogies of one's own when those he used himself have caused so much controversy. But one cannot expect to get at his meaning without analogies of some sort because he makes it clear that he cannot provide a literal account. What our analogy attempts to illustrate is:

1. the dialectical method as set out in the *Phaedo*;
2. the role of final causes, as desiderated in the *Phaedo*;
3. the position of the Form of the Good as ἀρχή ἀνυπόθετος, unpostulated first principle.

It may be used, with caution, to illustrate some of the things Plato says in the *Republic* about the Form of the Good. We are told that 'of the objects of knowledge not only their being known comes from the Good, but their existence and being also come from it, though the Good is not itself being, but transcends even being in dignity and power' (VI 509b6). Part of what this means can be illustrated by the analogy:

(a) The design as a whole is the cause of each part being known for what it is. The capital considered in itself is a lump of stone curiously carved. It cannot be known to be a capital until its place in the total design is known.

(b) The design as a whole is the cause of each part being the thing it is: a piece of stone curiously carved is a capital only as part of an entire building.

Can we also make sense of 'transcends even being in dignity and power'? An answer is to be found in an illuminating discussion of the passage in H.W.B. Joseph's *Knowledge and the Good in Plato's Republic*.[24] According to Joseph what fully displays goodness is 'the νοητός κόσμος, (*noetos kosmos*), the system of ideas, the eternal plan, perhaps we might say, imperfectly realized in the sensible world'. But, he goes on, 'the Form of the Good then is not one among the other Forms, to which being belongs and which are objects of knowledge. From one point of view, reality is exhausted in them: that which is good and the goodness of it are the same, for nothing of what is good fails to contribute to that goodness which consists in its being just all that it is. From another point of view its goodness is something beyond everything contained in our description of what is good. For we describe it by running over its constituent parts; and its goodness is none of these'.

If this interpretation is right, Plato's metaphysics resembles the 'axiarchy' which John Leslie advocates according to which the ultimate answer to the question why something should be so is that it is good for it to be so.[25] Leslie offers it as an alternative to theism and attributes it to Plato. But there are indications in the *Republic* of the Good's having a more substantial being than Leslie's formula suggests. The sun, after all, is a conspicuously independent being in its own right and, if this is simply an exigency of the parable, there is

---

[24] Oxford, 1948, pp.21f.

[25] J.Leslie, *Value and Existence*, Oxford, 1974.

also Mind, νοῦς, in the *Phaedo*. On the other hand, in the *Timaeus*, when God is explicitly introduced, his role is confined to that of a craftsman, δημιουργός (*demiourgos*), who constructs the universe on the patterns of the Forms out of pre-existing matter. However much Plato's argument seems to require it, it is hard to find full-blooded theism in the *Republic*.

Nevertheless there can be no doubt about the religious significance of the work. As Gregory Vlastos (one of the few modern commentators to acknowledge it) says of the vision of the Forms: 'Thus in one and the same experience Plato finds happiness, beauty, knowledge, moral sustenance and regeneration and a mystical sense of kinship with eternal perfection'.[26]

This provides the answer to Annas who claims that 'the ascent out of the Cave offers no personal interest or fulfilment'. The vision of the Good is the equivalent of the beatific vision in Christian theology, an intuition of the divine essence which alone gives the soul supreme satisfaction. The Form of the Good provides the answer to the two questions which human beings insistently ask: why are things as they are? how should we live?

This comparison helps solve another problem in Plato's account: how can the good life be thought to lead to the individual's supreme happiness if it entails sacrifice like the guardians; descent into the Cave? The answer would seem to be that no one can enter into the state of supreme blessedness who has not ceased to make himself the centre of the universe, but the blessedness he then enjoys is at the same time the fulfilment of his deepest desires. Plato's guardians will not be happy unless they are also dutiful, and duty demands their descent into the Cave.

If further proof is needed of the religious character of Plato's thought it can be found, as Vlastos notes, in passages where Socrates associates philosophy with the divine: 'In one passage in the *Republic* the philosopher is pictured as gazing daily at the Forms, which are "orderly and ever constant, neither wronging nor being wronged by one another, but abide in harmony and the rule of reason", and, as he does so, finds that his character takes on the impress of theirs. "Or do you think", asks Socrates, "it would be possible not to imitate that with which one consorts in love". "Impossible", says Glaucon, and Socrates concludes that "the philosopher, consorting with the divine and harmonious, will himself become as harmonious and divine as any man may" ' (VI 500c2-d1).[27] This being so, it is no accident that the myth of Er, with its vision of a life to come, provides the culmination of the *Republic*.

---

[26] Gregory Vlastos, 'A Metaphysical Paradox' in R.Kraut, ed., *Plato's Republic: Critical Essays*, Lanham, 1997, p.150.

[27] 'Understanding and the Good', *op.cit.* p.158.

The Rational Grounding of Morality

There is an obvious problem which attends any attempt to give a coherent account of the Sun-Line-Cave sequence and whatever else Plato says about the Form of the Good and the search for it. In the entire passage he is clearly conducting an argument, but what sort of argument on his own terms can it be? It is, in effect, a lengthy parenthesis, and yet it is plainly meant to be of crucial importance. Plato emphasizes that it is not the investigation that is ideally needed. That would require a different and more lengthy approach, ἄλλη γὰρ μακροτέρα καὶ πλείων ὁδὸς (IV 43543), the longer route he is unable to undertake. This implies that it is not itself an instance of the dialectical method as he is recommending it. But it manifestly does not fit anywhere else in the Line. The image of the Cave is a very powerful one which has gripped the imagination of subsequent ages, and Plato thinks it comes somewhere near the truth, which is not the case with εἰκασία, conjecture, or μίμησις, artistic representation, as described in Book X.

It seems that Plato, like many philosophers after him, has been so fascinated by the example of mathematics with its ideal of an entirely formal axiomatized system that he is unable to recognise the informal, persuasive method of reasoning which he himself employs so effectively. Indeed, Charles Taylor is led by Plato's insistence on mathematics as a preparation for knowledge of the Good to hold him partly responsible for the modern tendency to look for a conception of morality which can be fitted into a scientific picture of the world, itself arrived at with no consideration of ethics.[28] We are suggesting, however, that Plato is open to a different interpretation.

At this point our earlier analogy between philosophical argument and the process by which scholars seek to determine the meaning of a text becomes relevant. So long as Plato holds fast to his ideal of dialectic as a development of mathematical method, it is incompatible with the method he actually pursues in attempting to persuade us of the truth of his vision of the Good and its explanatory power and significance for conduct. However, what he actually tells us about the procedure of dialectic both in the *Phaedo* and in the *Republic* strongly suggests a more informal, cumulative style of argument. What is looked for in the scholarly debate and in metaphysical argument alike is an overall account which will make sense in the one case of the various constituent elements of the text, and in the other of our antecedent knowledge of the world and of morality.

Vlastos in his sympathetic and perceptive acknowledgement of the mystical element in Plato's thought is unhappy with Plato's confidence that he could prove it.[29] But, as we noted earlier,[30] for Plato to have abandoned all

---

[28] C.M.Taylor, *Sources of the Self*, Cambridge, 1989, p.69.

[29] 'Understanding and the Good', *op.cit.* p.194.

[30] Chapter 4, p.57.

concern with proof would have not only, in Vlastos' words, 'radically altered Plato's metaphysics'. It would have deprived it altogether of its character as metaphysics. And this is not dispensable. It is essential to Plato's enterprise in the *Republic* that morality requires the backing of reason and that reason seeks to discover, and can in principle discover, an order in the universe which explains why δικαιοσύνη, morality, is what it is, and why it is able to command our love and allegiance.

Chapter 8
Morality and Happiness

The Challenge Met?

Plato takes great care to formulate precisely the challenge which Glaucon and Adeimantus put to Socrates at the beginning of Book II of the *Republic* and is equally precise when, in Book X, he claims that the challenge has been met. Socrates is to commend δικαιοσύνη, morality, or righteousness, for the real benefits it brings its possessor compared with what ἀδικία, wrongdoing, or immorality, does, and leave it to others to dwell on rewards and reputation. He is to prove 'not only that δικαιοσύνη, morality, is superior to ἀδικία, immorality, but that, irrespective of whether gods or men know it or not, one is good and the other evil because of its inherent effects on its possessor' (II 376d2-e5). And at the end he claims, 'I think our argument has fulfilled the conditions you laid down and, in particular, has avoided mentioning the rewards and reputation which δικαιοσύνη, integrity, (*dikaiosune*), brings, as you complain Homer and Hesiod do' (X 612a8-b1).

In spite of this commentators have found it difficult to grasp his meaning. In some cases this is because Plato is not addressing the question which chiefly interests them or is asking a question which they regard as simply wrong-headed. Thus M.B. Foster and J.D. Mabbott debate whether Plato is a utilitarian, although Plato is not asking the question to which utilitarianism offers an answer, *viz.* 'what are the criteria of right action?' And H.A. Prichard accuses Plato of misdirecting himself by looking for reasons why we should do our duty, although Plato is not thinking in terms of duty at all. He is interested in δικαιοσύνη, morality, as a condition of a person's *psyche* and argues that what benefits someone most is to have a properly ordered *psyche* no matter what his external circumstances.

On the face of it there are two familiar claims, either one of which he might have been making: virtue is its own reward; or honesty is the best policy. He is undoubtedly closer to the former than to the latter. Nevertheless he is not saying, as Kant did, that the only thing good beyond question is a good will, or with Prichard that to do one's duty without reason given is the only thing that matters. He undertakes to show that δικαιοσύνη, morality, is good in itself and on account of what it does to the *psyche*, the two being distinct but indissolubly connected. Still less is he vindicating δικαιοσύνη, morality, in terms of its consequences as these are commonly understood. Reference to these is explicitly ruled out.

Cross and Woozley make the helpful move of distinguishing between consequences and results.[1] Although he dismisses consequences, Plato does attend to the results of virtue, those things that follow necessarily or naturally from it. What these results are is apparent from his description of the way δικαιοσύνη, integrity, operates in the *psyche* of the moral man as contrasted with what happens to the *psyche*s of those who fall short of δικαιοσύνη, integrity. The harmony in the *psyche* of the δίκαιος, well-integrated, man is not only good in itself but enables him to satisfy the needs of the whole *psyche* in such a way that each part of the *psyche* gets its own satisfaction. Only the fully δίκαιος, integrated, man achieves this benefit, but, in the ideal city, the lives of those who are not guardians are so regulated that they are enabled to approximate to this condition as far as their limited capacities allow. This implies that the lesser fulfilment of the non-philosopher is, nevertheless, so far as it goes, a good worth having, as it could not be if Plato intended by δικαιοσύνη something akin to the Kantian good will which has to be entirely autonomous.

A Kantian Plato?

John Howes has suggested,[2] taking his cue from the verb εὐδαιμονίζειν that the basic sense of εὐδαίμων, (usually translated 'happy') is 'worthy of ultimate congratulation' and that, accordingly, recognition that the δίκαιος is εὐδαίμων involves an ultimate value judgement which Plato invites Socrates' interlocutors to join him in making. He accordingly criticizes Plato in his treatment of θυμοειδής for providing as a support for δικαιοσύνη something which is an entirely inadequate and inappropriate substitute for the 'reverence' which Kant sees to be necessary. In this way Howes presents us with a Kantian Plato who regrettably fails consistently to carry through his Kantian insights. There is undoubtedly much in the *Republic*, and elsewhere in Plato's writings, to recommend such an interpretation but it fails to take full account of the metaphysical background to his ethical thinking which is fundamentally teleological. It is not just that, when we understand what δικαιοσύνη. is, we cannot but prize it above everything else, but that the economy of the individual *psyche* reflects the economy of a universe in which everything is ordered by the Form of the Good.

A serious difficulty for the project of a Kantian Plato is the extent to which he endeavours to show that the moral man's life is superior to others also in terms of pleasure. This surely suggests that pleasure is, in some essential way, involved in εὐδαιμονία as is indicated by Aristotle's remark that ἐμπλέκουσι

---

[1] R.C.Cross and A.D.Woozley, *Plato's Republic: A Philosophical Commentary*, London, 1966, pp.66-68.

[2] In conversation with one of the authors.

τὴν ἡδονὴν εἰς τὴν εὐδαεμονίαν [3] 'men associate pleasure with εὐδαιμονία, happiness'. The force of this consideration is not lessened by the fact that Plato's treatment of pleasure in the *Republic* is far from satisfactory, and is not greatly assisted by the fuller discussion in the *Philebus*. There is some merit in his distinction between pure and impure pleasures and between true and false pleasures, but he makes no consistent attempt to show that the life of the δίκαιος, moral man, (equated at this point with that of the philosopher) contains a higher proportion of pure and true pleasures than that of the immoral man, or that what pleasures he has are intrinsically related to his δικαιοσύνη, morality. Clearly what he wants to maintain is, in the words of John Newton's hymn, that:

> Solid joys and lasting treasure
> None but Zion's children know.

In order to make good such an argument he needs something like Aristotle's doctrine of pleasure according to which pleasure completes an activity 'like the bloom on the face of youth' (one of Aristotle's rare flashes of poetry).[4] Aristotle here concentrates on the sense of 'pleasure' as enjoyment. With its aid Plato could have maintained, as Aristotle does, that the value of enjoyment is proportionate to that of the activity which it completes and serves to enhance.

Howes dismisses the relevance of this, however, by treating the entire discussion of pleasure as simply an *a fortiori* argument. And there is some warrant for this in the text. Plato does say after all: 'and if the good and moral man is so much superior to the bad and immoral man in terms of pleasure, will his superiority not be infinitely greater in terms of grace and beauty of life and of excellence' (IX 588a7 ff.). Moreover, Howes argues, by the time the topic of pleasure is introduced, the herald has already been summoned and Glaucon has already acknowledged defeat. So the argument as so far stated, without reference to pleasure, must be taken as sufficient in itself to establish the conclusion that the δίκαιος, righteous, man is εὐδαίμων, happy and the meaning of εὐδαίμων must be such as to fit this argument taken by itself.

A close look at the text, however, seems to rule this out. The argument from pleasure is presented as co-ordinate with the one that has gone before: 'Well, here is one of our proofs', I said, 'Let us see what you make of the second one' (IX 581d). The word translated 'proof' is ἀπόδειξις and it is plain that both arguments are reckoned to be demonstrations. This must mean that each must be taken independently to establish the conclusion that the δίκαιος, righteous, man is happy and that the meaning which we give to

---

[3] *Ethics*, VII, 1153b15.

[4] *Nicomachean Ethics*, X, 1174b33.

εὐδαίμων must be one that each allows it to bear. We cannot take εὐδαίμων overall, to mean something which either one of the two 'proofs' would not let it mean.

There is, however, a difficulty for this interpretation if we try to carry it through. It arises from the claim that the δίκαιος, moral, man is εὐδαίμων even in extremity of suffering as when tortured or impaled. We are prepared to grant that in such a desperate situation, indeed especially in it, he is 'worthy of ultimate congratulation', if he remains obedient to the claims of δικαιοσύνη, righteousness, but to say that he finds it in any sense pleasurable is manifestly absurd. So, assuming that εὐδαιμονία has some connotation of pleasure, Aristotle remarks that 'those who assert that the victim on the wheel or the man who falls into great misfortunes is εὐδαίμων so long as he is good, are, whether they mean to or not, talking nonsense'.[5] Hence, it is argued, εὐδαιμονία as it figures in the conclusion of the first proof cannot be identical with εὐδαιμονία as it figures in the second, and the first must be taken as definitive of the meaning of εὐδαιμονία in the *Republic*.

But even apart from the argument from pleasure, Plato is in difficulty in establishing his case so long as the effects of δικαιοσύνη, integrity, in the *psyche* (its 'results') are brought into the reckoning. For these too are lacking to the man in extremity. He cannot, in that predicament, be enjoying intellectual activity to the full, or indeed at all; still less can the other parts of his *psyche* be receiving the satisfactions due to them. Only if εὐδαιμονία is conceived as the Stoic ἀπάθεια, complete absence of desire and complete indifference to one's situation, can the moral man still be reckoned εὐδαίμων.

Here again the clue is to be found in Aristotle: for him εὐδαιμονία is to be judged over a whole life. Aristotle would not, of course, be prepared to call a man εὐδαίμων if his life ended in an ignominious death, but Plato considers a life to be εὐδαίμων in spite of its bitter ending if the individual continues to act δικαίως, morally, so long as it is in his power, so long as he maintains his integrity. The same is true with the imputation of δικαιοσύνη. The individual is held to be well-integrated in accordance with the constitution of his mind as it has come to be firmly established over time. He does not cease to be well-integrated because under torture he is deprived of his faculties. The case is clearest if considered in terms of the comparison Plato is making with the life of the ἄδικος, wrongdoer. The δίκαιος, righteous, man is more εὐδαίμων than the ἄδικος, wrongdoer, who seeks to save himself by betraying his friends and in so doing hazards his *psyche*.[6]

---

[5] *Ethics*, VII, 1153b20.

[6] Richard Swinburne writes: 'In connection with the holocaust it is important to realize that the greatest evil was not that suffered by the Jews, but that suffered by the concentration camp guards. The Jews lost only their lives, the guards lost their souls (in the sense of any desire to pursue the good)'. *Religious Studies*, vol.36, No.2, p.224. Swinburne's assertion is entirely platonic.

But would it not have been better for him if he had never had to face this test and had been free to enjoy the natural fruits of δικαιοσύνη, integrity? The question was much debated in the early Church in relation to martyrdom. Was it right to seek martyrdom since so great a glory attached to it? The majority opinion was that the Christian should submit to martyrdom if that was the only way open to him of witnessing to his faith, but that he should not go out of his way to seek it, but rather lead the Christian life as fully as possible. It was God's gift and should not be gratuitously thrown away. Unless Plato takes essentially the same line there is no reason why he should insist on the need to establish the ideal republic at all. Life in the world as it is, disordered and unreformed, would afford all that is needed for the achievement of δικαιοσύνη, morality, and εὐδαιμονία, happiness.

However it does seem to follow that the εὐδαιμονία, happiness, which is achievable in the imperfect conditions of ordinary life is less than complete. Socrates has shown that even in such conditions, with all the accidents and all the wrongdoing attached to them, whatever happens to him, the δίκαιος, righteous man, is more εὐδαίμων, happy, than the ἄδικος, wrongdoer, but he has not shown him to be as εὐδαίμων, happy, as he ideally could be; not because he lacks rewards and other desirable consequences, which remain irrelevant to εὐδαιμονία, but because of the constraints which limit the unimpeded activity in which εὐδαιμονία, happiness, consists and which are removed only in the ideal city.

But, perhaps, this is too rash a judgement. In a moving passage at the end of Book IX, Plato appears to suggest that it does not matter whether the ideal city exists anywhere or will ever exist. It will in any case be a παράδειγμα ἐν οὐρανῷ ἀνακείμενον, a pattern laid up in heaven, which the good man will model himself on. 'His conduct will be an expression of the laws of that city and of no other' (Lindsay).

One thing is plain. Whether or not the ideal city exists the good man will live in the spirit of its constitution and will be to that extent εὐδαίμων. The question is whether the passage implies that he is in that case as fully εὐδαίμων as it is possible to be. Lee avoids the problem by translating τὰ γὰρ ταύτης μόνης ἂν πράξειεν, ἄλλης δὲ οὐδεμιᾶς 'in it alone and in no other city will he take part in public affairs', (IX 592b4-5) but Lindsay's translation is a more plausible rendering of the Greek which literally means 'he will do the things of that city and of no other'. Plato's consistency can perhaps be saved by translating διαφέρει δὲ οὐδὲν not as 'it does not matter' but as 'it makes no difference', *i.e.* it makes no difference to the behaviour of the δίκαιος, good man. He will adhere to the principles of the ideal republic just the same, although, of course, he will be less completely εὐδαίμων than he would be if he were living in the ideal republic.

The entire question has recently been addressed by Annas.[7] She maintains what she calls 'the sufficiency thesis', that in Plato's view virtue is sufficient for happiness no matter what the circumstances. This interpretation she contrasts with that offered by Irwin, 'that the virtuous person is happier than the non-virtuous, but may fail to be happy if external circumstances are bad.'

Is Plato's Argument Broken-backed?

But even if it is granted that Plato has shown, in his own terms, that the righteous man is happier than the wrongdoer, the entire *Republic* remains open to the objection, voiced by H.A. Prichard in his inaugural lecture, 'Duty and Interest', and reiterated recently by David Sachs,[8] that its entire argument is 'broken-backed'. For Plato fails to show that the δίκαιος man in the sense of the man whose *psyche* is properly ordered, will act in ways generally taken to be moral. In Sachs' phrase there is no connection made between 'platonic justice' and 'vulgar justice'. To be sure, Plato does claim (IV 442e4 ff.) that the δίκαιος man—the man with his *psyche* properly ordered—would refrain from doing the things commonly regarded as wrong, but neither then nor later does he justify the claim.

Before considering this criticism, it is worth noticing that Plato, in Book I of the *Republic*, does not in any case unreservedly endorse common notions as expounded by Cephalus and Polemarchus. He rejects the commonly accepted idea that it is δικαίον, right, to do good to friends and evil to enemies and provides a reason for doing so, *viz.* that it is wrong to make people worse. However the critic can still complain that whether Plato endorses 'vulgar justice' or corrects it, he fails to make it clear how 'platonic justice' determines either process. He seems to take it so much for granted that he gives it only the most cursory treatment.

Nevertheless the fact that Plato is prepared to revise the accepted morality is significant. Prichard like the other Oxford intuitionists of his time, such as Ross and Carritt, assumes that we know what our duty is; the difficulty is only to bring ourselves to do it; how to adhere steadfastly to the principle, 'Do your duty whatever your duty may be'. Theirs is a moral philosophy suited to the ethics of a stable society. Plato, however, is confronted by a society in turmoil in which customary moral certainties are being called in question. He seeks a more secure foundation for ethics than can be afforded by the conscience of the ordinarily decent person. If then he is to be defended against critics who

---

[7] *Platonic Ethics: Old and New*, Cornell University Press, Ithaca, 1999, pp.89ff., discussing T.Irwin's *Plato's Ethics*, Oxford, 1995, p.192.

[8] 'A Fallacy in Plato's *Republic*' in R.Kraut, ed., *Plato's Republic: Critical Essays*, New York, 1997, pp.1-16.

complain that his argument is 'broken-backed' it will have to be in terms of a metaphysic of ethics which goes beyond what Aristotle calls τὰ ἔνδοξα and which we might call, following Galbraith, 'the conventional wisdom'. This is what in the central books of the *Republic* he sets out to provide. The answer to the critics must be found in Plato's description of the philosopher's encounter with the Form of the Good and his subsequent wrestling with the problems of δικαιοσύνη, morality, and ἀδικία, immorality, in the everyday world. This is made clear in his account of the reasons why the guardians must play their part in politics: 'You must, therefore, each descend in turn and live with your fellows in the cave and get used to seeing in the dark; once you get used to it you will see a thousand times better than they do and will distinguish the various shadows, and know what they are shadows of, because you have seen the truth about things admirable and just and good', διὰ τὸ τἀληθῆ ἑωρακέναι καλῶν τε καὶ δικαίων καὶ ἀγαθῶν πέρι (VII 520c1-6). Someone might make the same sort of complaint about Christ's summary of the Law: 'Thou shalt love the Lord thy God with all thy heart and with all thy mind and with all thy *psyche*, and thy neighbour as thyself'. Why, it might be asked, should it follow from my loving God that I also love my neighbour? And why, if I love my neighbour, should I tell him the truth, keep my promises to him, and so forth?

These are all proper questions for students of Christian ethics and one can see roughly how to go about answering them. One is to love one's neighbour because he is created in the image of God and the object of God's love. One's more particular duties to others are bound up with their fundamental needs as the kind of creatures they are and which have the same claims upon one as one's own. It would be reasonable to complain that Christian ethics was broken-backed only if the entire Christian world-view was held to be fallacious. J.L. Mackie is able to acknowledge a Christian warrant for traditional Christian ethics as objectively 'required by the universe' but nevertheless rejects it because he thinks that a purely naturalistic world-view is more credible than a theistic one.[9]

Plato's ethics are similarly bound up with his entire metaphysical scheme and have to be, in his view, because morality otherwise lacks a secure foundation. He is convinced that it is possible to know what actions are right only if one knows what δικαιοσύνη essentially is, and one can know that only if one understands how δικαιοσύνη is also good, that is to say if one becomes acquainted with the Form of the Good. As the simile of the Sun makes clear the Form of the Good is the source of the reality of objects within the intelligible world and of their being known. Since the sun itself is the 'offspring of the good' and is the cause of the processes of generation, growth and nourishment in the physical world, we have the makings of a thoroughly teleological view of

---

[9] J.L.Mackie, *Inventing Right and Wrong*, Harmondsworth (Penguin), 1977.

the world whose ethical implications emerge in subsequent theories of natural law. Surprisingly enough they are to be found also in Kant's account of the supreme principle of categorical imperatives. Although Kant believes that to reject any of his categorical imperatives involves a purely logical contradiction, it is plain that in some instances there is no logical contradiction unless a teleological component is presupposed. The duty of cultivating one's talents, for example, depends upon the assumption, which Kant actually states, that they are given one for a purpose. And the same is true of his prohibition of suicide. The presence of this element of teleology in an ethical system which is deliberately designed to dispense with any such metaphysical baggage is a curious testimony to its lasting influence in European thought.

It must be conceded that Plato does not spell this out and it may be the case that he is unsure how to do it in any detail. The central books of the *Republic* provide a prospectus for a metaphysics of ethics but do not go far in working it out. It is its political rather than its ethical implications which are given extended treatment.

Chapter 9
Plato and Pluralism

The Different Faces of Democracy

Plato has long been thought the enemy of democracy, but the issue has been confused because he—and we also—use the word in several different senses. Plato, with some reason, thought ill of the political regime in the Athens of his day. Democratic follies had lost Athens the Peloponnesian War, and democratic intolerance had condemned Socrates to death. But Plato was much more a critic of the theory of democracy. Democracy was egalitarian and pluralist. It extended equality before the law, ἰσονομία (*isonomia*), to an absolute equality, which held that all men were equal in all important respects, and maintained that one man's opinion was as good as another's. If all choices were equally valid, each man should be free to make up his mind as he pleased, and follow his own inclinations. A democratic society must, therefore, be a permissive one, recognising no objective standards of right and wrong.

Our contemporary understanding of democracy is equally confused. Many use the word simply as a term of commendation without descriptive content. Communist regimes have unblushingly described themselves as democratic, and in debates on the future composition of the House of Lords, a government spokesman resisted, in the name of democracy, proposals that the members should be elected; and plebiscites together with open town meetings in New England have often been criticized as undemocratic. Democracy as understood in the West, is what was fought for in the Second World War, and is defined negatively: democratic is what the Axis powers were not.

The dispute between Plato and modern democracy is, therefore, not a simple one. There are several different issues, and while on some Plato can be severely criticized,[1] he is able to make valid points against many modern proponents of democracy.

Plato Against Athenian Democracy

Athenian democracy was not as bad as Plato made out. It had prosecuted some wars successfully. It had allowed itself to be guided by Pericles. It had nurtured the high peak of Greek civilisation. But it had thrown away

---

[1] For example by Christopher Taylor, 'Plato's Totalitarianism' in R.Kraut, ed., *Plato's Republic: Critical Essays*, New York, 1997, ch. 3.

117

the Peace of Nikias, almost committed genocide in Mytilene, actually committed genocide in Melos, and in the end, through its own wilfulness, lost the Peloponnesian War. These disasters were not accidents. After Pericles' death the Athenians became very hard on their leaders. Distrust of leaders doomed the Sicilian expedition. After the battle of Arginusae, the admirals, who had won the battle for Athens, were blamed for not having picked up survivors from Athenian ships that had been sunk. Instead of their being put on trial, an Act of Attainder was moved, that is to say a motion in the ἐκκλησία , the Assembly, that they should all be put to death. Some argued that this was illegal, whereupon there was a great uproar, τὸ δὲ πλῆθος ἐβόα δεινὸν εἶναι εἰ μή τις ἐάσει τὸν δῆμον πράττειν ὃ ἂν βούληται, the plebs roared that it was terrible if anyone did not let the people do whatever it wanted.[2] It so happened that Socrates was in the chair on the day. He refused to put the motion to the vote, since it was unlawful; but the next day a more compliant individual occupied the chair, and the motion was put, and the admirals executed. We should agree with Socrates: not everything the people want is, for that reason alone, right. There are principles of politics, arising out of the nature of government, which hold good independently of what the majority wants. Although in the middle of the Twentieth Century it was fashionably said that self-government was better than good government, subsequent events have shown the cruel price that bad self-governments have exacted from those unfortunate enough to be subject to them.

Plato goes further. Government is nothing but a skill, like steersmanship. The ship of state should be steered by experts, who not only know how to run things, but also, guided by the Forms, know where to aim for.

> O'er forms of government let fools contest,
> Whate'er is best administered is best.

No one today wants to defend Plato's own ideal.[3] It suffers, as Christopher Taylor[4] has argued more temperately than Popper,[5] from a failure to acknowledge autonomy or attach any value to it; and autonomy is basic to any political system we are prepared to accept. But Plato's criticisms of modern versions of the dogma *Vox populi, vox Dei* remain trenchant. We have much to learn from his questions, even if we cannot accept his answers.

---

[2] Xenophon, *Hellenica*, I,7,12.

[3] But many have rediscovered some of Plato's arguments against liberal permissiveness; for example, Anne Atkins, *The Daily Telegraph*, July 17, 2000, p.20.

[4] 'Plato's Totalitarianism' in R.Kraut, ed., *Plato's Republic: Critical Essays*, New York, 1997, ch. 3.

[5] *The Open Society and its Enemies*, London, 1945, vol. I.

Plato Against Egalitarianism

Many Athenians were egalitarians. The word ἰσονομία (*isonomia*), suggested not only equality before the law, νόμος (*nómos*), but equality of distribution. The concept seems to have originated at the time when colonies were being sent out. It would make sense then to discuss how the pasture, νομός (*nomós*) in the new colony was to be distributed (from the verb νέμω (*nemo*)), and to agree that each colonist was to have an equal share, and concomitantly an equal say in determining the laws of the new colony. ἰσονομία (*isonoma*) remained an influential concept throughout the Fifth Century BC, with strong egalitarian overtones, suggesting not only that like cases should be treated alike, but that all cases should be treated the same, which would preclude the recognition of the fact that circumstances alter cases, and the rational requirement to take all relevant factors into consideration.

Plato accepted the former as being of great cogency among gods and men, but reckoned that the latter led to the anarchic absurdity of assigning equal shares to equals and unequals alike (VIII 558c5-6). He was able to draw the necessary distinction in consequence of his mathematical researches. He wanted to axiomatize geometry.[6] Euclidean geometry, as we have it, is based on the axiom of parallels. But it can be characterized by similar triangles instead of the parallel postulate.[7] In non-Euclidean geometries, such as that on the surface of a sphere, if the angles of a triangle are given, so is the length of their sides. For example, if a triangle in spherical geometry has each of its angles a right angle, we know that its sides are each one quarter of the circumference (like that on the earth's surface whose vertices are the North Pole and the two points on the equator where it intersects the meridian of Greenwich and longitude 90° East). And whereas the proof of Pythagoras' theorem in Euclid I 47 is difficult, it is far easier and more intuitive to prove it by similar triangles. Plato was inhibited from doing that because of not having a satisfactory account of the irrational numbers, but was aware of the importance of similar triangles. Similar triangles are equiangular, but not congruent: they are the *same* shape, but not the *same* size. Corresponding angles are equal, but not corresponding sides. Sameness and equality are thus shown to be not simple dyadic relations, relating just two terms, this triangle and that triangle, but more subtle triadic relations, relating three terms, this triangle and that triangle, in respect of shape, or alternatively, size. Plato made much of the distinction between 'geometrical equality' (same

---

[6] See above, ch.6.

[7] Proved much later by John Wallis, '*De Postulato Quinto*", *Opera Mathematica*, Oxford, 1693, vol.ii, pp.669-678; and Gerolamo Saccheri, *Euclides ab omni naevo vindicatus*, Milan 1733, tr. George Bruce Holland, Chicago, 1920.

shape, corresponding angles equal) and 'arithmetical equality' (same size, corresponding sides equal).[8]

Aristotle took over the distinction, and elucidated justice in terms of 'proportionate equality', based on lengths, not numbers, in which good things were distributed to people not equally but in proportion to their ἀξία, worth, merits. The distinction between geometric and arithmetic equality allowed that δικαιοσύνη was a sort of equality, treating like case alike (the principle of universalisability); but it did not require that every case be treated the same, acknowledging that circumstances altered cases. Egalitarianism thereupon faded out in the ancient world, and only Pyrrhonian sceptics supposed that all opinions were equally valid, or that all men were equally good at judging what was true or what ought to be done.

Pluralism

Like εἰκασία (*eikasia*)Plato's δημοκρατία (*demokratia*) has now come alive for us. We have become familiar with a type of liberalism or 'pluralism' which seeks to found a liberal society solely on freedom for its members to choose how they shall live and what for them shall count as right or wrong. As Plato says of his democratic city: 'First and foremost they are free: the city is full of liberty and freedom of speech and there is permission for everyone to do what he wants' (557b5). In this city 'each man will arrange his life to suit himself'. Plato believed that democracy, so understood, was the eventual outcome of any departure from his own ideal of an authoritarian meritocratic regime, and that it would decline into tyranny.

Pluralism, by contrast, maintains that autonomy not only is an indispensable good but is the sole good which requires to be universally acknowledged, together with toleration which is necessarily implied by recognition of the autonomy of others. So understood pluralism requires us to reject not only Plato's authoritarian scheme as set out in the *Republic* but also certain assumptions which Plato shares with all but his most recent critics, and which hitherto the West has accepted from the Platonic-Aristotelian tradition. They are:

1. that there is a good to which all human beings aspire;
2. that life is or ought to be governed by reason, which enables one to discern the good and order one's life in accordance with it.

Democrats in this tradition have added:

3. that the common good is most likely to be realised in a democratic society both because autonomy is a good in itself and because freedom of thought and expression are necessary conditions of the discovery of truth and the pursuit of happiness.

---

[8] *Gorgias* 508a; *Laws* VI, 757.

This third claim is a comparatively recent development of the tradition. Indeed it has only been formally accepted by the Roman Catholic Church since Vatican II, with its Declaration of Religious Freedom. Until then it was commonly accepted that 'error has no rights', as Plato himself maintained.

Contemporary engagement with Plato must lead us to consider whether liberal democracy is best defended in terms of the new 'value pluralism' with its echoes of his own conception of δημοκρατία (*demokratia*) or in terms of the older rationalism which largely derives from him. But is it at all fair to compare this new pluralism with Plato's δημοκρατία, which is defined by its place in Plato's hierarchy of political systems. The 'democratic' individual is portrayed as someone who has no controlling philosophy of life and is consequently at the mercy of his animal appetites. The pluralist, on the other hand, sees people as self-creators who devise a variety of differing patterns of life each of which represents a possible ideal, and these varying ideals are incommensurable. There is no question of their forming a hierarchy, except one constructed from the unique standpoint of one such pattern. The pluralist counterpart of Plato's δημοκρατικός, libertine, would not be someone whose life is entirely unregulated but rather someone who deliberately chose to savour every possible experience. Similarly the other life-choices which figure in Plato's descending hierarchy would appear as alternative individual ideals affording their own peculiar satisfactions, and these the pluralist will refuse to grade in the way Plato does, or in any way at all.

It would be wrong to suppose that, for the pluralist, reason, in something like the traditional sense, plays no part in the elaboration and practice of such life-styles. The very notion of an individual ideal or form of life implies something in the nature of a plan or project which can be conceived and executed more or less successfully and this must involve some exercise of the creative imagination and critical control which are traditional attributes of reason. The adherent of any such ideal will be subject to temptations to abandon it or modify it inappropriately. The principled hedonist may be tempted by the love of a good woman in a form that resists assimilation into his chosen life-style. Nevertheless, the scope of reason is limited. Reason may tell him to what extent this new experience can be accommodated but not whether he should abandon his chosen life-style altogether and adopt one in which fidelity to one woman is preferred to continual experiment. Indeed to stand for one's convictions unflinchingly while acknowledging their relative validity is a primary pluralist virtue.[9] To change them demands not a reasoned choice but a non-rational existential decision.

Somewhat similarly, reason has a subordinate part to play in the life of Plato's democratic man and the other lives in his descending hierarchy. It

---

[9] cf. John Gray, *Berlin*, London, 1995, p.142.

is implied that, at each stage in the individual's descent from the ideal meritocratic state, reason is overcome by love of honour, or wealth, or sensual
appetite, but nevertheless continues to operate in an instrumental way to
organize living in accordance with these inferior values. Reason retains the
function of seeking the good of the whole person; it is just that it steadily
loses the capacity to discern where the good actually lies. So what is in one
sense a usurpation of reason is, in another, its corruption.

Diversity and Toleration

One of the most persistent and most attractive themes in contemporary value
pluralism is its celebration of diversity and cultivation of tolerance.[10] Plato,
in the *Republic*, has little time for either. Though his imaginative sympathies
were wide, as is apparent in the *Symposium*, they appear in the *Republic*
chiefly as temptations to be resisted. Traditionally-minded admirers of Plato
have deprecated this and sought to save him from himself and enlist him in
the service of democracy by repudiating his obsessive puritanism while still
retaining his cardinal insistence on the objectivity of good.

It is maintained, however, by pluralist thinkers that it is this very insistence on the objectivity of good which generates Plato's intolerance. For if
there is an objective truth about what is good, and if it is known, rulers are
entitled and even obliged to impose acceptance of it upon society as a whole.
Hence the only sure way to defend freedom is to challenge this basic platonic
assumption and the conception of reason that goes with it.

John Gray sums up Berlin's pluralism in a final paragraph which demon-
strates clearly his decisive break with the metaphysical tradition initiated by
Plato: 'Berlin's central idea of pluralism in ultimate values denies human beings the metaphysical comfort, itself answering to a nearly universal human
need, whereby their particular forms of life are accorded a universal authority by being underwritten or guaranteed by a rational or natural or historical
order. Berlin's thought does not satisfy, or seek to appease, this human need
for metaphysical consolation'.[11]

In the face of this challenge, it remains to consider whether liberal democracy is best defended by reference to certain positive beliefs about human
nature claiming universal scope or by a value pluralism which regards all
such beliefs as having only relative significance.

The objectivist case for liberalism comes in a specifically Christian form
and in a secular form, both resting on firm metaphysical foundations. The
Christian form is based upon a conviction about the nature of man as made in

---

[10] cf. John Gray, *Berlin*, London, 1995, *passim*.

[11] *op.cit.* p.168.

the image of God and having an eternal destiny. Freedom to follow one's conscience is a necessary condition of developing our full humanity and therefore requires to be protected. The secular form is non-committal about religious claims and takes as the supreme values of human life the discovery of truth and the achievement of happiness, it being assumed that there is a truth to be discovered and that happiness is in principle recognisable and achievable. These values, it is argued, can be fully realised only in conditions of freedom. Thus, although liberalism developed in opposition to the then authoritarian tendencies of the Christian churches, it inherited from them its basic metaphysical assumptions about the objectivity of good.

By contrast with both of these the pluralist case is based upon the concept of human beings as self-creators who generate schemes of life which have value for them but are incommensurable. Since they cannot be ranked in any order there is no warrant for preferring one to another and the state is bound to give all of them as much freedom as is compatible with the maintenance of minimum public order.

The discussion so far has been exceedingly abstract and has paid no attention to the basic requirements of democratic government except for 'freedom' or 'autonomy' expressed in the most general terms. But there are other more specific requirements which need to be taken account of:

1. In a mature democracy people can as a rule be relied upon to behave well independently of anything the state might demand of them. This calls for a common morality which most people understand and support. The need for this is evident from the extreme difficulty of introducing liberal democracy to Russia after the collapse of the Soviet regime. For several generations under that regime people were encouraged to identify morality with the law of the state and the edicts of the party which together purported to govern the whole of life. In the sudden absence of these authorities they are left with little sense of personal initiative or social responsibility.

2. Administrators are for the most part incorrupt, acknowledging a professional ethic which inhibits them from pursuing their private interests at the expense of society at large. There is an ideal of public service.

3. The military and the police observe a strict code of political neutrality which forbids them to take control of the state or manipulate its operations in their own interest.

4. There is an impartial judiciary. Jurisdictions vary, and lawyers disagree, as to how freely judges can initiate or interpret legislation, but their powers are strictly defined.

5. Politicians too accept an obligation to pursue the common good and not to use the opportunities of office to promote their own interests. They are not simply delegates, but are expected to make up their own minds about what policies are best.

6. Majorities recognise limits to their power and take account of the interests of minorities.

7. All parties subscribe in principle to canons of rational debate and are open to criticism through the operation of a free press.

The first and the last of these would seem to presuppose that there is a capacity on the part of people in general to determine by rational reflection by what laws and through what institutions they can best live together. Such accommodations are normally the product of tradition and accepted as such, but, if they are challenged, the assumption is that they can be assessed by reasoned arguments which are in principle accessible to all who take the trouble to consider them. We wish, then, to argue that these features of a mature democracy depend fundamentally upon a 'platonic' conception of an objective good together with a human capacity to recognise it. Pluralists cannot view the matter in this way, because they hold that it may always be the case that, when people disagree, there is in principle no way in which their disagreements can be rationally resolved. Hence, their critics urge that, to take the most intractable case, if a particular group rejects the liberal ideal of toleration itself, the liberal society cannot appeal to reasons of universal scope but can only coerce the dissidents or secure their compliance in some non-rational way.

Pluralist thinkers are understandably reluctant to accept these implications and tend to modify their doctrine to admit of some limits upon what is acceptable in a form of life. Their attempts to do this are among the least successful elements in the varying statements of the pluralist case. Gray, in his study of Berlin's thought, refers to this tendency as his 'minimal universalism'[12] and, like Strawson in his seminal essay 'Social Morality and Individual Ideal',[13] Berlin seeks to base it on certain fundamental human needs which must be respected in anything which is to count as a morality at all. Stuart Hampshire similarly sees the need for 'a bare minimum concept of justice, underlying all the distinct, specific, and substantial conceptions' which he holds 'is indispensable, if there is to be a peaceful and coherent society'.[14] Hampshire is wary of any suggestion that fundamental human needs be brought into the reckoning since in his view all substantial conceptions of the good are bound up with local and particular forms of life and these are incommensurable. It follows that any universally acceptable concept of justice must be 'thin' and purely procedural.

It is clear from this brief survey what the basic problem for pluralism is. If, with Hampshire, the pluralist limits the scope of any universal principles

---

[12] John Gray, *Berlin*, London, 1995, p.157.

[13] *Philosophy*, **36**, 1961, reprinted in P.F.Strawson, *Freedom and Resentment*, 1974.

[14] *Innocence and Experience*, Harmondsworth (Penguin), 1989, p.73.

of morality to something purely formal and procedural, the result is too 'thin' to provide any defence against the chief objection to pluralism, namely that in the end it reduces to relativism or 'blank subjectivism', and affords no basis for a coherent society. If, on the other hand, the universal principles are given substantial content by some reference to fundamental human needs, this affords room for rational comparison between rival forms of life and their conceptions of the good in terms of their comparative ability to satisfy these basic needs, a mode of reasoning which is thoroughly platonic.

Hampshire builds into his account of minimum procedural justice a readiness to engage in reasonable argument, and in this he is clearly right. But in so doing he does not escape the pluralist's dilemma. For either he accepts, with Alasdair MacIntyre,[15] the contention that 'principles of rationality' vary from one culture to another, in which case procedural justice loses its capacity to monitor inter-cultural disputes; or there is room for rational comparison even here, with the possibility in principle of eventual agreement.

Gray seeks to minimise the problem by insisting that what the pluralist rejects is not a rational ordering of values within a recognised form of life but only the claim that 'there is a common measure or overarching principle, whereby conflicting values can be arbitrated'.[16] He gives as an example of how a liberal society might justify curtailing liberty and suppressing a particular form of life the case of a traditionally monogamous society which refuses to recognise polygamous marriages. This it might justify 'not by any claim about the peculiar value of monogamous marriage, but by the role monogamous marriage has in a particular way of life that is worth renewing'.[17]

This is one way in which the problem can be dealt with, and it has considerable initial plausibility. On any showing there is often a marked difference between cultures, each of which has made a more or less coherent selection of the values open to it, whose comparative merits are notoriously difficult to assess. But it does not guarantee unlimited toleration; for each of these distinctive societies will have generated in this way its own moral standards and will need to set limits on the conduct of minorities who are at odds with the standards set. However much a modern liberal democracy may wish to allow ethnic minorities freedom to maintain their own way of life, it will not be prepared to tolerate practices which according to its own standards involve the exploitation of women and children.

---

[15] *Whose Justice? Which Rationality?*, London (Duckworth), 1988.

[16] John Gray, *Berlin*, London, 1995, p.155.

[17] *op.cit.*, p.153.

Rational Decision Between Forms of Life

There are, interestingly enough, occasions when such decisions have to be taken entirely *de novo*. In the newly independent state of Kenya the government appointed a commission to recommend whether monogamous or polygamous marriages should be recognised in the new state.[18] Although the traditional pattern in this instance was polygamous the commission reported in favour of monogamy, with the proviso that existing polygamous marriages should remain valid for the time being. The sort of considerations which carried weight with the commission were the greater opportunities and dignity afforded to women and the greater cohesion of the two-parent family with consequent benefits for the children. These considerations are entirely general and relate to the basic needs of women and children anywhere of the sort that must figure in any catalogue of fundamental human needs. Plato's own proposed arrangements for the procreation and care of the guardian's children are open to criticism for his relentless subordination of the needs of women and children to his political ends.

In such cases the appeal to an 'overarching principle' having to do with the welfare of women and children is clear. But on close consideration it is apparent that, whatever allowance is made in particular cases for variable cultural factors, such universal principles remain in the background ready to be brought into play. The tight family structure of an Indian village with its strong patriarchal authority provides a context into which arranged marriages fit and this is reinforced by a craft-based economy in which skills are traditionally nurtured within an extended family and may be linked to a particular caste. In these circumstances it is felt to be essential for the family as such to exercise tight control over the admission of new members who will have access to the secrets of the craft. Normally there is no occasion for this system to be compared in its entirety with the much looser and freer social organization of the typical 'western' country in which a high level of autonomy is demanded both for the self-realization of the individual and for the development of the economy. When, however, a boy or a girl comes back into a traditional village with a university education there is a tension between the traditional order and their desire to exercise freedom of choice in their selection of a marriage partner. As a rule it cannot be resolved because in that culture there is no tradition of free discussion of such matters. The young people have no alternative in practice but to yield to local custom or return to the city. But when they come to found a family of their own they will need to reconcile the two demands of stability and freedom, both of which have universal validity.

---

[18] *Republic of Kenya: Report of the Commission on the Law of Marriage and Divorce*, Nairobi, 1968.

When Indian families settle in Britain there are unavoidable demands by the young for the freedom to choose their marriage partner, which is taken for granted by their British contemporaries. Some kind of accommodation has to be made. In these circumstances, where the surrounding culture encourages freedom of discussion, the resulting inter-generational debate does not have to be a matter of sheer uncomprehending confrontation. The stability of the Asian family is, so far as it goes, a virtue worth holding on to. Indeed it is to some extent worth imitating when contrasted with the breakdown of many British marriages with its demonstrable ill effects upon the children. But the greater freedom of the immigrant children, as they grow up, to make choices for themselves is of benefit to them in their personal life as well as fitting them for an economy in which individual initiative will be increasingly demanded.

Of greater relevance to the present discussion than the Kenya example is the decision of the British in India and in their colonial territories elsewhere to introduce the rule of law based upon an independent judiciary and the elimination of corruption in the public services. Although these were undoubtedly alien importations the successor governments have chosen to maintain them in the conviction that they are of universal validity and in spite of a strong traditional insistence upon the individual's right and responsibility to exercise the prerogatives of office to the benefit of tribe, family and friends.

Our argument has been that modern democracy depends for its successful working upon a number of assumptions of a broadly platonic kind, designed to ensure that self-government is also good government in which the interest of the governed are adequately taken care of. The requirements we have been dealing with so far (numbers 1 and 7 on pp.123-124) are entirely general. But the more specific requirements (numbers 2-6) also present a problem for pluralism. They demand in each case a definite professional ethic to which civil servants, the military, the police, the judiciary, and politicians must adhere. This cannot be a matter of individual choice once the particular public role has been undertaken. Nor is it enough for a stable democracy that only those with the relevant commitment should observe the ethic in question. Respect for them needs to be widely diffused among the general public. This is compatible with their being open to lively criticism, but not with a climate of opinion in which, when competing views are at issue, the assumption is that 'anything goes'.

It may seem perverse to be enlisting Plato in a defence of democracy in a sense different from his own against a pluralist philosophy which has only a slight analogy with his own δημοκρατία. But there is a fundamental issue at stake here in which what is under attack is recognizably platonic in inspiration, a conviction that human life should be governed by reason and that reason aims at an objective good. That he is right about this should not be obscured by the fact that his argument in the *Republic* is open to the traditionally brought against it to the effect that he is insensitive mands of freedom and to the diversity of human personalities and cultures. Modern readers of the *Republic* will not be prepared to give up the insights of the Romantic movement. Any defence of the platonic conception of an overarching good must allow for the rich variety of the ways in which that good can be realised and for the role of the imagination in comparing and assessing them. It is a tragic feature of human life that universal goods are not always combinable, a feature which gives rise to painful dilemmas. But it does not follow from this that they are not objective goods or that we cannot, in principle, provide a coherent account of how or why they are good.

Autonomy and Objectivity

Plato can be criticized for ignoring the importance of autonomy in moral judgement, but modern advocates of autonomy are open to more damaging criticisms still. The concept of autonomy is itself in part to blame. It is unclear what it is. On one interpretation it requires each of us to make up his mind for himself on every occasion, and never to do something because someone else has told him to. At the other extreme it requires only that at some stage a man should have made a conscious decision to accept some code or person as an authoritative guide. The first interpretation is attractive, but unrealistic. We do not have the time or the ability to think out each problem for ourselves. Good behaviour, like language, is largely learned from others. On occasion we may have to deliberate and reach a conscious decision on what we ought to do, but for the most part we act unthinkingly, in ways we have been schooled to act so as to avoid harming others or disappointing their expectations. Nor is this due solely to our lack of time and understanding. Once I recognise that I am not the only moral agent making decisions, I have to limit my freedom of action by abiding by conventions in order that other agents may know what I am going to do without fear that I may autonomously reach a different decision. As they approach a roundabout, they do not want me to act solely on some maxim that I can at the same time will to be a universal law of nature; they want me to keep to the highway code, made up by some gentleman in Whitehall without any input from my autonomous will. Nor are conventions the only constraints on my freedom of action: other people are too. If I am loyal to my friends, I shall often do not as I will but as they will. Loyalty is a paradigm of heteronomy, but a virtue none the less.

Loyalty is a virtue, but not an absolute virtue. I ought to be loyal to my family, my friends, my college, my church, my country, but not in all circumstance or without ever being prepared to question whether it really is right to do what they lay down. A German who failed to carry out an order to kill some Jews, may have been disloyal, but was right in his disobedience. A moral agent aware of his own weakness of understanding, may well be right to be guided by his father, the Government, or the Church, but does not escape thereby the ultimate responsibility for doing what he does. It was his decision to be guided.

Plato is criticized for not acknowledging the need for this minimal degree of autonomy. The critics may be right. Plato nowhere shows himself sensitive to the importance of each person positively accepting and endorsing any scheme of values worked out by others in order to make them genuinely his own. But the critics may be unduly harsh in making out that Plato is treating the members of his ideal society merely as means and not also as ends in themselves. He believes, perhaps wrongly but not wrong-headedly, that all would subscribe to the ideal of a just society that sought to discover what was good and to do it. Monasteries sometimes have lay brothers, who are not deemed worthy of holy orders, and have no say in the running of the institution, but are accredited members none the less, and could well have made a conscious choice to serve a God they only dimly knew, by doing what they were told by those they believed to understand the will of God better. Not all *kibbutzniks* fully understand the *rationale* of the *kibbutzim*, but can still sensibly decide to go along with the policies of their own *kibbutz*. Sartre was caustic about a waiter who, suffering from *mauvaise foi*, tried hard to be a good waiter. But a Jew who had escaped from a communist country and had landed up in a *kibbutz* could authentically wish to be a good waiter, seeing that as his contribution to a society whose values, so far as he understood them, he endorsed.

Autonomy is not only a matter of accepting ultimate responsibility. It is a matter also of cherishing and encouraging individual choice. Plato did not see the point of this, because he thought his objectivism ruled it out. He thought that the only important question about a moral judgement was whether it was right or wrong, with the way in which it was arrived at being completely irrelevant. But objectivism does not require that every moral judgement is either right or else wrong, but only that some are. We can agree with Plato against the sophists that it is not just a matter of opinion whether it was right or wrong to massacre the inhabitants of Melos, while allowing with Berlin that in some situations it is impossible to achieve one good without forgoing another, and that sometimes there is no saying which choice is the right one. There can be objective values without their being arranged in a single, uniform, monolithic order.

The moral decisions we are called upon to make are important partly on account of the consequences that ensue from them simply regarded as actions bringing about events, but partly also as significant indications of states of mind. Where actions involve injury, or are likely to bring about other bad consequences, there is little doubt that they are wrong; and then we are much more concerned that an agent should be inhibited or pressured from doing them, than that he should make a free autonomous choice. Better that he heteronomously abstains from murdering me for fear of punishment, than that he autonomously gives rein to his atavistic impulses. But sometimes assessment of consequences gives no clear guidance, and often the action is significant on account of what attitude of mind it reveals rather than for any event engendered by an impersonal nexus of cause and effect. If it is a question of not having the soup poured down my neck, I would rather be served by a waiter suffering from *mauvaise foi*, than by one authentically asserting his proletarian independence of mind: but my full appreciation for his concern for my comfort and enjoyment of the meal depends on the assumption that his concern is genuine, and not something machined into his false consciousness.

Plato is ambivalent about individual judgement. Implicit in his account of discussion, διαλεκτική, is an acceptance of its importance: but for the most part, and especially with regard to those who are not guardians, he fails to see the importance in decision-making, of τὸ τὰ αὑτοῦ πράττειν, each doing his own thing. This failure to take account of autonomy is a serious defect in his political philosophy, but it does not invalidate his insistence on the importance for good government (of any kind) of the capacity to make a rational assessment of objective good.[19]

---

[19] For a modern depiction of the deficiencies of Plato's ideal, see John Christopher, *The Guardians*, London, 1996.

Chapter 10
Sex, Self and Power

Plato's Feminism

Plato was the first feminist. Women were the same as men, only—in general—not so good. But though women were on average less strong and generally less good than men, that was only a generalisation, which did not hold in every case. Some women were just as good, indeed better, than some men (V 455d). Whether a particular woman was suited to a particular task should be decided on the merits of the case, not on any general assumptions about woman-kind as a whole. There was no fundamental differences between the sexes which unfitted women from useful toil. The guardians were to rise above their sexual prejudices. They might feel that the sight of old women exercising in the nude was ridiculous, but that was only a matter of custom, and should be overcome (V 452). It was a waste of woman-power to seclude women in their homes, when they could be performing useful tasks in the factory or the office. Women should be used, just as men were, for the benefit of the community. They should exercise the same as men, be educated the same as men, go to war the same as men, and generally be treated exactly the same, except that not so much should be expected of them (V 457a10). Differentiation in treatment between one guardian and another should be based on difference of talent, not on difference of sex (VII 540c5-9). The only function sex was relevant for was the breeding of children (V 454de). In modern terms Plato holds that while a guardian's chromosomes are highly relevant to his suitability for various social roles, the possession of a Y-chromosome rather than a second X-chromosome is not.

Plato offers no justification, or account of how any justification might be obtained for his factual claim, but none is needed in the context of his argument. It is an indisputable fact that some women are stronger than some men, though women in general are less strong. Once it is allowed that the good of the community overrides all other considerations, it follows that in filling jobs we should seek to have the best person for the job without regard to sex. Whether a particular female candidate is better or worse than a particular male candidate is a question to be decided in each individual case on the basis of the merits they are found, on examination, to have. Sex is irrelevant to everything save sex, and it is only where specifically sexual functions are in issue that any differentiation can be justified.

Sex is relevant to the architect of the ideal society on two counts: it is the means of producing new guardians, and it is emotionally charged and potentially divisive. Motherhood cannot be abolished if there are to be guardians

131

in time to come, and motherhood is time-consuming. Plato could not want his female guardians to opt out of motherhood altogether, because that would be dysgenic. Once a rigorous selection-procedure is adopted whereby all the best people are identified and promoted to being guardians, they cannot be allowed to opt out of parenthood, or the gene-pool would be rapidly depleted of the best genes. Children will be born to female guardians, and will have to be cared for. But it would be a great waste of valuable administrative and academic talent to have top-class females acting as nursery maids. So there must be *crèches*. Our society has a similar problem, when career women decide to start a family. In time past it was possible for them to hand over nursery functions to nannies, recruited from the lower classes, but in the second half of the twentieth century it has been difficult to accept that some women should look after other women's babies, because it implies, or is thought to imply, lower status. It is often felt that the solution we should adopt is that the father should stay at home and be an *au pair* boy, but Plato could not have countenanced that, because eugenic breeding would require that top-class females should mate with top-class males, who could no more than their spouses be spared for nursery duties. Even so, even if all the chores of looking after children are left to others, women have hitherto been obliged to give up time to gestating and giving birth, and have been correspondingly less available for career jobs. Now, however, modern technology has come to Plato's aid. *In vitro* fertilisation and surrogate motherhood would enable Plato's female guardians to pass on their genes to the next generation without having to waste time away from their high-powered jobs on maternity leave. Lower-class women, who were not capable of anything better could bear children for their upper-class sisters in much the same way as they used to nurse them in the past. The occasional visit to the surgery for egg-extraction would no more interfere with a guardian's usefulness than her male colleague's occasionally having to go to the insemination centre to donate sperm.

Plato is led to the community of children and their communal upbringing in communal *crèches* simply on the economic grounds of getting the greatest possible amount of work out of female workers, in much the same way as the communists did: it is a consequence of his principle τὸ τὰ αὑτοῦ πράττειν: there must be no πολυπραγμοσύνη among the guardians in respect of child-rearing any more than in any other sphere of life. But that is not his only reason. It is not only that motherhood takes time and effort, but that mating is emotionally charged and family affection dangerously disruptive of corporate solidarity. It is a commonplace observation that men are more likely to fall out over the possession of women than for any other cause, and that not even the closest friendship can withstand the rivalry of courtship and the jealousies of love. Once partnerships are countenanced, competition and jealousies will ensue, and the unity of the ruling class will be destroyed by dissension: and once families are legitimised, family pull will be exerted to divert the operation of meritocratic selection procedures in favour of sons and nephews, and the unity of the ruling class will be riven by dynastic rivalries and feuds.

Emotional Involvement

The community of wives and children solves both problems. Sex is marginalised. In the *Republic* it is only an animal appetite, not a personal affection leading to lifelong exclusive commitment. And family affection is universalised behind a veil of ignorance. Sex is an appetite most men happen to have, and one which we need on occasion to gratify in order to secure the continuance of the species. If men could restrain their appetite, so much the better, but if they cannot, then it should be gratified in a casual, uncommitted way, without forming couples who would distinguish themselves from the rest of the guardians by an exclusive commitment to each other, which could make some other guardian jealous. I need not be jealous of Jill going out with Jack tonight, if I know that it means nothing and my turn will come tomorrow. We can slake our passions as they arise, without our temporary liaisons meaning anything much that anyone else could mind about. Those who have the grace of continence should be continent: those who cannot aspire to so high a standard, should sleep around as need be, being careful to avoid any issue or emotional entanglement. Better sow sterile wild oats than marry.

Homosexuality

Plato's homosexuality has often been cited as the reason for his low esteem of the married state, and at one level this is undoubtedly true. He was attracted to boys and young men, although he became increasingly puritan about the physical manifestations of sex. The saying he reports of Sophocles is illuminating (I 329bc): sexual attraction was a biological fact, to be restrained as much as possible, and otherwise treated as a mere animal necessity, necessary for the generation of guardians, and unavoidable for those who have not the requisite self-control, but not something he could live with emotionally or integrate into his scheme of life. But deeper explanation is called for: it is not simply that he had never experienced the love of a woman, and did not know how much he was asking the guardians to forgo. He knew the power of erotic love, and in the *Symposium*, and later in the *Phaedrus*, likens it to divine ecstasy, reaching out to Beauty itself, an ultimate principle of all things, of which the fundamental explanation is, in Aristotle's phrase, κινεῖ ὡς ἐρώμενος, it moves as being the object of love. But he draws back. It is the same as with poetry. The purveyors of divine inspiration in the *Ion* are by Book X of the *Republic* to be banished from the borders of the Ideal Society. The man who was trying to curb his poetic genius and schooling himself to be properly prosaic could well have reckoned that he should also subject the irrational leap of love to the cold calculations of eugenics. And perhaps at this level his homosexuality should be seen as a symptom rather than a cause. There is, furthermore, especially in the *Republic*, a pervasive sense of turning away from this wicked world, a sense that in the real world real politics is a dirty business, the good man fares ill, and things are inevitably going from bad to worse. The Seventh Letter reveals the biographical background: Plato was emotionally driven out of the Athens that had killed Socrates and the Syracuse that had nurtured Dion; he turned back from the commitment and responsibilities of heterosexual love, to the less deep and more transient fellow-feeling of the adolescent peer-group. His homosexuality represents a certain regression, a turning his back on the world as he found it and seeking solace in the cosiness of a small community in the company of yes-ful youths. He did not just happen to be a homosexual who could therefore forget about the power of love for women, but was one because he could not afford to allow his self to be vulnerable as a lifelong lover and beloved.

The Abolition of the Self

The community of wives and children is part of a more ambitious programme—the abolition of the self. Plato's ideal is that we shall all cease using the pronoun ἐμόν, 'mine', in its customary, divisive use, and instead use it only as we now use 'ours' (V 463e5–464d5). Only so, he thinks, can the ruling class be made a complete unity, in which nobody is conscious of himself as a separate entity; and only so shall we each be able to transcend our natural selfishness, and come to lead a moral life. The problem of morality was that we were all rationally inclined to πλεονεξία, selfishness, and Plato's solution for selfishness was selflessness.[1] It was only if we could completely escape from the self that we should be able to avoid the ultimate autism of the self-centred life. But marriage is an obstacle to this process: marriage is peculiarly self-enhancing. Each partner is unique in the eyes of the other, and so comes to have a strong sense of intrinsic value and individual identity. It bolsters the awareness of the self, and strengthens its self-image as something existing in its own right and being of inherent value. Marriage separates off the married couple, surrounding them with glass walls, and encouraging them to think of themselves as a unit, as something different from society at large, and espousing values not necessarily the same.

The abolition of the self is a difficult enterprise, and in his concern for the family and the generation of children, he showed himself sensitive to the key factor in the evolution of the self. Organisms have evolved a sense of self because all the genes in the phenotype have a common interest in its survival. The ultimate evolutionary entity, the self-replicating gene, cannot afford to be entirely a selfish gene, because its only chance of replicating itself lies in the

---

[1] See above, ch.2, pp.23-24, and ch.3, pp.38-39.

survival of the organism to an age when it can reproduce its kind. In sexual reproduction each of my genes has as good a chance as any other of being passed on to my offspring, and there is no way for one to compete with another to obtain a better chance of being passed on. With individual members of a species it is different. Although some co-operation may be beneficial, there is an element of competition in leaving successful progeny behind, and those who lose out in this competition have no posterity to carry on their line. For this reason we have come to care very much about our own children, and to strive to do well by them. If we are guardians, and believe that being a guardian is a great good, we shall want our children to be guardians too. Often, of course they will be, since we shall mate with guardians, and the result of our union will inherit good genes from both parents. Often, but not always. There is in any population, even among children of exceptional parents, a tendency to regress to the norm. Sometimes the children of the guardians will themselves have a less than golden genetic make-up. And then their parents, if they know that they are their parents, will be reluctant to see in their offspring anything less than golden promise. We are partial to our progeny, and will try very hard to secure that they pass their examinations and take their place in the top stream and remain on course for admission into positions of privilege and power. Unless our family pushiness is curbed, the seamless fabric of social unity will be tied into dynastic knots, and evolutionary pressures will continue to operate against true selflessness. Plato needs to place the generation of children behind the veil of ignorance, in order that none shall know who his offspring are, and be thus unable to give them a selectively helping hand.

We may question whether the programme is either feasible or desirable. Surprisingly, it is feasible, being exemplified by a certain species of African mole-rat (*Heterocephalus glaber*), which live in colonies occupying tunnels in the banks of rivers, where it is difficult to re-identify one's previous partner or recognise one's offspring.[2] There is no occasion for sexual jealousy, no feeling for family, no preference for one's own progeny. The care of the young is a communal responsibility, and each individual identifies with the whole community, not knowing any other entity to identify with. The life-style of the African mole-rat is not pleasing, and Plato's own arrangements are distasteful, not to say disgusting. On a charitable view, we can ascribe them to the technological inadequacies of his time. In the modern world we can, or at least

---

[2] Information about this curious beast is most easily obtained from the web. At the time of writing http://natzoo.si.edu/Animals/nmrats/datasht2.htm works and is informative, with a webcam offering a glimpse of the beasts themselves. But web sites can be as ephemeral as mayflies. A more permanent reference is J.U.M.Jarvis, M.J.O'Riain, N.C.Bennett, P.W.Sherman, *Trends in Ecology and Evolution*, 1994; 9 (2) pp.47-52. We are indebted to Dr Anne Magurran, of the University of St Andrews, and Sir Richard Southwood, FRS, Fellow of Merton for these references.

can envisage our being able to, separate the emotionally charged operation of copulation from the clinical business of conception and gestation. In the first place, contraception enables us to have the former without the latter. A modern-day Plato would have no need to countenance abortion or infanticide: vasectomy and the pill would ensure that there were no unwanted results of the guardians disporting themselves. Artificial insemination would enable the bureau of eugenics to select for desirable qualities of character and intellect without resort to deception. There would however be a danger of their giving preferential treatment to their own sperm. That could be prevented by certain institutional arrangements; or it might be better to eschew selective eugenic breeding among the guardians, mixing the semen from all donors so that there was a random selection of the successful spermatozoon, thus assimilating the reproductive process of the πόλις, as a whole to that of the individual organism. And, as we have seen, even gestation may be separated from genetics. Not only would the division of labour be complete, but the veil of ignorance between one generation and the next would occur naturally and without deception or concealment.

Dynasties and Power

Plato's solutions are repugnant, but they are attempts to solve real problems, and we can better appreciate his proposals if we consider how other societies cope with the family and the transmission of power. Some make no attempt, and experience disastrous dissension as dynasties compete for power. With the passage of time the regression to the norm reasserts itself, and the families in power become incompetent, until defeat or revolution supervenes. Other societies, especially those imbued with social ideals, attempt to ensure that family divisiveness does not have it all its own way. The Israeli *kibbutzim* come nearest to Plato's ideal; they countenance marriage, but insist on the communal rearing of children. There has been some evidence that children do not thrive in the absence of traditional family life: they need fathers, and especially mothers, to relate to. It has proved difficult to continue that arrangement into the second generation in the face of that evidence and the natural affections of husbands and wives—who already constitute a fundamental division among *kibbutzniks*. St Augustine relates how, when he was thinking of setting up a select community of like-minded friends, he abandoned the idea on the grounds that their wives would be sure to quarrel, and in due course the monasteries dealt with the problem of sex by banning it altogether. Had Plato known of the monastic movement, and its success in sublimating men's sexual urges, he might well have enjoined celibacy on his guardians too, were it not for the problem of replacing guardians when they die. The monasteries' response is to recruit novices from the outside world and to recognise their own essential incompleteness, as only one facet of the church, whose *raison d'être* lies beyond the monasteries themselves, and encompasses the non-monastic world. Plato could not envisage his ideal society being similarly dependent on the outside world for its supply of new guardians. Such novices would bring with them many corrupt practices and ideas from the non-ideal world, and would infect the πόλις, with dangerous thoughts. If in any existing city all those over ten years of age were to be got rid of in order to ensure that society could start afresh with a clean slate (VII 540e-541a), it clearly would not do to keep on re-infecting the body politic with new arrivals. The mediaeval Western Church had a further problem, that of nepotism. Not all the bishops were chaste as well as celibate (and, even if they were, sometimes had genuine nephews whom they were tempted to promote); hence the prohibition in Canon Law, which survives to this day, on anyone illegitimate becoming a bishop.

The Roman Empire allowed the Emperor to marry, but thanks to the fortunate fact of neither Julius Caesar nor Augustus having a son, developed a policy of adoption, whereby the Emperor chose his successor and made him his nominal son. But family ties proved too much for the otherwise excellent Marcus Aurelius, who allowed his biological son Commodus to succeed him. Neither Rome nor Byzantium ever solved the succession problem for the Emperor himself, and after a few generations of hereditary succession there would be a violent displacement of one dynasty by another. Byzantium, however, went some way to solving the wider problem of power by castrating its civil servants. Eunuchs were excellent. They were disturbed by no sexual jealousies, nor diverted from their work by family commitments. They were often devoted to the public good, and though sometimes given to nepotism in the strict sense, did not push the interests of their relatives with true parental zeal. But they were proverbially power-hungry, and we might well think that children were worth having if only to siphon off successful men's urge to achieve yet further success, and to console the unsuccessful with the prospect of being able to spend more time with their families.

Jowett admired the *Republic*, and sought to make Britain a meritocracy after Plato's heart. He had a fair measure of success. Although there is a dignified part of the constitution in which Parliament plays a key role, and democratic elections take place at intervals, power has been steadily leaking away from Westminster to Whitehall. The Departments of State pay nominal obeisance to their Ministers, and when there is an inter-departmental dispute the Cabinet can exercise real power; but for the most part the Minister has neither the time nor the knowledge to make his Department do what it does not want to do. In that sense the real power in contemporary Britain is substantially exercised by civil servants, themselves selected by examination after a rigorous academic course, often in philosophy. Civil servants, though sometimes said by MPs to be political eunuchs, are not real eunuchs, and have wives and families to prove it. But their wives and families play no part in their public lives and have no political power. Although the wife of a top civil servant is addressed as 'Lady', she has much less pull than the ladies, or even the mistresses, of previous ages. She is kept in *purdah* in the suburbs, well away from the corridors of power. Nor from the career point of view is it any advantage to be the child of a civil servant. Britain is an enthusiastic meritocracy, and parental pull is rigidly excluded from all selection processes. We deal with the problem of sex by legitimating it but separating it from everything of public importance. A rigid separation between public and private life ensures that amorous ambitions and family loyalties have no influence on the course of events. (It should be noted that the dignified part of the constitution is not totally ineffective. Parliament still has some real power. It should also be noted that the hereditary principle is in practice still strong even in the House of Commons, where many MPs, including many Labour MPs, are descended from the politicians of a previous age.)

The Real Origin of Sin

Plato is dealing with a real problem. We cannot say that we or other societies have dealt with it well, but still we may have qualms about his solution. He himself expresses some doubts: he was more realistic than most in seeing that the problem of succession was one that proves fatal to most regimes, and in the dark passage at the beginning of Book VIII fears that it will be the undoing of even the ideal society. But he fails to identify the source of the difficulty. He lays down that the guardians should have everything in common except their bodies (V 464d9), but this is the wrong exception. Their bodies are not to be peculiarly their own, since they are to be at the disposal of the πόλις, for child-bearing and child-begetting: it is their minds that are inherently their own, and it is their minds that need to be excepted from individual determination, if the community is to be completely at unity with itself. And this is difficult. Each of us has a mind of his own, which he can, and sometimes must, make up for himself: that is what it is to be an autonomous agent. The guardians, although acknowledging the supremacy of reason and engaging in free and frank discussion and open-ended argument (VII 534c1-3, 539c5-d1), cannot be guaranteed to reach agreement on all matters, since, as Plato elsewhere notes, there is no decision-procedure for evaluative disputes.[3] The guardians will sometimes disagree about what ought to be done, and however much they are anxious to reach agreement and not to quarrel, each will think that it would be better if they agreed with him than if the general consensus went the other way. I necessarily think that what I think is true, and that others ought to agree with me more than that I should agree with them. Although sometimes I shall be convinced by their arguments, and

---

[3] *Phaedrus* 265a.

then gladly exchange my own previous false opinions for those I now see to be true, and sometimes they will be convinced by my arguments, and be argued out of their mistaken views, we shall not always reach a common mind on all matters, and then the decision we take, whatever it is and however it is taken, will leave some of us not thoroughly convinced. Someone will be left with a nagging feeling of having been right but not properly attended to; a prophet, temporarily without honour in his own generation, but due to be vindicated in the fulness of time, when others will come to see how right he was, and how much better it would have been if only they had heeded him when he told them so. In that sense there is bound to be a contest for power. I cannot give my mind to the question of what ought to be done—or, often, to the question of what ought to be believed—without wanting my views to carry the day. Although I may change my mind under the influence of argument, discussion, friendly criticism and debate, and the different opinions of different thinkers may converge towards a common mind, we shall not always reach complete agreement, and in so far as we do not, each of us will be ineliminably anxious that his own views should prevail. And this is an inherent source of dissension among the guardians, quite independent of the rivalries of love and quarrels about family possessions. In the decline of the constitution of societies and individuals, Plato sees the competition for *prestige* and the competition for wealth as the first two stages on the downward path, but does not see that the guardians, even though they may have eschewed all pursuit of money or of glory, are still bound, of necessity, to compete for power. Many abbots in the middle ages and many civil servants in our own times have been notably unconcerned with securing wealth for themselves, and have been quite content to stand out of the limelight and let others take the acclaim for what they have done, obtaining their own satisfaction simply from the knowledge of their job well done; but, once their power is threatened, they have fought like tigers to ensure that whatever else happens, it shall be they who have the decisive say about the way things go. The hunger for power is the last infirmity of high-minded men, because it is power that enables them to put their good intentions, based on high aspirations and well-reasoned judgements, into effect. I can keep my bodily appetites under control, and can even curb my family pride for the sake of the community, but to give up power is to give up altogether in the great project itself. To abdicate is to forgo having any say in what shall happen, and to have no share in trying to make the world a better place. It is for this reason that power struggles are more likely to occur among committed intellectuals than sexual jealousies or family feuds, and are more disruptive and deep-seated. Plato thought that having wives and children in common would remove all cause for dispute, and would enable the guardians to dwell together in unity as a band of brothers sharing their joys and sorrows, because they all had the same aim and were of one mind (V 464d), but failed to see that he had not excluded the chief source of dissension among high-minded men.

Plato's moral and political ideals are at odds with his intellectual methodology. He wants his guardians to have all things in common, but believes that truth comes out of the clash of different opinions. We do not all have the same apprehension of the truth. If we did, there would be no need for διαλεκτική (dialektike), argument and probing examination of one another's views. IF there were a strict decision-procedure for moral questions, so that initial misapprehensions would be seen to have been wrong even by those who had at first laboured under them, THEN, perhaps, they would not take it too much amiss that they had been shown to be wrong: there are relatively few people who, having once imagined that the square root of two was a rational number, or that π was exactly equal to $3\frac{1}{7}$, cherish a grievance at having been shown to be wrong. But the illumination that comes from διαλεκτική comes more sparingly, and may not come at all to some, who may continue in error, sincerely believing that they alone are right, and that everybody else is too pig-headed to recognise the fact. The convergence of opinion on moral matters, which is the most that Plato can reasonably hope for, is neither quick enough nor universal enough to ensure that the guardians are all of one mind about them, and free of all tendencies to *stasis*. But this is only a contingent truth. Although it is a defining mark of our being separate selves that each of us can make up his own mind differently from others, it is not the case that he has to. And hence, though the absence of a decision-procedure for evaluative disputes means that Plato cannot rely on our all becoming like-minded on all questions, there is some tendency for wise men to think alike, and over the ages a consensus has emerged on some moral questions. It could be the case that disagreements, though real, were not so widespread or long-standing as to pose a serious threat to the unity of the state. At least, it did not seem so much a forlorn hope in Plato's time as it does now after two millennia of dissension. Plato's political methodology, although flawed, was not obviously incapable of working. But Plato assumed it was bound to work, because it was based on a programme—the abolition of self—which ruled out the possibility of our making up our minds differently. If I do not even have a mind of my own, I cannot be permanently at odds with my fellow guardians. We may have different perspectives initially, reflecting our different points of view, but we shall soon discount all subjectivity of approach, and see the Forms as they really are, and not as they had at first sight appeared to be. And this programme, we may now conclude, is inherently unattainable; however much we try to put off our selfhood, the old Adam will resurrect himself in new and original ways. But our complaint is not that Plato's programme is incapable of achievement: rather, it is not one we ought to attempt. Granted that πλεονεξία, seeking always to get more for oneself, is wrong, it does not follow that the only way of being right is not to consider oneself at all. The opposite of selfishness is unselfishness, not selflessness. As the lyre-string argument in Book I (349a-350e) shows, a man acts wisely and well in not grabbing too much for himself rather than in insisting on assigning to himself nothing at all.[4]

There is a danger of selflessness masking, and becoming a vehicle for, self-hate, and the moral selfless person often is as hard on others as he is on himself, and unhealthily eager to impose sacrifices on all under the guise of seeking the common good. The Judaeo-Christian commandment that one should love one's neighbour as oneself presupposes that one ought actually to love oneself. Although any concern for others must sometimes require the abridgement of one's own interests, and involve a degree of self-sacrifice, the point of the sacrifice is the good of others, not the abnegation of oneself.

Plato had two problems: the problem of sons and the problem of lovers. They are real problems that any political or social philosopher must address. Those with power want to hang on to it, and to leave it to their family or friends when they die; and the pair-bond, most fully realised in marriage, creates units within the community with values not all identical with those of the community itself. Other societies have adopted different solutions to these problems, but none of them satisfactory. Plato's solution was radical and all-encompassing, but did not get to the root of the problem, which was the self's concern with power rather than sex. Modern technology might make a quasi-Platonic scheme work so far as sex was concerned, but would place the natural affections of most men and women under intolerable pressure, and would not solve the problem of power and political dissension. Our most serious criticism, however, is of his seeking to exalt the community by deflating the self. Although the pair-bond is exclusive, and does indeed create glass walls around married couples, the community can afford to be that amount divided into separate sub-units; and the self is better to that extent when it is fulfilled in loving and being loved than if it is entirely cut down to communal size.

Modern Feminists and Plato[5]

Feminists have ambiguous attitudes to Plato. They approve his giving women equality of opportunity, but do not like his assuming that that will not secure equality of outcome. A few domestic occupations apart, Plato claims that men generally outperform women. But, feminists feel, the factual basis is shaky, and in any case Plato has skewed the playing field by concentrating on 'agonistic' male pursuits like warfare and dialectical philosophy. Women

---

[4] See above, ch.1, pp.11-13.

[5] A helpful and balanced account is given by G.Vlastos, 'Was Plato a Feminist?', *Times Literary Supplement*, no.4, 485, March 17, 1989, pp.288-289, reprinted in R.Kraut, ed., *Plato's Republic*, Lanham, Maryland, USA, 1997, pp.115-128.

are being judged less good than men because they are being judged by men using male criteria of excellence. If instead of setting questions on dialectical philosophy, the Civil Service Commissioners selected on the basis of consensual skills, like securing agreement, our mandarins would be more equitably chosen and more representative of the people they ruled.

There is some force in this criticism. There is an element of *machismo* in Plato's ideal of human excellence, and the militarist tone of the *Republic* grates on our ears. In his defence Plato could argue that the guardians had to guard the freedom of the city. Situated in the Balkans in a violent age, the city was under constant threat of attack, and an ability to defend it by force of arms was a prime requisite. We may concede to Plato that military prowess and bodily strength are a qualification for exercising rule over others; but they are not the only ones: other forms of courage are equally essential— fortitude for instance, and in particular the moral courage needed for taking difficult decisions, and in a less troubled world more weight can be given to less Spartan virtues, such as empathy and sensitivity to the feelings of others. Empathy and sensitivity to the feelings of others are often claimed as peculiarly feminine virtues, and they might in fact be so. But Plato could accept that. Although he has a low view of the general run of women, he is not a principled misogynist—he is equally scathing about the general run of men. Helen was fickle, and there may have been many would-be Helens around him; but Penelope, Alcestis, Antigone and Iphigenia all showed great courage and firmness of purpose, and would have been ranked ahead of most male candidates as outstandingly well-qualified to guard the city.

Plato can be argued with about the virtues needed for being a good guardian. The Civil Service Commissioners do not set examinations only in mathematics and philosophy, but in literature and history too, reckoning that humane letters confer a breadth of comprehension and depth of judgement that are as valuable as precision of thought and penetration of understanding. Plato, if he could have been reconciled to the poets, and not insistent on differentiating his Academy from Isocrates' finishing school, would have acknowledged the value of empathy and intuitive understanding generally. And if female candidates turned out to be better, they would have been chosen. But he would have set his face against regarding specifically female excellences as desirable virtues in guardians simply because they were female. There would have been no paper in Women's Studies. The criteria of selection would have been set solely by the needs of the job, not by the orientation of the candidates. Some modern feminists are outraged.[6] Plato

---

[6] See, e.g., J.Annas, 'Plato's *Republic* and Feminism', *Philosophy*, 51, 1976, pp.307-321. J.Annas, *An Introduction to Plato's Republic*, Oxford, 1981, pp.181-185. A.W.Saxonhouse, 'The Philosopher and the Female in the Political Thought of Plato', *Political Theory*, 4, 1976, 195-212, and C.D.C.Reeve, 'The Naked Old Women in the Palaestra', both the latter reprinted in R.Kraut, ed., *Plato's Republic*, Lanham, 1997, pp.95-113, and 129-141.

is not showing concern with women's natures as *they* perceive them, but subordinating them to the interests of the community as *he* perceives it. Instead of securing to women the right to abort their foetuses if they so chose, and ensuring that conditions of employment were family-friendly out of regard for women's reproductive role, Plato plays down the fact that women alone can bear children, reckoning that irrelevant to their employment (even among the non-guardians).

Plato would be unworried by these criticisms. Having himself formulated the Law of Non-contradiction, he would see that he could not hope to meet the feminists' demands. We can note his unconcern with women's rights—but note also his equal unconcern with men's rights. Plato's exaltation of the community at the expense of the individual is, indeed, unpleasing. We would like him to combine his moral objectivity and sense of communitarian values with a respect to the individual and kindness to the self. But that would require the *Republic* to be a very different book—indeed, a book that has never yet been written.

Chapter 11
Plato and Education

Jowett's Ideal

In the heyday of the British Empire education in Britain had a distinctly platonic character. Universities deliberately aimed to train an élite, the sort of men who could be relied upon to take their rightful place in the administration of the empire, of which the jewel in the crown was India. It is no accident that the members of the Indian Civil Service were commonly referred to as the guardians; nor that Benjamin Jowett, the influential Master of Balliol College, Oxford, was a leading authority on Plato. The curriculum of Greats at Oxford comprised Greek and Latin language and literature, philosophy and ancient history. Students were thoroughly familiar with the culture of the classical world, and the study of philosophy was firmly based on Plato's *Republic* and Aristotle's *Nicomachean Ethics*. The public schools from which most of them came gave them a thorough grounding in the ancient languages and, beyond that, saw it as their primary function to train character; hence the emphasis on team games.

All of this has now disappeared along with the imperial order it was designed to serve. It is surprising, therefore, that the rhetoric of official documents about education still preserves a distinctly platonic phraseology. The *Education Reform Act, 1988*, states that the aims of education are to 'promote the spiritual, moral, cultural, mental and physical development of the pupils; and to prepare such pupils for the opportunities, responsibilities and experiences of adult life'. Here are all the main elements of Plato's scheme in the *Republic*.

Nevertheless, in spite of this official declaration, the dominant educational philosophy of our time is opposed to Plato's in almost every respect. Plato took it for granted that it was essential to select for his education those who were best fitted to be rulers or to assist the rulers, and to provide them with an education designed to fit them for their role. Modern educationalists agree to selection only reluctantly and the term 'élite' (and even more the adjective 'élitist') have acquired a pejorative sense in educational circles. Although entry to higher education in Britain is highly competitive and government-inspired league tables reveal that levels of achievement vary greatly as between different schools and universities, public discourse tends to insist on parity of esteem as between institutions of higher education in a way that is not the case in the USA. Moreover, although strenuous efforts are made to ensure that only the ablest and best qualified candidates are admitted to the schools and universities which are most sought after and that tests for admission are transparently fair, there is a distinct reluctance to admit that their products are *prima facie* better qualified for key positions. There is an unresolved tension between meritocracy and egalitarianism. In an increasingly complex and technological society it becomes more and more important that institutions are honestly and effectively administered, but there is an unwillingness to accord the administrator an elevated status or prestige.

The tension could be resolved by a Judaeo-Christian understanding of relationships in society, but this is rarely given public acknowledgement. It involves the recognition that all are equal in the sight of God and can serve him equally, but there is a diversity of gifts in virtue of which some are able to achieve more than others. In the absence of such an overall vision the temptation is strong either to identify human worth with individual achievement or, by way of resistance to this, to regard all achievements as of equal worth. The educational imperative of enabling all children to develop their gifts to the full is readily interpreted as requiring that all opinions are of equal value.

Plato did not believe that all human beings are of equal worth, so that he is able to champion a hierarchical society without any sense that it may threaten other important values. By contrast the modern tendency is to stress equality to such an extent that the need for hierarchy in certain contexts is only grudgingly admitted.

Indoctrination and Censorship

Plato's educational scheme is open to the charge of indoctrination. The early education of the guardians is designed to prepare them physically, emotionally and intellectually for the reception of a pattern of virtue whose authority is unquestioned. The best short summary of his educational philosophy occurs in a passage in which he is explaining how his ideal regime differs from that of Thrasymachus. The governed are ruled not to their hurt but because it is better for every man to be ruled by divinity and insight, θείου καὶ φρονίμου. He goes on to instance the way in which children are ruled: 'We don't allow them to be free, until we have set up a constitution in them, as you might in a city, and until by nourishing the best in them we have provided a guardian to bear rule within them which is like and can take the place of our ruling principle; and then we give them their liberty' (IX 590e2-591a3). Julia Annas[1] rightly defends Plato against the charge that education as he conceives it is a form of brain-washing. This is incompatible with the attention he pays to character training. But she continues:

> All the same it is undeniable that his educational system aims to impose on children a set of values in such a way that they will not be seriously sceptical about them either at the time or later in life. We feel unhappy about this;

---

[1] J.Annas, *An Introduction to Plato's Republic*, Oxford, 1981, p.89.

and most educational theorists would hold that this cannot be the proper function of education. Education, it is widely held, must aim to produce people who are autonomous in that they can think independently and can ask themselves whether they find it better to hold the values in which they were brought up, or choose to live by another set of values.

But Plato, as we have seen,[2] does not set a high value on the autonomy of the individual. And this is undeniably a serious defect in his entire system. But this very fact compels one to consider just what difference it would make to his thought if autonomy were given the significance it merits. What part should autonomy play in any satisfactory theory of education?

Plato's neglect of autonomy is nowhere more apparent than in his readiness to make use of censorship, which stems in part from his understanding of literature,[3] and in part from the ambiguity of the Greek word ψεῦδος, which can mean both falsehood and fiction. The *Iliad*, for example, incurs his strictures, for conveying the wrong moral, for being morally false, whereas his own γενναῖον ψεῦδος,[4] his mythical account of the origins of his ideal city, (III 414b) is to be promulgated because, although literally false, it communicates a fundamental truth. Whereas Plato has no misgivings about the exercise of censorship, even for adults, modern educators regard it as a necessary evil which is appropriate only for children. In Britain the clearest example of this distinction is the so-called nine o'clock rule which governs television programming. It is assumed that any programme screened before nine o'clock at night may be watched by children, and that, therefore, material deemed unsuitable for children should be held back until later in the evening. There is general agreement that such a convention is necessary, but opinions differ as to the reason why. Some people, no doubt, have a broadly platonic view that it is desirable to prevent children, so far as possible, from developing into adults who will think wrongly and behave badly according to certain commonly accepted standards. This was undoubtedly the view of Lord Reith, the founding director of the BBC. But it is not, as a rule, the view of today's broadcasters, who are anxious to present 'adult programmes', which will represent a range of alternative life-styles, between which viewers are free to choose. Their position is that of Annas: the aim of education is to produce adults who will be free to decide for themselves what sort of people to be. It is common ground between these parties that children need to be kept from material which they are not yet mature enough to understand and to make responsible decisions about.

---

[2] Ch.9, p.118.

[3] See next chapter, pp.160.

[4] To be translated not 'noble lie', but 'glorious fiction', or 'moral myth', or even 'profound truth'.

It would be a mistake, however, to assume that from the more liberal standpoint of broadcasters there is no place for censorship of adult viewing, or that none of the censorship imposed upon children is to be maintained into adult life. When children may no longer read *Little Black Sambo* it is with the intention that they shall grow into adulthood free from racial prejudice; and when efforts are made in school to avoid distinction between boys' subjects and girls' subjects, it is intended that they will as adults avoid gender stereotyping. Hence in Britain there are laws against racial and sexual discrimination, and a discreet but firm censorship is imposed on certain uses of language.

The fact is that in contemporary society there are ambivalent attitudes to censorship. Traditionally there were certain areas in which a more or less strict censorship was imposed, notably in respect of sex and religion. Hence obscenity and blasphemy were condemned by law. Certain ideals of chastity and religious devotion were commonly accepted and it was taken for granted that children should be brought up to reflect these ideals in adult life. These ideals were challenged increasingly by a growing emphasis upon personal freedom and uninhibited self-realisation and so was the apparatus of censorship designed to protect them. Hence the word 'censorship' itself was associated with older, more traditional conceptions of what men and women should be like, and the fact that a considerable degree of censorship was being invoked in aid of the newer ideal was easily overlooked. It was noticed, however, by Edith Wharton, who wrote in her autobiography, 'There is always censorship of the same sort, though it is now at the other end of the moral register.'[5]

Hence the question which Annas raises in connection with Plato and his neglect of autonomy is less easy to settle than at first appeared. Plato is accused of wanting to impose on children a set of values in such a way that they will not be seriously sceptical about them either at the time or later in life. But it looks as if, with regard to certain values, the modern liberal educator does the same. Is his practice, too, indoctrinatory or is there some significant discrimination to be made?

What, clearly, would be objectionable is to impose values on children in such a way that they are incapable of criticizing them in later life, that is to say in such a way that they end up as adults with closed minds and restricted sympathies. But this is wholly compatible with their continued abhorrence of racism, given that the conviction that all human beings, whatever their race, are worthy of respect, is objectively true and can withstand criticism. There would be point, as J.S. Mill insisted, in subjecting even this conviction to criticism in order better to understand its implications and the reasons for maintaining it.

---

[5] *A Backward Glance,* London, (Everyman), 1993, p.92.

But, if this is so, it follows also that Plato, if only he were to be persuaded of the importance of autonomy, could be defended against the charge of indoctrination. What is wrong with his educational theory is not that he aims to induct the young into a continuing pattern of virtuous conduct, but that he fails to see that an essential element in the virtuous life is a free choice as to how to live. In other words, it is not the project of developing virtue as such which is mistaken, but the defective conception of virtue which he adopts.

In considering Plato's use of censorship, it is important also to remember the context of his discussion. He is talking about the education of the young, in a small community whose members are dedicated individually to a life of integrity and communally to the search for truth. Plato's ideal society is much closer to a monastery, a seminary, or a college: the argument is not about imposing censorship on unwilling subjects, but about what set texts to have in the syllabus, or what pictures to have on the common-room walls. Those are decisions which have to be taken. Plato thinks they are important decisions. He thinks that people are influenced by what they see and hear. Many people today believe this to have been the case with some modern TV dramas or the film 'Clockwork Orange'. TV producers deny this. They say that there is no evidence that television affects viewers' attitudes and behaviour. Advertisers, however, think otherwise; and much of education is based on the assumption that pupils' outlook and behaviour can be influenced by what they see and hear. It is difficult to hold that Plato was wrong to think the curriculum and environment important factors in education. In San Marco in Florence almost every cell has a depiction of some scene from the life of Christ, including many Crucifixions, thereby expressing the communal *ethos* far more powerfully than if there had been no pervasive theme of decoration. And again it is difficult to hold in the name of freedom that communities have no right to adopt and express a communal *ethos*.

Plato can be criticized, however, for an unduly protective attitude towards the minds of the young. He recognises that as regards physical dangers, we should not be over-protective. We stunt our charges' growth if we wrap them in cotton wool; and it could be that a diet of monotonously 'improving' literature might not foster the critical and independent spirit he wants the guardians to possess. An argument against Plato's prescriptions could be developed along these lines, but it would be an argument about means, not about ends. The curriculum would still need to be carefully controlled, even if it included some subversive texts in order that pupils might learn to be genuinely critical.

Higher Education

Plato's scheme for the higher education of the guardians is designed to introduce them to those studies which will develop their intellectual and moral capacities to the full and enable them, in due course, to grasp the Form of the Good. These studies are not thought of by him as a means only to the apprehension of the Good, but rather as constituents of it. They are not, however, its only constituents, since knowledge of the Good enables the philosopher also to understand and satisfy the needs of people in society. Modern liberal societies have no synoptic vision of the Good. For this reason it cannot be said that, in them, higher education aims at the Good. The fragmentation of knowledge faces the university student with a bewildering variety of subjects and courses offered by specialist departments which have little contact with one another. Hence the often lamented gap between the sciences and the humanities; and the unity of science itself is no more than a pious aspiration. Within the natural sciences there are marked disagreements, and the social sciences and the humanities are notoriously fissiparous. In so far as an overarching theory is to be looked for, in the modern liberal university, it would seem to be in the province of philosophy, but professional philosophers in recent times have been reluctant to attempt such a thing, or even to countenance its possibility: philosophy has been regarded as another highly specialized discipline whose practitioners disown any more architectonic role.

Nevertheless it is possible to discern in public discussions a number of broadly speaking philosophical theories which implicitly or explicitly govern peoples thinking. One is materialism or scientism. It is assumed by many that the field of knowledge is coterminous with that of natural science; the world revealed by natural science is the only world there is. Given this assumption two possibilities would seem to remain for the humanities. Either such truths as are to be found in the humanities will turn out to be expressible in purely scientific terms; or the humanities must renounce any claim to objectivity. Presented with this dilemma some literary critics, moral and philosophical theorists and even some (though fewer) historians are prepared to accept their role as irremediably subjective and even to celebrate the creative freedom which they are thus enabled to enjoy. There is, however, an alternative open to the humanities, which is to stake out for them a claim to objective knowledge which is *sui generis*. It is not reducible to scientific knowledge and possesses its own independent criteria of truth.

Plato, as the *Phaedo* makes clear, is no materialist and the synoptic impulse in him is too strong for him to rest content in an ultimate dichotomy between two types of knowledge. The only remaining modern alternative which would capture Plato's insistence on the primacy of the Good is some form of theism. Theology, then, might provide an architectonic discipline, but in no British university does it still do so. Strenuous efforts were made in Oxford in the nineteenth century to maintain the dominance of Christian theology in its Anglican form, but they could not resist the demands of academic freedom and churchmen made no attempts to work out a coherent compromise. In contemporary universities there are three recognisable patterns:

1. The university may be entirely secular: no provision is made for religion.
2. No confessional theology is allowed, but religious studies are permitted on the understanding that they are religiously neutral.
3. Christian theology may be given an authorized presence but is otherwise left to float freely in an atmosphere of critical enquiry.

In Britain, the norm is (2), but Oxford, Cambridge, Durham and King's College, London exemplify (3). In all these three patterns the underlying assumption is that the university as such is devoted to free enquiry and it is left to individuals to develop their own philosophy of life. A good university will encourage an ethos of lively debate about fundamental questions. In pattern (3) the university ensures that Christianity is represented in the debate.

It might seem that Plato's scheme for the higher education of the guardians is, as Popper maintained, rigidly authoritarian and incompatible with such free debate. Since the Good is *ex hypothesi* known, both students and teachers must accept it as a basis for their inquiries. There is nothing for them to do but work out the practical and theoretical implications of what is already known. The Cave itself conveys the impression that the guardians will have all the answers.

However, there is no indication that in the ideal society the practice of dialectic is to cease, and the possibility cannot be ruled out that gifted individuals might continue to make discoveries of facets of the Good which have not hitherto been recognised. Either the Good itself may invite further exploration or new situations may demand fresh solutions in the light of it.

Whether this be so or not, the modern liberal university does share Plato's conviction of the power of reason to arrive at an objective truth. It presupposes:

1. that there are truths, independent of human minds, which human beings can aspire to learn;
2. that the human mind is capable, in principle, of attaining, or at least approximating to, these truths, so long as it employs the methods appropriate to each particular enquiry;
3. that the pursuit of truth is a difficult and exacting task for which a rigorous initial training and continuous discipline is necessary; it calls for creative imagination—the capacity to hit upon hypotheses which have a good chance of proving true; also for critical reflection and careful attention to evidence;
4. that the pursuit of truth is a cooperative task to be pursued by people in a community in which encouragement and criticism can both flourish.

These convictions are under attack in the culture war which rages in some American universities. From the standpoint of some postmodernist thinkers the liberal ideal itself with its concept of impartial investigation is to be repudiated as being the expression of a particular cultural bias. It is a product of the European Enlightenment, which exalted reason by making universal claims for it and suppressed or neglected other elements in the human make-up.

This critique of rationalism generally aims to undermine it by asking who stands to benefit by the appeal to reason itself and by the particular beliefs that reason is held to validate. Influenced by the great modern masters of suspicion, Nietzsche, Marx and Freud, it refuses to take rational arguments at their face value and seeks to probe the hidden unconscious psychological and political forces which motivate them. Thus, it is held, the rationalist tradition of the West has served as a cloak for imposing on the rest of the world an intellectualist philosophy which disparages the claims of indigenous cultures and renders them effectively mute. What is presented as a process of free enquiry into objective truth is, when properly understood, an exercise of raw power assisted by technological mastery.[6]

It is obvious that Plato's *Republic* has been enormously influential in promoting the concept of reason which is here under attack. In fact, by a curious irony, postmodernism is enabling Thrasymachus to turn the tables on Socrates by arguing that his sustained appeal to rational argument is itself an illustration of the thesis that justice is the interest of the stronger.

This critique finds expression in British universities, especially in departments of literature and the social sciences, but has had little impact on the way the university views itself. Like other British institutions universities are comparatively impervious to abstract ideas of any kind. American universities, by contrast, have in many cases succumbed to a severe lack of confidence in their traditional role and the academic ethic which underpins it. There is often a reluctance to impose standards of literacy and logical consistency out of a sense that these are class- or culture-bound; and faculty members sometimes even wonder whether they are entitled to outlaw cheating and plagiarism. For have not students a right to advance their careers by any means available to them; and in a competitive *milieu* are not these legitimate devices for the advancement of vulnerable individuals who for one reason or another may be at odds with the dominant *ethos* of the university? When traditional academic standards are taken to be no more than reflections of the dominant culture, the very notion of standards tends to be undermined.[7]

---

[6] This critique is explored, with special reference to Michael Foucault, in an article by Grace M.Jantzen, 'What's the Difference: Knowledge and Gender in (Post) Modern Philosophy', in *Religious Studies*, Volume 32, Number 4, December 1996.

[7] See J.D.Hunter, *Culture Wars*, New York, 1991; ch.10; Allan Bloom, *The Closing of the American Mind*, New York, 1987.

If American universities more than British ones have felt the impact of distinctly anti-platonic educational philosophies, they have also in some cases made more deliberate efforts to face the problem of the fragmentation of knowledge by devising projects like the Great Books programme which are designed to introduce students to past attempts to give coherent answers to the fundamental problems of human life. In Britain, more especially in England, there is a traditional reluctance to face such issues head on. It is left to informal agencies such as university societies and clubs to discuss such questions as how one ought to live, ὅντινα τρόπον χρὴ ζῆν (I 352d5). These used to flourish and to some extent still do, but as a result of the student movement of the 1960s and 1970s they have often been abandoned in favour of temporary like-minded huddles.

Modern universities face a basic problem in relation to the academic *ethos* itself. How are they to respond to the cultural diversity of contemporary society? Plato was not confronted by this problem (although he would have been if he had studied Herodotus carefully). It is not difficult to see what his solution would have been. If there are conflicting conceptions of the Good or if there are those who would dispense with it altogether, the choice between them must be determined by a thorough-going use of the dialectical method. And if dialectic itself is held to be a one-sided and defective method of reasoning, then a better must be found, which takes appropriate account of the genuine virtues of rival suggestions. If the generally accepted patterns of reasoning can be shown to be biased, then they must be corrected to eliminate the bias. But, Plato would insist, they must actually be shown to be biased: mere allegation of bias is not enough. Reason, now better understood, must still have the last word.

The Transmission of *Mores*

Plato was concerned with the question of how to make people good. In the *Meno* he asks whether virtue can be taught, or whether alternatively, it is instilled by habituation, ἐθισμός, or is an inherited niceness, or comes by some divine chance. In the *Republic* he comes down in favour of all these alternatives. The guardians are led to the knowledge of the Form of the Good by a course of sustained philosophical argument. But the early education of the guardians is intended to habituate them in the ways of virtue so thoroughly that no subsequent experience can leach virtue from their characters; they are to be dyed with a purple so fast that no subsequent bleach can wash it out (IV 429de). Only those with gold in their make-up are to be selected as members of the ruling class. And the language used of the mystical vision of the Form of the Good suggests that it is vouchsafed only to the favoured few, and may be denied to others equally assiduous in their study of metaphysics.

Nevertheless, Plato holds *au fond* that virtue can be taught. The other approaches are important ancillaries, and may, indeed, be necessary conditions, for the successful transmission of values; but it is philosophical argument which establishes the objectivity of values and the sovereignty of good. Aristotle evidently believed the same in his youth, but he lost his faith in the Form of the Good, and at the end of the *Nicomachean Ethics* quoted Theognis: if arguments were enough to make men good, they would be much valued, εἰ μὲν οὖν ἦσαν οἱ λόγοι αὐτάρκεις πρὸς τὸ ποιῆσαι ἐπιεικεῖς, πολλοὺς ἂν μισθοὺς καὶ μεγάλους δικαίως ἔφερον[8] concluding that we must habituate men in the ways of righteousness if we wanted them to be good thereafter. The dispute continued among Aristotle's successors, Dicaearchus continuing Aristotle's move towards the practical life and the practical control of education, while Theophrastus reverted to Plato's belief in the supremacy of argument, and the corresponding primacy of theory. Cicero after political failure confided to Atticus that he thought of abandoning politics for the βίος θεωρητικός.[9] The controversy continued throughout antiquity, and ended with St Augustine who held that virtue came neither by rational argument nor by being well brought up, but stemmed from the irresistible grace of God—a divine chance.

The typical modern view is that of Annas,[10] that the object of education should be to enable individuals to become autonomous, and choose whatever values they like. Hence the problem of how to make people virtuous does not arise. Liberal educationalists, as we have seen, are not generally consistent in their views. They are anxious to encourage certain virtues, like tolerance, and to discourage certain vices, like racism and sexism. We ourselves would argue that, whether education seeks autonomy alone, or, with it, other more substantive virtues, the aim cannot be achieved without providing the young with a coherent framework of belief, within which they can grow, and which they can, in due course, modify or reject, if in marturity they can see good reason. Since morality is deeply involved with our attitudes and emotions, this educational process has in the early stages to be pre-rational and sub-rational.

---

[8] *Nicomachean Ethics* X, 1179b4-6.

[9] Cicero, *Ep. ad Att.* II.16. See above, ch.2, p.34; see further for the three lives, W.Jaeger, *Aristotle*, Oxford, 2nd ed. 1948, Appendix II, pp.426ff.

[10] J.Annas, *An Introduction to Plato's Republic*, Oxford, 1981.

Chapter 12
The Quarrel with the Poets

Education and Drama

Plato famously quarrelled with the poets. It is strange, we think, because he was himself a poet, and evidently of great poetic sensibility. In this he differed from most philosophers, who have much to say about morals, politics, religion, metaphysics, logic, knowledge and meaning, but give to poetry barely a passing mention. But then most philosophers can afford to pass over poetry and art generally, for it means little to them. Philosophers tend to be grey men, tediously controverting what other philosophers have said or ordinary men think. Although a few can write well, for the most part they give the impression of having missed out on many of the experiences, and particularly the poetic and artistic experiences, of life. But not Plato. Not only was he a poet, but he was versed in literature, deeply responsive to it, and could not help writing well. He was susceptible to beauty. If in the end he wanted to banish the poets, it was because he knew their power. He was fighting himself. And the fact that the ancient quarrel was an internal one explains both the vehemence and the incoherence of his arguments.

In the *Republic* the issue arises tangentially in the course of the education of the guardians, and again in Book X in what appears to be an appendix—perhaps added in later editions as a rejoinder to criticisms. The arguments he uses change, and one crucial word—μίμησις (*mimesis*)—is used in a variety of meanings which change between the two passages. He also discusses the arts in other dialogues: the *Ion*, the *Symposium*, the *Phaedrus*, the *Philebus* and the *Laws* at considerable length.

Although initially in the *Republic* his ostensible purpose is, as we have seen,[1] to shield the young from unsuitable reading matter, he goes on to express grave reservations about literature generally. In the *Ion*, and again in *Republic* III, Plato criticizes dramatic performers because they pretend to be what they are not. In part it is due to his having no word for fiction. What is not fact is in his book not true. But, whatever other criticisms we may make of fiction on the score of lacking truth-value, we cannot seriously charge the actor, the playwright, or the novelist, with deceit. We know, or should know, perfectly well that Romeo and Juliet do not really die, and that Jennifer Archer did not really have an illegitimate baby. There is in all fiction a suspension of truth-value, recognised by speaker and audience, writer and

---

[1] See above, ch.11, pp.145-148.

reader alike. Nobody need be deceived. Plato has a deeper worry about literature, in as much as it involves μίμησις, which could be translated 'playing a part', or 'impersonation', or 'mimicry', or 'imitation', or 'representation'. No translation is adequate, because Plato changes his meaning in the course of the *Republic*: in Book III 'playing a part' or 'impersonation' is probably the best term to use, but in Book X, where he has the visual arts in mind as well, 'representation' might be better. The complaint in Book III is that much of Greek literature available in his time involved long passages in direct speech in which the narrator impersonated the character being portrayed. Sophocles puts words into the mouth of an actor pretending to be Oedipus. And the same is largely true of Homer. Plato has no objection in Book III to people playing the part of good men propounding improving sentiments, but thinks that if the young guardian impersonates unworthy persons in all their weakness and wickedness, he may identify with the character, and adopt his outlook and attitudes. We tend to scoff, but Plato has a point. If I am really to get inside the part of Iago, I must, at least vicariously, feel as he did. I need, if only for the duration of the play, to be envious and mean-spirited. And having experienced such emotions, I might find it no longer unthinkable to feel them for real. Worse, I might take Iago as my role model. If my performance in the school play had won wide acclaim, my vanity would regret my not putting on such a performance again, after the play was over. Young people need role models. Literature abounds with possible role models, many of them unsuitable. Amateur dramatics might lock some susceptible youths into inappropriate ones.

We can find this argument in Plato, but there are two others, more prominent in the text. They concern πολυπραγμοσύνη, doing more than one thing. The actor, or someone reading Homer to himself, takes on many parts. Instead of sticking to his last, he will be at one time Agamemnon, another Athene, and another Thersites. This does not seem to us to be anything to worry about, and it is reasonable to suppose that for Plato πολυπραγμοσύνη, doing more than one thing, covers a multitude of not-very-sinful-sins. In part it is the puritan's suspicion of anything that may divert the attention from the main object. Future guardians should not waste their time play-acting, when they might be studying the higher mathematics. But Plato is not as extreme as that. Perhaps, rather, he senses that amateur dramatics can take up too much of an undergraduate's time: the proverbial wisdom of tutors is that, even more than rowing, it can detract from a proper devotion to study. A different complaint is that in taking on a variety of different roles, an actor, or a reader of a work of literature, extends his ability to empathize at the cost of his own stable identity. It is not my habit to sacrifice my daughter, sulk in my tent, or tell crafty lies. But if I am to enter into the part of Agamemnon, Achilles, or Odysseus, I must see things from their points of view, suspending my own inhibitions, and putting my own views out of mind. If I do this much,

I shall begin to sit loose to my own opinions, and ultimately to forget them altogether. Actors and actresses are commonly supposed to lack firmness of purpose, especially in personal relations. The proverbial wisdom of tutors again counsel the young against falling in love with stage-struck contemporaries who will readily play the part of being in love in return, but without actual commitment to a real person, being more in love with being in love than offering constant fidelity to one particular individual.

These arguments are not negligible: in ancient Greece impersonation was much more full-blooded and immediate that it is with us: we read in the *Ion* how the rhapsode is completely taken over by the character he is portraying: in the USA television productions of star wars have been taken to be genuine news bulletins by viewers who had just switched on. But such arguments can be countered. Plato himself recommends the use of indirect rather than direct speech as diminishing the immediacy of the words and their apparent claim to truth. In the modern world, although some novelists report that they are taken over by the characters they are writing about, we mostly exercise a suspension of reality when in the theatre or reading a novel.

At a first reading Plato seems to be banning bad characters altogether from the curriculum. But that cannot be so. It would belie his own practice. His Socratic dialogues are dramas with different participants talking in their own persons (perhaps it was some uneasiness on this score that led him to cast the middle dialogues into indirect speech, sometimes at considerable stylistic cost). He needed bad ideas to be expressed forcefully (as they were by Thrasymachus) in order to be able to show that they were bad, and bring out the rationale of the true alternative. And similarly in life we need to be given examples of wickedness in order to see how wicked it is, and the pre-eminent attractiveness of the alternatives. The young guardians were to be apprised of this in indirect speech, so that they should not be seriously tempted to follow suit. Our criticism of Plato as regards his scheme of education, is not that it is totally wrong, but that it is too protective, suitable for those under ten, but not for those verging on adulthood, who need already to have some intimation of the real choices that lie ahead.

Copy of a Copy

Plato discusses poetry and the arts again in Book X. The leading arguments are bad, so bad as to make us wonder how Plato came to include them, the more so as the topic does not fit into the overall scheme of the *Republic*.[2] There is also, at the end of the passage, a note of apology, as though Plato were defending himself against criticisms, whose force he could not altogether counter. It looks as though Book X is a sort of appendix, added on to later

---

[2] Plato's arguments in Book X are criticized trenchantly, but fairly, in Julia Annas, *An Introduction to Plato's Republic*, Oxford, 1981, ch.14, pp.335-344.

editions of the *Republic*, in which Plato sought to rebut criticisms that had been made of earlier editions, and tie up what had been seen as loose ends.

What criticisms could Plato have been trying to rebut? He argues that art is at a third remove from reality, only a copy of a copy. The contention to which that would be a pertinent rejoinder is that art is only one remove from reality, being a direct copy of the Forms. This was maintained, later, by Aristotle in the *Poetics*. In chapter nine he distinguished literature from history: whereas history reports the things that actually happened, literature portrays the sort of things that happen. As Plato moved from an adjectival theory of Forms to a substantival one, all the time maintaining that the Forms were more real than their earthly copies, it would have been an attractive move to argue that fiction, although factually false, was in a deeper sense true, since it mimicked the Forms of life instead of their mere, untidy and imperfect, actual manifestations. Faced with this counter, Plato might have retorted that art did not copy the Forms themselves, but only copies of them. It is not a very convincing argument even with regard to the visual arts, but if Plato by then had primarily geometrical shapes in mind as the paradigm Forms, he could have thought it telling. It is tempting to speculate—it is but a speculation— that earlier versions of the *Republic* were discussed in the Academy, and that after the addition of the metaphysical books, V, VI and VII, the brightest of the students, young Aristotle, argued that if the Forms alone were really real, then fiction's lack of factual truth-value ceased to be a demerit, since instead of representing what had actually happened, it represented the *sort* of things that happen, the Form of human affairs. The middle-aged Plato, caught on the hop, gave a quick answer, which pride prevented him from withdrawing on further consideration. Instead, it is buttressed in Book X by a quite different argument from the primacy of final causes, which picks up the ἔργον (*ergon*) argument of Book I: many of our concepts—sickle, razor, food, fuel—are defined in terms of their function, not their appearance, composition, or origin; with them the consumer is the final arbiter, and the producer—ποιότες (*poiotes*)—is subject to the consumer's judgement as to whether he has done his work well or not, and the *rapporteur*, wordsmith, ποιότες (*poiotes* from which our word 'poet' is derived), is even less in a position to pass judgement. In Plato's time such a line of reasoning constituted some sort of argument against the tendency to cite Homer as an authority on everything—we sometimes quote Shakespeare on medical matters, but would not prefer his authority to that of medical evidence—but it constitutes no argument whatsoever for banning the poets altogether.

The Appeal of Art

Plato has two further arguments (X 602c4-606d) against art. He claims that it appeals to inferior aspects of the personality. The first argument (X 602c4-603c3) depends on a contrast between Appearance and Reality. Art represents appearances, and appearances are illusory. But the meaning of 'appearance' depends on what it is being contrasted with. It is importantly true that most literature gives, either directly or vicariously, a first-personal view. Keats describes his feelings on first reading Chapman's Homer:

> Much have I travell'd in the realms of gold,
> And many goodly states and kingdoms seen;
> Round many western islands have I been
> Which bards in fealty to Apollo hold.
> Oft of one wide expanse had I been told
> That deep-brow'd Homer ruled as his demesne;
> Yet did I never breathe its pure serene
> Till I heard Chapman speak out loud and bold:
> Then felt I like some watcher of the skies
> When a new planet swims into his ken;
> Or like stout Cortez, when with eagle eyes
> He stared at the Pacific—and all his men
> Look'd at each other with a wild surmise—
> Silent, upon a peak in Darien.

And Shakespeare similarly remembers his experience of the English weather and his own life:

> Full many a glorious morning have I seen
> Flatter the mountain-tops with sovereign eye,
> Kissing with golden face the meadows green,
> Gilding pale streams with heavenly alchymy;
> Anon permit the basest clouds to ride
> With ugly rack on his celestial face,
> And from the forlorn world his visage hide,
> Stealing unseen to west with this disgrace;
> Even so my sun one early morn did shine
> With all triumphant splendour on my brow;
> But out! alack! he was but one hour mine,
> The region cloud hath mask'd him from me now.
> Yet him for this my love no whit disdaineth;
> Suns of the world way stain, when heaven's sun staineth.

Much of literature is concerned with expressing a personal view-point; the author is telling us how things are with him. It is an appearance—it tells us how things are from his point of view, that is, how they appear to him, but it is not an appearance in the way that sticks appear bent when partially immersed in water. The latter, and illusions generally, are how things appear to *us*, in contrast to how they really are. The sticks appear bent, but are really straight; things appear large or small, seem heavy or light, but when properly measured or weighed, we know objectively how large or how heavy they are.

The appearances the poet relates, by contrast, are not how things seem to us, but how they seem to him, though he hopes thereby to enable us to share his experience. The contrast is not with a reality to be discovered by a reliable error-proof method, but with how things seem to other people. A school-boy doing Chapman's Homer for an exam might be unenthused, wishing he could be eating a hamburger at MacDonald's now instead of reading about beef barbecues a long time ago. Plato cannot fault the account the poet gives of how things appear to him on the grounds of its being in need of subsequent correction. Homer seldom gives exact measurements. He would be an inadequate guide to a shipwright or someone wanting to give gale warnings for the Mediterranean many years ago. But that does not mean that he cannot convey truthfully what it was like to be a seafarer. An Impressionist painter may not give the details about the stamens and pistils that someone illustrating a flora should, but he may none the less convey what it was like for him to be in a garden in France on a spring afternoon. The poet and the artist deal not with matters of fact that can be checked by any competent observer, but with human responses and emotions, which once articulated, have a universal resonance.

Plato does not distinguish the different senses of appearance and the different contrasts that define them. All appearances are fickle fleeting, unreliable and unreal. As we have seen,[3] even the inter-subjective, non-illusory, carefully monitored observations of the astronomers are downgraded in favour of an austerely mathematical reality whose warrant is its rational appeal rather than any congruence with observation (VII, 529). Under this characterization, no representation of reality is possible. We may come to understand the Periodic Table or Hilbert Space, but we cannot picture either. An academic who is serious about reality has no time for reading novels, and should work in an austere office with a steel filing cabinet, fluorescent lights and Venetian blinds covering the plate-glass windows of a campus tower-block, and take care always to refuse social engagements, and hasten away from Common Room or Faculty Club in order to get back to the computer print-out. Reality thus understood demands aesthetic puritanism.

Plato's argument against appearances (X 602c4-603c3) does not work, although it reveals one source of his puritanism, a source he shares with Judaism and Islam together with the iconoclastic tradition in Christianity. His second argument (X 603c4-606d8) is a deeper and much more serious one, developing his critique of $\mu\ell\mu\eta\sigma\iota\varsigma$ (*mimesis*) in Book III. Art panders to, and encourages, the inferior, because irrational, aspects of the personality. In appreciating art we suspend our critical faculties, and allow ourselves to enter into the artist's world and see things the way he sees them. It is not just that we blur our vision and are content with an impression of a riot of flowers,

---

[3] Ch.6, p.80.

instead of counting the stamens and pistils as a proper botanist should, but we allow ourselves to feel with Clytemnestra and Medea, instead of keeping the awfulness of their crimes firmly in focus. Empathy breeds sympathy, and if we sympathize with criminals, we shall soon cease to condemn their crimes. The 'feelie feelie' approach erodes moral judgement, and a non-judgemental guardian cannot give guidance on what ought to be done.

Plato has a point. For one thing, there is an inevitable absence of social censorship. The poet shares with his readers his first-personal and therefore uninhibited point of view. Whereas a well brought-up man does not display his grief or fears to others, a poet does just that in articulating how things really are with him. It is not only the absence of the stiff upper lip: equally important in social life are the inhibitions of tact, prudence and decorum. In real life I may on occasion have felt like telling a colleague what I really thought of him, or murdering a particularly irritating pupil, but have desisted from doing so, or even showing that I was minded to, with the consequence that people who know me only through my actual social responses are hygienically ignorant of my real inclinations. But once literature is allowed, they become privy to men's private thoughts, and may be infected by their bad ones.

Modern debates about TV drama have a similar concern. The characters have to be articulate—or the play loses its point; but if they are articulate, they articulate motives and inclinations few would admit to in real life, and few viewers would come across in the course of their normal existence. Many, therefore, are shocked. Many, though shocked, are fascinated. Ratings go up, as programmes come down market, morally speaking. And that is a Bad Thing. A glance at a book stall in an airport shows the same tendency at work, and authors of those nineteenth-century novels we still read often bewail the popular preference for trashy alternatives to what they themselves had to offer.

Plato is presenting two arguments, which need to be assessed separately. The first is that, in revealing uninhibitedly the bad emotions that are part of our human condition, a play may evoke similar feelings in people who will then act on them.[4]

Rather than argue, implausibly even if fashionably, that art and literature have no social effects, we should look for countervailing benefits that offset the danger of instigating bad behaviour. Many men have seen it as a great virtue of literature that it widens our sensibilities, as Dr Johnson put it. That surely is a benefit to be set against the fact that in widening our sensibilities, it not only makes us more cognisant of the power of evil, but may induce us to act on it. I may indeed be led to imitate the hero in his weakness and folly as well as his greatness: I may find the villain so sympathetically portrayed

---

[4] See above, ch.11, p.148.

that I identify with him, and make his principles of action my own. Plato sees the danger, but not the countervailing benefit: we may acknowledge the danger, but reckon the benefit worth it.

Literature not only widens our sensibilities, but deepens them. We not only come to know what makes other men tick, but understand ourselves better. In a sympathetic representation of character we acquire a means of articulating our own feelings and emotions. We find it, for the most part, difficult to formulate what we feel, and find ourselves flooded with feelings we cannot control because we cannot say what they are. But Shakespeare can. He puts into the mouths of his characters words which we also can use to express our emotions, and we can gauge our reactions by reference to their responses. Literature makes us all articulate about ourselves. And to be articulate is the first step towards self-control. If I know that it is envy or jealousy that is moving me, I have a better chance of resisting or discounting it than if I am simply suffused by a fury I know not what. Psychiatry has made great advances this century in applying the insight of Freud that often we do not know ourselves, and are crippled by our lack of knowledge. If literature induces self-knowledge, it may help to cure both our anguish and our bad behaviour. Although in introducing me vicariously to many unadmirable states of mind, it may sometimes stimulate undesirable emotions, it will be mostly introducing me to myself, and by enabling me to recognise my emotions for what they are, will enable me also to master them rather than be carried away by them. Plato takes too animal a view of our lower nature. Most of our sins and most of our failings are specifically human faults. Pornography and sadism apart, there are few forms of representation that simply stimulate our emotions. Most forms of representation portray specifically human situations, and enable us to sympathize and identify with them only in so far as they describe them in a way that engages our human sympathies. Any bad effects from representing human diverse characteristics must have set against them the good effects of increasing our self-awareness and our capacity for self-control.

To know oneself is not always to control oneself. Literature may hold a mirror up, but need not purify thereby. Aristotle hoped that it would. He argued that in drama we experience *catharsis* of our emotions,[5] and indeed, sometimes a play, an epic, or a novel, not only gives good characterizations, but shows how aspirations and attitudes and actions work themselves out. We are engaged by the characters and recognise in them part of ourselves: but by the end of the affair we want also to disengage ourselves, for we could not rationally want to own all the actions and consequences that ensued. We *were* caught up. But we see, more fully than before, where such anger, where such avarice, where such ambitions, led. We have not only articulated something

---

[5] In ch.6 of *Poetics*.

in us, but have then distanced ourselves from it. We are purified, and could not have been so unless something in us had been, as it were, crystallized and then separated out. Literature can be cathartic. But that it should always be so has not been established by either empirical evidence or *a priori* argument. Aristotle has at best only a partial answer to Plato's charge.

We have parried Plato's complaint that literature nourishes the lower elements in the personality by claiming—in terms of the social metaphor—that it is good to make these lower elements stand up and be counted. The more we know them for what they are, and the likely consequences of their being indulged, the better able we shall be to rein them in, and keep them under control. But that is an empirical claim for which the evidence is uncertain. We rely more on the assumption that to widen and deepen our sensibilities is in itself a good thing, sufficient to outweigh the damage done by disseminating models of bad behaviour. But this Plato denies. He believes that in expanding our sensibilities and opening ourselves to artistic influences we are indulging a liking for ποικιλία, variety, that is at variance with the single-minded pursuit of truth and goodness (X 604e1 and 605a5). It is a common complaint. Voltaire complained that Shakespeare offered us a huge variety of characters, but with no underlying theme to order them, or enable us to pass a uniform judgement on them. There is a necessary permissiveness of someone who wants to enter into the minds of other men. *Tout comprendre, rend très indulgent.*[6] There is a tension between the suspension of judgement we need to exercise if we are to widen our sensibilities, and the firmness of judgement of someone who needs to know his own mind in order to know what ought actually to be done. Good listeners are often bad decision-makers, and decisive leaders are often insensitive to the feelings of others. But Plato overdoes the tension. I cannot lead unless I have some awareness of what those I am leading are likely to think, and, contrary to contemporary opinion, I cannot be a counsellor unless I can make firm value-judgements, and help the person in distress to see what he needs to do. Our knowledge of other minds depends crucially on having some idea of what we might be inclined to do were we in the other's position.

Moral judgement is not all of one piece. In deciding what to do, we have to consider *cons* as well as *pros*. Although in the end I decide on one course of action, in my earlier deliberations I become fully aware of reasons for doing something else. Of course Clytemnestra should not have murdered her husband, but Agamemnon was pretty awful, and we can see her point of view, just as we have on occasion felt inclined to murder colleagues or pupils, while not actually doing it. Although in the end we have to reach a definite decision, in the process of doing so we go through a number of intelligible indecisions which enable us to appreciate the considerations which could lead someone

---

[6] Mme de Stael, *Corinne*, lib.iv, ch.3.

to act in some other way. Hence, in reading Homer or watching Aeschylus, we can see why they felt as they did, construed their situation in a particular way and reacted to it appropriately. 'Appropriately' does not necessarily mean 'rightly'. I can understand the actions of Agamemnon, Clytemnestra, Achilles, or Paris, without approving of them. Yet even to understand is to recognise some propensity in myself, if situated as they were, to act as they did. And Plato fears that in as much as they are portrayed sympathetically, the propensity to identify with them and endorse their values is increased. It is not obvious that he was wrong. Many readers of *Paradise Lost* come to see Satan as its hero.

The Rationality of Literature

Plato's rejection of literature's variety, ποικιλία, is a facet of his puritanism. It is due in large part to his failure to develop an adequate theory of moral reasoning, giving weight to the *cons* as well as *pros*. He is beguiled by the all-or-nothing proofs of mathematics, and seeks a similarly black-and-white moral universe in which good and bad are kept firmly apart. We can share his yearning for the white radiance of eternity,[7] but claim that the many-colouredness of life does not stain but is constitutive of whiteness.

Plato's understanding of rationality excludes not only the variety of goods that literature is sensitive to, but the whole canon of literature. He convicts it of irrationality, and believes that in opening ourselves to artistic influences we are abjuring the use of reason. Art has a message, but it communicates it in an irrational way. The proper vehicle for the communication and apprehension of truth is the μέθοδος διαλεκτική, the dialectical method, as he came to understand it:[8] art does not use the dialectical method: art therefore is suspect.

Plato is on to something. It is possible to hold *The Satanic Verses* blasphemous in a way that would be clearly inappropriate for an academic critique of Islam. If I adduce arguments against Islam, I lay myself open to counter-argument: my arguments invited criticism, and can be controverted. Works of art make truth-claims of a sort, but cannot be similarly rebutted. They insinuate their message, rather than stating it explicitly and openly. And whereas truth is great and will prevail over open challenges, we fear it may be eroded and undercut by sub-rational fifth-column activities.

The dialectical method that Plato inherited from Socrates encourages criticism. Suggestions can be controverted; indeed, they are subjected to a destruction test before being accepted. But if I lay myself open to art, I shall be subject to all sorts of influences which I shall not separately recognise, and cannot separately assess. I shall find my perceptions altered in all sorts

---

[7] Shelley, *Adonais*, LII.

[8] See above, ch.6.

of ways I know not, and my understanding and reactions subtly changed. After going to a play by Shakespeare or seeing a picture by Rembrandt I am a different person, not only emotionally but intellectually. I have a different apprehension of truth. But this difference is not due to my having accepted, after careful examination, a new proposition. Although after going to many plays or seeing many pictures, I may become something of a critic and be able to articulate some aspects of the play or picture in question, my first and continuing response to a work of art is one of acceptance, seeing it as a whole, and taking it for what it is. I cannot interrupt Hamlet's soliloquy with a Socratic question or apply a tape measure to a statue of Phidias without destroying the artistic effect. Obviously in fiction there has to be suspension of unbelief: but more generally in all art there has to be a suspension of the give-and-take of conversational interchange. I may not be entirely passive, but I have to be in an accepting frame of mind before I can appreciate. If I persist in interrupting, if I insist on examining each detail in depth, I make myself unable to respond to what the artist is trying to communicate, and forfeit my capacity to respond to it as a whole. But if I forswear interruption and abandon the dialectical method altogether, I lose the touchstone of truth, and may accept as artistically true something that is not. In the *Laws* Plato re-iterates his banishment of the poets on the grounds that they are offering a rival artistic vision, whereas he is offering the true one. If dramatists ask to be allowed to come and perform, they should be told:

> ὦ ἄριστοι τῶν ξένων, ἡμεῖς ἐσμὲν τραγῳδίας αὐτοὶ ποιηταὶ κατὰ δύναμιν ὅτι καλλίστης ἅμα καὶ ἀρίστης: πᾶσα οὖν ἡμῖν ἡ πολιτεία συνέστηκε μίμησις τοῦ καλλίστου καὶ ἀρίστου βίου, ὃ δή φαμεν ἡμεῖς γε ὄντως εἶναι τραγῳδίαν τὴν ἀληθεστάτην. We are dramatists too, honoured sirs, and our drama is the best we can produce: our whole constitution is a production (μίμησις) of the best and finest life—and that, we maintain, is really the truest drama.[9]

Homer and the tragedians have a message, but it is not a true one, since it has not been communicated dialectically, and therefore must not be heard in the ideal society.

Plato's criticism is a serious, though confused, one, and is echoed in contemporary attitudes. Many modern thinkers are, as he was inclined to be, puritans, with an austere view of truth, confining it to the literal truth, and consigning any artistic message to the realm of emotional expression, without cognitive content. If society is founded on rational principles, then subversive propaganda may well be banned, for fear that it will weaken the respect in which the constitution is held by the weaker brethren. In the United States of America the Stars and Stripes is an emblem of national identity, founded

---

[9] *Laws* 817b2-5.

on the self-evident truths of the Declaration of Independence, and public dis-respect of the flag is punishable by law. While the weaker brethren need to be protected, those who can think for themselves will be unmoved by mere symbols, accepting only what has been validated by cogent argument.

Such a position is taken by many modern thinkers, but it is not one Plato can take. In spite of his own austere account of cogent argument, he spectac-ularly fails to confine himself to piecemeal analytical reasoning. Analogies, allegories, parables are pressed into service to convey his deepest convictions. The brilliant portraits in Books VIII and IX of the deteriorating characters of individuals and societies fail to conform to his canon of logical argumentation, but are convincing none the less. Truth is not necessarily prosaic, and is not confined to what can be apprehended by analytical reasoning. In the end, as we saw in Chapter Six, διαλεκτικὴ (*dialektike*), argument, could not be adequately explicated in terms of deduction alone, but had to be something more, though Plato was unable to give a clear account of what extra was involved. The Form of the Good, although apprehended only after a rigorous course of question and answer, is actually apprehended itself through some flash of holistic intuition, when the different pieces are seen to fit into one architectural whole.[10]

If knowledge of the Form of the Good transcends prosy discussion, other sorts of knowledge may do so too. It is possible for there to be artistic truth communicated not exclusively through seminars. It is at least possi-ble that I respond to some messages receptively or meditatively rather than argumentatively, holistically rather than analytically: certainly this is how we sometimes respond to some features of our environment which are not necessarily messages. I do not have to be saying 'but' all the time, but can take some things for granted some of the time. Even where a message can be adequately articulated in propositional form, I do not have to examine the propositions one by one, but can also consider the set of them together, and ask whether together they are consistent, coherent, or true. Sometimes, indeed, it is the only way we can usefully consider them. Newton's three laws of motion constitute his theory, and only together can be regarded as true or false. Although philosophers may argue about the exact status of some one of Newton's laws, they can do so only against the background of the others. We can be analytic about Newtonian mechanics, but must be holistic too.

Much the same is true of art, but with very different emphasis. On suitable occasion, I can interrupt the soliloquy and count the syllable, can get out my tape-measure, and calculate the statue's proportions. But I must also, and antecedently, listen, look, and accept as a whole. I must first lay myself open to understand the artist, let myself get his message. But having done this, I may subsequently criticize it. I may scrutinise it in detail, as most critics do,

---

[10] See above, ch.3, pp.38, 42, ch.6, pp.86-87, ch.7, p.104.

or I may accept or reject it *in toto*, as ordinary viewers or readers are wont to do. I do not have to go on accepting it, merely by virtue of having had to accept it initially in order to understand it. If some works can be admired as expressing deep artistic truth, others may be rejected as facile and false, and others again, although allowed to be sincere expressions of authentic experience, may still be judged ultimately unacceptable, because ultimately false. Plato, although himself an acute critic, fails to see the importance of literary criticism in enabling us to judge the truth of literary productions in something of the same way as the dialectical method allows us to do so with philosophical propositions. It may not be as rigorous, but it is enough to secure that the truth claims of the dramatists do not have to be accepted uncritically, but can in due course be subjected to rational appraisal. If that is so, Plato was wrong to banish the visiting dramatists. They should be welcomed, like visiting academics who bring new ideas for discussion. In either case what they bring may turn out to be no good. But even if the new is less good than the old, it will invigorate the old by challenging it, and forcing us to re-think our reasons for preferring it.

There is, of course, a risk that we may be misled. Having had to suspend criticism initially in order to appreciate and understand, I may continue to do so by reason of my infirmity of judgement. Often in fact I am taken in by a novel or a play or a picture, just as often in fact I am taken in by the conventional wisdom about matters of prosaic truth. We cannot escape the possibility of error. Plato's ideal of absolute intellectual autonomy is as impractical as Descartes', and as unreasonable. I cannot doubt everything and rebuild the edifice of knowledge on sure foundations, but must stand on other men's shoulders if I am to attain to any serious truth. Inevitably, then, I must pay the price of believing some false propositions, taken on trust second-hand; but only by running the risk of being sometimes wrong can I hope ever to believe anything true. What I must do, in the face of the fallibility of my own opinions, is to be ready to scrutinise any belief I have which falls under suspicion. Equally with my moral beliefs and way of life, and the images, stories, dramas and legends which form my cultural inheritance. ὁ ἀνεξέταστος βίος οὐ βιωτὸς ἀνθρώπῳ, the unexamined life is not worth living. But I have to live my life as well as examine it, and can only examine it in so far as I have already lived some of it. I cannot stop living until I have decided how to live; I should not stop believing until I have decided which propositions I may safely believe: and similarly I should not have a policy of excluding all artistic communications until I am sure I can exclude all false ones. Rather, in each case, I should recognise the possibility of error, and accept the fact that I shall sometimes live on unexamined, and wrong, principles, sometimes believe uncriticized, and false, prosaic propositions, sometimes accept subliminally and be influenced by works of art which convey artistic falsehoods. But I should not thus rest content with the error, but be alert to recognise it and banish it, and thus seek an ultimate, though not initial, purity of life, intellectual belief and artistic response.

Envoi

Everyone must make his own interpretation of the *Republic*. One cannot read it without responding to it, and each reader's response will be different. If what we have written carries conviction with you, we are happy. If, having read it, you are led to interpret Plato and assess his arguments differently, we are still content. It is a large part of the spell of the *Republic* that it admits of many different defensible interpretations, and this is the reason why it is not only a great work of philosophy, but a great work of art.

Schematic Analyses of Text

Plato had no chapter headings, and the form of a dialogue makes him appear to wander from topic to topic aimlessly, often with digressions and sub-digressions. These analyses, given in increasing detail, are intended to help the reader find his way round the text. Digressions and sub-digressions are indicated by indentations and indentations of indentations. The suggestion that there were many editions of the *Republic* is controversial. Many scholars think that the *Republic* was conceived as a whole, but we find it helpful to view the text as having been written in stages.

Short Schema of the *Republic*

1. **Book I** Perhaps originally a separate Socratic Dialogue:
Περὶ Δικαίου (*Peri Dikaiou*), *On Honesty*

2. **Books II, III and IV** Perhaps originally a first edition of
ΠΟΛΙΤΕΙΑ (*POLITEIA*), *Republic* (or *The Constitution of Society*)
Book I Prologue
357-367 Glaucon and Adeimantus restate the challenge of moral scepticism.
368-369 Introduction of *Πόλις* (*Polis*) analogy
369-434 *Πόλις* (*Polis*) analogy. Cardinal virtues of a society identified
434-435 Discussion of *Πόλις* (*Polis*) analogy
435-444b Tripartite psyche: virtues of an individual identified
444c-445b The value of *δικαιοσύνη* (*dikaiosune*)
(first climax of the *Republic*)

   3. Books V, VI, and VII (IV 449b-VIII 543c) Digression (added in third edition)

4. **Books VIII and IX(i)** (445c-449a, 543c-580c)
The four bad types of constitution, social and individual (added in second edition of *The Constitution of Society*)
445c-449b Introduction: four bad types of constitution
543c-580 The decline of the constitution, social and individual
580a-c The superiority of *δικαιοσύνη* (*dikaiosune*) again vindicated
(second climax of the *Republic*, second edition)

      5. IX 580d-592 Appendices I and II (? added in fourth edition ?)

      6. X 595-608b Appendix III (? added in fifth edition ?)

      7. X 608c-621 Epilogue (? added in fifth edition ?)

Further Analyses

Republic I

Perhaps originally a separate Socratic Dialogue Περὶ Δικαίου *On Honesty*

327-331b   Introduction. Scene setting. The Good Life.

  331c-336a Inconclusive Socratic Dialogue with Cephalus and
  Polemarchus on what δικαιοσύνη (*dikaiosune*), honesty, is.

336b-339e Thrasymachus' intervention:

δικαιοσύνη, morality, is simply the interest of the stronger;

Socrates probes ambiguities of 'interest' and 'stronger',

and traps Thrasymachus in self-contradiction.

      340 Cleitophon's amendment—rejected by Thrasymachus

340d-341a   Thrasymachus restates his proto-Marxist position.

    341-348 Inconclusive Socratic Dialogue with Thrasymachus
        on whether honesty really is the best policy.

348c-e Is morality/honesty/humanity merely good-natured stupidity?

349-354 Three concluding arguments:

1. Lyre strings should not be tightened too much.

2. Even among thieves honour is needed.

3. Humane behaviour is the true function of human beings.

354b-c Conclusion: the argument has been inconclusive; more thought needed.

Republic II-IV

  369-434 Πόλις (*Polis*) analogy

    369-374 Origin and nature of society

      369-371 Mutual help essential

      371-374 Structure of complex communities

    375-376 Guardians needed for government

      376e-412b Education of Future Guardians

        376e-400c The Curriculum

          376e-392c Literature

            392c-398b The Dangers of Dramatics

          398c-400c Music

        406c-403c Aims of education

        403c-412 Physical education

      412-427 The Guardians

    427-434 Excellencies of the Πόλις (*Polis*)

  434-435 The application of the Πόλις (*Polis*) Analogy

  435-441c Analysis of the individual personality

  441c-445b Integrity is psychological health. QED

Republic V, VI and VII

Digression added in third edition: ostensibly about the collective life of the guardians. In fact, chiefly concerned with metaphysical and epistemological issues:

451c4-471c The Unity of the Community

451c4-457c Community of wives and children
    451c4-453b1 Equality of women
    453b2-457c2 Inferiority of women
  457c-461e Eugenics
462-466d5 Abolition of Self
  462a-463e Reform of Language
  464a-465b4 All interests shared
  465b5-466d5 The bliss of the selfless
466e-471c Usages of War
  466e-467e Female and child soldiers
  468a-469b4 Penalties and rewards
  469b5-471c Hellas

471c-540 The Intellectual Guardian

471-474 Political power and intellectual commitment must be united
474b-480 The realm of the intellect
  474b-475e Definition of the intellectual
    475e-480 Nature of knowledge as contrasted with belief
      475e-476 Forms
      476-480 Knowledge and belief
VI 484-502c Government by intellectuals
  484-487a Need for knowledge
  487b-489c Academics unacceptable as governors
  489c-497a The treason of the intellectuals
  497a-502c The possibility of good government
502c-511 The Good
  502c-506b Goals of human life
  506c-509c The Sun
  509d-511 The Line
  VII 514-521b The Cave
521c-540e Academic education
  521c-535a Brochure for the Academy
    521c-531c Mathematics
      524d-526c Arithmetic
      526c-527c Geometry
      527d-528e Solid geometry
      528e-530c Particle dynamics
      530c-531c Theory of vibrations
    531c-535a Philosophy
  535a-540 Moral requirements of the intellectual life
540e5-541 Replacement of the existing gang by the uncorrupted young

Republic VIII and IX(i)-580c

445c1-547c4 Prefaces:

445c1-449b1 (1) Need to discuss inferior constitutions as a foil to the best

543a-545c7 (2) Recapitulation after long digression

545c8-547c4 (3) Number of the Beast: transition from ἀριστοκρατία (*aristokratia*) to τιμοκρατία (*timocratia*)

547c5-550c3 Τιμοκρατία (*Timocratia*) (English 'Aristocracy')

   547c5-548c5 Aristocratic society

   548e6-550c Aristocratic individual

550c4-555b Ὀλιγαρχία (*Oligarchia*) (English 'Plutocracy')

   550d-551b7 Transition from aristocracy to plutocracy.

   551b8-553a Plutocracy.

      553a-553e Transition from aristocrat to plutocrat

   554a-555b Plutocrat

555b-562a Δημοκρατία (*Democratia*) Permissive Society

   555b-557a Transition from plutocracy (cf. 572) to permissive society

   5557a-558c6 Permissive society ('democracy')

      598c8-561a Transition from plutocrat to libertine cf. 572c1-d4

   561a-562a Libertine

562a-576b Τυραννίς (*Turannis*) Autistic Autocracy

   562a-566b Transition from permissiveness to totalitarian dictatorship

   566d-569c Totalitarian dictatorship

   (IX)571a-573b5 Transition from libertine to autistic autocrat

   573b-576b Description of autistic autocracy

576b-580c Evaluation of Autistic Autocracy:

Morality Much Better than Selfishness

Republic IX(ii)

580d-588a Two Appendices on Pleasure and Recapitulation (added in fourth edition)

      580d-583b Philosophy is fun.

   583c-587b Pleasure not really pleasurable

587b-588a Life of the φιλόσοφος (*philosophos*) 729 times as pleasant as that of the autistic autocrat.

588a-592b Recapitulation of argument of second edition of the *Republic*

Republic X

Perhaps added in fifth edition

X 595-608b Appendix on Art. Refutation of Critics. Expulsion of Poets

X 608c-621 Epilogue. Myth of Er

Index